The Collected Courses of the
Series Editors: Profe
Profe
Prof
Europe
Florence

VOLUME XI/3
Accountability in the European Union

The Collected Courses of the Academy of European Law
Edited by Professor Philip Alston, Professor Gráinne de Búrca,
and Professor Bruno de Witte

This series brings together the Collected Courses of the
Academy of European Law in Florence. The Academy's mission is to
produce scholarly analyses which are at the cutting edge of the two
fields in which it works: European Union law and human rights law.
A 'general course' is given each year in each field, by a
distinguished scholar and/or practitioner, who either examines the
field as a whole through a particular thematic, conceptual or
philosophical lens, or who looks at a particular theme in the context
of the overall body of law in the field. The Academy also publishes
each year a volume of collected essays with a specific theme in each
of the two fields.

Accountability
in the European Union

CAROL HARLOW

Academy of European Law
European University Institute

OXFORD
UNIVERSITY PRESS

OXFORD
UNIVERSITY PRESS

Great Clarendon Street, Oxford OX2 6DP

Oxford University Press is a department of the University of Oxford.
It furthers the University's objective of excellence in research, scholarship,
and education by publishing worldwide in

Oxford New York

Auckland Bangkok Buenos Aires Cape Town Chennai
Dar es Salaam Delhi Hong Kong Istanbul Karachi Kolkata
Kuala Lumpur Madrid Melbourne Mexico City Mumbai Nairobi
São Paulo Shanghai Taipei Tokyo Toronto

Oxford is a registered trade mark of Oxford University Press
in the UK and in certain other countries

Published in the United States
by Oxford University Press Inc., New York

© Carol Harlow 2002

British Library Cataloguing in Publication Data
Data available

Library of Congress Cataloging in Publication Data
Data available

ISBN 0–19–924593–2 (hbk.)
ISBN 0–19–924597–5 (pbk.)

1 3 5 7 9 10 8 6 4 2

Typeset by Kolam Information Services Pvt Ltd, Pondicherry, India
Printed in Great Britain on acid-free paper by
T.J. International Ltd., Padstow, Cornwall

This book is dedicated to my children, Antony and Rhiannon, and their partners, Helen and Stephen, in token of the invariable suport they have given me through the trying period during which this book was written.

Preface

This book originated as a series of lectures at the European University Institute, given in Florence for the Academy of Law in July 2000. I owe my thanks to the Directors for giving me the opportunity to explore a subject which I have found of absorbing interest. The Academy provided a first opportunity for debating and discussing accountability and its problems with students from every EU Member State plus several of the Enlargement States. This was especially important because accountability is a concept with many meanings, differently understood, as it was to turn out, in different EU legal systems. Their linguistic skill and knowledge of other constitutional systems were, therefore, invaluable. Later, the ideas as they were developing in the book were presented at several workshops and seminars, in Hamburg, Toledo, and a valuable session in Brussels, at which Commission officials were present, organized by the European Policy Forum and British Council. In addition, I owe some of the ideas in the last chapter to the LSE European Administrative Law Group, and the discussions surrounding its Response to the Commission's White Paper on European Governance.

The Academy also provided an opportunity to publish the lectures as a short monograph with the Oxford University Press. I must record my thanks to John Louth, whose patience with the many delays, for the most part occasioned by my participation in the Research Assessment Exercise, has been exemplary. My thanks are due to many friends and colleagues for help and advice, especially: Michael Barzelay, Simon Hix, Michael Power, Richard Rawlings, Joanne Scott, Adam Tomkins. Paul Dimblebee of the NAO helped with material on audit. I have also had the help of several researchers, primarily Keith Vincent, to whom I am particularly grateful, but many thanks go also to Katie Pritchard, Stijn Smismans, and Magda Tovar-Gomis. Finally, my thanks to my secretary for many years, Elizabeth Durant.

To OUP's anonymous reviewer, I owe a particular debt. Not only did s/he struggle with an incomplete and badly presented manuscript, but s/he pointed to several omissions and corrected errors and misunderstandings of EC law. Later, s/he kindly read a re-draft of Chapters 2 and 3.

Finally, a small point concerning terminology. The term 'Community' has largely been superseded by 'European Union', legally not always correct. Wherever possible, I have used 'European Union' or 'Union' when the contrast is with the national levels of governance. In Chapter 6, which deals with the judicial system, I have adopted the term 'Community courts', in general use by lawyers, to cover the ECJ and CFI. Otherwise, I talk of the 'EU' legal system, without too much regard to technicalities.

CAROL HARLOW
Richmond on Thames
May 2002

Contents

Tables of EU Legislation and Cases

Treaty Articles

Declarations and Protocols

Primary and Secondary Legislation

Case law (listed alphabetically)

Introduction

I take a sceptic to be someone who is unwilling to go along with prevailing fashion or orthodoxy, or unquestioningly to accept the assumption that the world is round. A sceptic demands proof. She tests dogmatic assertions, asks Socratic questions, and seeks so far as possible for empirical evidence. In this sense, this tries to be a sceptical book about 'accountability' and its place in the 'governance' of the European Union.

Until recently, accountability was not a term in common use, nor did it figure as a term of art outside the financial contexts of accountancy and audit. Today, Richard Mulgan notes,[1] the word 'crops up everywhere performing all manner of analytical and rhetorical tasks and carrying most of the burdens of democratic "governance"'. Accountability regularly figures in lists of values chosen by bureaucrats and transnational bodies as essential characteristics of 'good governance'. The first chapter of this book sets out to track the various meanings of the term and its progression in the world of European governance. We shall find it again in the Commission's White Paper on European Governance,[2] where it is given a somewhat misleading and idiosyncratic interpretation.

This book aims to give accountability a proper place in the debate over European democracy and democratic deficit, dominated as this tends to be by the concepts of legitimacy and sovereignty. At this level, the public is of course concerned with the question of who makes the rules and how it can participate. Currently the preference seems to be for small-scale government, evidenced at the ballot box, where nationalism has ceased to be a dirty word. This contrasts with the preference of rulers for global and multi-national solutions, and poses problems for the legitimacy of all transnational systems of governance. It raises serious questions too about the nature and machinery

---

[1] R. Mulgan, ' "Accountability": an Ever-Expanding Concept?' (2000) 78 *Public Administration* 555.

[2] Commission White Paper on European Governance (COM(2001) 428 final [2001]) OJ C287/1.

of democratic accountability. The answers to these questions are seen as lying within the terrain of politics and constitutional law.

This book, however, is written by an administrative lawyer interested in more lowly aspects of accountability. The notorious 'Three Es' of public management[3] represent a response to popular concern over waste, inefficiency, and the apparently self-serving nature of the 'public service'. Economy, Efficiency and Effectiveness figure high on the list of qualities deemed by the general public to be important. The public wants to know how it is governed;[4] it wants in particular to know how public money is spent and to receive assurances that it has been well spent.[5] These are the managerial aspects of accountability. Nowhere did this truth emerge more clearly than during the 'Santer scandal', which led to the resignation of the Commission following an investigation into allegations of corruption and malpractice. Eurostat figures record a rise of 8 per cent in the visibility of the European Parliament in the year of this affair. A White Paper on Reform of the Commission[6] quickly followed, but, two years later, when the Santer Commission is forgotten and Santer has taken up new work as a delegate to the Constitutional Convention, all we have are promises and position papers.[7] The fall of the Santer Commission however marks the start of my personal interest in accountability in the European Union.[8]

This book originated as a set of lectures given at the European University Institute in Florence for the Academy of Law in July, 2000. With some hesitation, I have decided that their structure should be preserved. The institutional structure I adopted was easily comprehensible to the law students of many backgrounds who made up my audience. The institutional analysis is familiar to all EC lawyers, and follows the pattern also of national systems of constitutional law. For this reason, the book developed around three institutional studies of legislatures, courts, and audit systems, retained as Chapters 4, 5, and 6. Knowledge of the the Commission and machinery of EU governance was able largely to be assumed. In this book, however, a sketch of the constitutional structure and administrative machinery is necessary and will be found in Chapters 2 and 3. Chapter 2 makes an attempt

---

[3] C. Hood, 'A Public Management for All Seasons' (1991) 69 *Public Administration* 3.

[4] D. Osborne and T. Gaebler, *Reinventing Government* (New York, Addison Wesley, 1992).

[5] M. Power, *The Audit Society, Rituals of Verification* (Oxford, Oxford University Press, 1997).

[6] European Commission, *Reforming the Commission*, COM (2000) 10 final.

[7] See L. Cram, 'Whither the Commission? Reform, Renewal and the Issue Attention Cycle' (2001) 8 *Journal of European Public Policy* 770.

[8] I am grateful in this respect to my colleague and collaborator Adam Tomkins and his note on Santer: A. Tomkins, 'Responsibility and Resignation in the European Commission' (1999) 62 *MLR* 744.

at mapping the complex contours of the EU. It sketches the policy- and rule-making machinery, but only so far as is necessary to identify gaps, or potential gaps, in accountability. The Byzantine corridors of the Comitology and the growing resort to agencies are both considered. The chapter also focuses on the machinery of the Third Pillar and other areas which fall outside the standard EU machinery for accountability, where Member States co-operate on an informal basis, in this way evading democratic scrutiny. The book does look briefly at the European banking system but makes no attempt to deal with the EU external affairs or security functions. Chapter 3 deals in similar selective fashion with the Commission and its function as an organizer of administrative networks.

This somewhat traditional approach has the disadvantage of tending towards a mind-set in which Europe is seen as being in a state of flux. The Member States are moving progressively outside their statal framework, in which our modern notions of accountability were devised, towards a destination defined in statal terms: a constitutional haven of federation, perhaps, with which we are familiar and comfortable. This is an integrationist vision, which leaves little room for alternatives; in particular, the possibility that the EU will never transmute into a state or adopt statal institutions falls out of sight. The statal approach again tempts the reader to prioritize the traditional, statal forms of accountability: election, representative institutions, and the opportunities these offer for calling politicians and officials to account. Expressed in terms of legitimacy, the argument could then be made that the 'democratic deficit' is supplied by the election of a responsible government[9] or when directly elected parliamentary institutions are in place.[10] The sceptic should question this assertion, seeking assurance that the machinery functions.

It is perfectly possible, as many writers argue, that the 'Union' will remain a 'Community' of nations; a collaborative international regime comprised of nation states, whose sovereignty is recognized by the others.[11] It would then constitute the first distinctive system of 'transnational governance', and might, as with the European Convention of Human Rights, become the pattern for many more. Some theories of governance in the European Union accept this premise. In this context, the EU has been presented as a

---

[9] S. Gustavsson, 'Defending the Democratic Deficit' in A. Weale and M. Nentwich (eds.), *Political Theory and the EU, Legitimacy, Constitutional Choice and Citizenship* (London, Routledge, 1998).

[10] J. Lodge, 'The European Parliament' in S. Andersen and K. Eliassen (eds.), *The European Union: How Democratic Is It?* (London, Sage, 1996).

[11] W. Wallace, 'Less than a Federation, More than a Regime: The Community as a Political System' in H. Wallace, W. Wallace, and C. Webb (eds.), *Policy-Making in the European Community* (Chichester, John Wiley, 1983).

regulatory system,[12] or as a set of policy networks, open to a variety of different actors, public and private, at subnational, national, and transnational levels.[13] If European government is to be non-majoritarian,[14] a rather different institutional framework for accountability might be selected. Experts, functioning through the 'comitology' and variants, or perhaps inside a network of agencies co-ordinated by the Commission, would play a leading role.[15] Amongst students of regulation, horizontal or 'multi-polar' systems of accountability have been suggested.[16] The most sophisticated effort to work out such a model comes from Scott,[17] whose ideas have been used as an alternative benchmark for assessment throughout the earlier chapters of this book. Scott's theory is evaluated in the final chapter. Whole-heartedly to adopt a network theory or systems analysis of European governance would have necessitated a set of detailed sectoral case studies, covering the core competences of the European Union, along the lines suggested by the reports of the Committee of Independent Experts. This was beyond my capabilities as a social scientist.

Whether courts possess a role in ensuring accountability is a moot point. As we shall see, lawyers prefer the language of rule of law. A role for courts is usually assumed, though never defined too clearly. Some, like Majone, equate accountability with a strong system of judicial review; others, like Lord,[18] focus on the mechanics of law enforcement. I have chosen to focus on the role of the European Court of Justice in building a European legal system, but also on the principles of procedural due process. Important in classical judicial-review systems, this is becoming a neglected area of administrative law. The Community Courts have, however, made an important contribution to administrative accountability, which has impinged on the practices of EU institutions and spilt over also into national administrations.

[12] G. Majone, 'The Rise of the Regulatory State in Europe' (1994) 17 *W. European Politics* 77 and *Regulating Europe* (London, Macmillan, 1996).

[13] K.-H Ladeur, 'Towards a Legal Theory of Supranationality—The Validity of the Network Concept' (1997) 3 *European Law Journal* 33. See also W. Wessels, 'An Ever Closer Fusion? A Dynamic Macropolitical View on Integration Processes' (1997) 35 *Journal of Common Market Studies* 267; G. Marks, F. Scharpf, P. Schmitter, W. Streeck, *Governance in the European Union* (London, Sage Publications, 1996).

[14] R. Dehousse, 'Constitutional Reform in the European Community. Are there Alternatives to the Majoritarian Avenue?' (1995) 18 *W. European Politics* 118.

[15] See J. Vervaele, 'Shared Governance and Enforcement of European Law: From Comitology to a Multi-level Agency Structure' in C. Joerges and E. Vos (eds.), *EU Committees: Social Regulation, Law and Politics* (Oxford, Hart Publishing, 1999).

[16] C. Hood, 'The Hidden Public Sector: the "Quangocratization" of the World' in F.-X. Kaufmann, G. Majone, and V. Ostrom, *Guidance, Control and Evaluation in the Public Sector* (Berlin, de Gruyter, 1986).

[17] C. Scott, 'Accountability in the Regulatory State' (2000) 27 *Journal of Legal Studies* 38.

[18] C. Lord, *Democracy in the European Union* (Sheffield, Sheffield Academic Press, 1998).

The 'Santer affair' has now been demoted, though, given its significance in the mythology of the accountability, I have retained a short account as a basis for discussing the problems of the Commission in Chapter 2. It has been replaced as a subject for complaint by the supposed failures of the Nice Council and discontent with President Prodi. Hope for the future rests in the recent White Paper on European Governance, published as the final draft of this book was taking shape, in turn supplanted by the establishment of the Convention for an EU constitution which has sparked off an enthusiastic, if not always well-informed debate over the future of Europe. Over everything hangs the shadow of enlargement, a threat to accountability with which this book cannot hope to deal.

1

Thinking about Accountability

I TOWARDS A DEFINITION

Even in the British system of government where it is probably best ensconced, the terminology of accountability may be a relatively recent arrival. The term used in classic British constitutional theory is always 'responsibility', denoting the relations between Ministers of the Crown with, on the one hand, their departments and, on the other, Parliament. In the great nineteenth-century works of Dicey,[1] the idea of a 'balanced constitution' depends upon the two pillars of political responsibility of ministers to Parliament on one side and, on the other, the personal legal liability of all public officials before the ordinary courts of the land. This was Dicey's idealized vision of the Rule of Law. And however much the author may have denied it, this balance reflects Montesquieu's classical, triadic division of functions,[2] a principle which has been, and remains, influential in European constitution-making.

In a thoughtful study of accountability in the modern British constitution, Dawn Oliver describes the concept as creating:[3]

a framework for the exercise of state power in a liberal-democratic system, within which public bodies are forced to seek to promote the public interest and compelled to justify their actions in those terms or in other constitutionally acceptable terms (justice, humanity, equity); to modify policies if they should turn out to have been ill conceived; and to make amends if mistakes and errors of judgement have been made.

It is with this general conception of accountability that this book is concerned.

In Oliver's definition, however, accountability is linked both to '*state power*' and '*liberal-democratic*' systems, both ideas which, as briefly indicated

---

[1] A. V. Dicey, *Introduction to the Study of the Law of the Constitution* (10th edn. by E. C. S. Wade, London, MacMillan, 1959).

[2] M. J. C. Vile, *Constitutionalism and Separation of Powers* (Oxford, Clarendon, 1967), chap. IV.

[3] D. Oliver, *Government in the United Kingdom: The Search for Accountability, Effectiveness and Citizenship* (Milton Keynes, Open University Press, 1991), 28.

in the Introduction, may be considered unsuitable for a study of 'governance' in the EU. At a very general level, however, it must be true to say that *constitutional* debate in the western world has centred around a small number of fundamental principles which are associated with liberal democracy. For present purposes, it is pertinent that the Preamble to the Treaty of European Union confirms the attachment of the signatories to 'the principles of liberty, democracy, and respect for human rights and fundamental freedoms and the rule of law'. In slightly different phraseology, the same principles are reiterated as common provisions in TEU Article 6(1), which this time adds that the principles are 'common to the Member States'. This does not necessarily imply, however, that the terminology is to be given an identical interpretation or possesses equal resonance in every Member State that felt able to sign up to the Maastricht Treaty.[4] Given the tendency within the Treaties to make reference to common constitutional traditions and principles, it is important to bear in mind that much room is left for divergent traditions within a very general commitment to common ideals of the type listed here. It is again pertinent that this list, which could be considered to represent the constitutional state of play at the end of the twentieth century, contains no reference to accountability.

Richard Mulgan notes how 'a word which a few decades ago was used only rarely and with relatively restricted meaning (and which, interestingly, has no obvious equivalent in other European languages) now crops up everywhere performing all manner of analytical and rhetorical tasks and carrying most of the burdens of democratic "governance"'.[5] So where did the *arriviste* term come from? Accountability, alongside transparency, its *alter ego*, attained considerable resonance during the last decades of the twentieth century as values representative of popular democracy, though whether these are yet constitutional values worthy of inclusion with the more traditional liberal-democratic values mentioned in the Preamble is a moot point. Certainly, both figure high on the list of values on which the common law is said by modern Anglo-Saxon writers to be based and, as we shall see, make an appearance in codifications of such values used to promote principles of good administration.[6] It would not be unduly radical in some common law countries to describe accountability as having joined the classical constitutional trilogy of sovereignty, rule of law, and separation of powers as directive principles of constitutional law, while transparency or, more usually, freedom of

---

[4] See the country reports in J. Schwarze (ed.), *Administrative Law under European Influence* (London, Sweet & Maxwell/Nomos, 1996), at 479.

[5] R. Mulgan, ' "Accountability": An Ever-Expanding Concept?' (2000) 78 *Public Administration* 555.

[6] See, for example, M. Aronson and B. Dyer, *Judicial Review of Administrative Action* (Sydney, LBC Information Services, 1996), 1. But note that D. Oliver, 'The Underlying Values of Public and Private Law' in M. Taggart (ed.), *The Province of Administrative Law*

information, is a highly rated constitutional value in several European constitutions, notably that of Sweden, where it dates back to the Swedish Constitution of 1766.

What are we to understand by 'accountability'? Is it a term of art with a
semblance of fixed meaning or is it, as Mulgan suggests, a catch-all term,
beloved of the media, its use to castigate modern governments for their many
failures? *Democratic* accountability is a term familiar in political science, and
one with considerable resonance in western society. This is a simple definition of accountability in terms of suffrage: the principle according to which
it is possible to replace the holders of political office through general elections. In this sense, accountability is the framework of government and
precondition for all democratic rule. As Christopher Lord observes,[7] 'it is
political responsibility that ensures that the terms on which political power is
authorized are duly observed; and it is the need for power-holders to compete
for re-election that gives them an incentive to be responsive to the public'.
This definition does not in practice take us much further. In the present
context, indeed, it implies on the one hand that the European Union can
never be accountable unless and until we move to an elected government or,
on the other, that the installation of an elected government is the panacea for
accountability deficits. Such an interpretation would invite a rerun of the
somewhat sterile 'sovereignty' debate over the democratic deficit and the
European Parliament.[8]

Dawn Oliver also prioritizes political accountability, though admitting
that 'it is not as effective as it should be'.[9] Political accountability is premised
on representation; it exposes its subjects 'to politically motivated control, to
public censure through elected institutions'.[10] 'Public accountability' is defined somewhat traditionally by Oliver in terms of the ballot box and
representation rather than in terms of transparency (a term admittedly only
just beginning to make its mark when she wrote), while the role of the press
or media in providing access to information, making it the central institution
for assuring accountability to the public, is seriously discounted in her study.

As already noted, Oliver views accountability as essentially public in
character, accepting the intrinsic connection with 'the exercise of state
power'; there is, for example, no discussion of any possible need to hold

---

(Oxford, Hart Publishing, 1997), 225, does not list accountability as one of the five key values
of public law (autonomy, dignity, respect, status, and security), although she takes Nolan's
'Seven Principles of Public Life' (n. 23 below), where it is listed, as her starting point.

   [7] C. Lord, *Democracy in the European Union.* (Sheffield, Sheffield Academic Press,
1998), 80.

   [8] S. Williams, 'Sovereignty and Accountability in the European Community' (1990) 61
Political Quarterly 299.

   [9] Oliver, n. 3 above, 24.

   [10] Ibid., at 23.

private corporate bodies accountable. This discounts the role and steady advance of regulation as a technique for ensuring accountability in modern public law. It might also undercut Majone's view of the European Union as a vehicle for safeguarding accountability through regulation. In many areas of EU activity, accountability at national level has arguably been increased through the EU's standard-setting activities, used to bring multi-national corporations to account.[11] More controversially, Oliver classifies 'consumer accountability' under the head of 'public accountability',[12] though even to include the term was, at the date she wrote, an innovation. The direct participatory rights of citizens (e.g., parents as school governors) are grouped together with the rights of sections of the public as consumers of public services under devices such as Citizens' Charters, then just coming into fashion in the United Kingdom. These two types of right are, however, clearly separable. Rights of participation are democratic in character and relate to representative democracy, though they may seek to modify its forms. True consumer accountability is derived from the market and is essentially a means whereby individuals seek redress on their own behalf. It may of course be translated into a hierarchical tool of the so-called 'New Public Management' and be used to secure the effectiveness and better operation of public services. Yet Oliver groups much of the new scrutiny machinery, including the machinery for audit, in her fourth class of 'administrative accountability'. In these respects, her analysis begins to look outdated.

Oliver gives further body to her concept of accountability when she says that it 'has been said to entail being liable to be required to give an account or explanation of actions and, where appropriate, to suffer the consequences, take the blame or undertake to put matters right if it should appear that errors have been made. In other words, it is explanatory and amendatory'.[13] This definition has three main elements, though the last two are conflated: explanation or the giving of an account, blame and censure, and redress. This seems to borrow from the traditional constitutional notion of ministerial responsibility. It overlaps also with Hood's definition of 'control' as the 'periodic checking and examination of the activities of public officials by external actors possessed of formal or constitutional authority to investigate, to grant *quietus* or to censure, and in some cases even to punish'.[14] Here again, we find the elements of explanation, the giving of an account, together with insistence on censure, blame, and punishment. There is too the sense of absolution and closure. Both writers see accountability as essentially

---

[11] C. Scott, 'Accountability in the Regulatory State' (2000) 27 *Journal of Legal Studies* 38.

[12] Oliver, n. 3 above, 24.

[13] Ibid, at 22.

[14] C. Hood, 'The Hidden Public Sector: The "Quangocratization" of the World' in F.-X. Kaufmann, G. Majone, and V. Ostrom, *Guidance, Control and Evaluation in the Public Sector* (Berlin, de Gruyter, 1986), 766–7.

retrospective, and Hood makes explicit reference to externality. There is a link here with Mulgan, who adds as part of the 'core sense' of accountability, 'rights of authority', by which he means that external actors are 'asserting rights of superior authority over those who are accountable, including the rights to demand answers and to impose sanctions'.[15] We can perhaps conclude that accountability does contain elements of authority, such as is found in the classical doctrine of parliamentary sovereignty, and externality. Hierarchy, an alternative to external control is, on the other hand, more evident as a feature of *managerial* control, further discussed below.

Although control may be very close to accountability, the terms are not entirely synonymous. If, indeed, the primary element in accountability is the giving of an account or explanation, then it must be essentially retrospective.[16] This suggests that, in its financial sense, the term would cover book-keeping and audit rather than the setting of budgetary targets. Only an extended definition of accountability can embrace the notion of control through rules and the rule-making process. I have, however, argued elsewhere that standard-setting is a vital element in the process of securing accountability.[17] In this book, I shall hold to this expansive usage, giving accountability a prospective dimension to embody the 'fire-watching' function of legislation and regulation.[18] A similar idea is implicit in Oliver's description of accountability as 'a framework for the exercise of state power', within which public bodies are forced to justify their actions. Oliver has remarked[19] that 'accountability cannot be effectively imposed if the criteria against which conduct is to be measured in the process of calling to account are not made clear', a formulation which suggests that, if standards, values, and principles are not contained in the notion of accountability, then at the very least they are an essential aspect of its context, setting in place the framework against which political and administrative actors are judged. Standards, principles, and rules create the framework for evaluation of administrative policies and decisions, while those who make the rules are rendered accountable as much by the structure of procedural requirements for rule-making as by the political and electoral processes. Here there is a strong parallel with the argument that administrative law can, through the imposition of procedural controls,

---

[15] Mulgan, n. 5 above, 555.

[16] C. Scott, 'Accountability in the Regulatory State' (2000) 27 *Journal of Law and Society* 38, 39.

[17] C. Harlow, 'Accountability, New Public Management, and the Problem of the Child Support Agency' (1999) 26 *Journal of Legal Studies* 150.

[18] C. Harlow and R. W. Rawlings, *Law and Administration* (2nd edn., London, Butterworths, 1997), 75–8.

[19] D. Oliver, 'Standards of Conduct in Public Life—What Standards?' [1995] *PL* 497.

contribute a democratic element to governance. This is an argument rooted in participatory rather than representative democracy.[20] The development of procedures by which this can be achieved is an important function of modern administrative law, discussed further in Chapter 6. In the EU, where a *representative* democratic deficit is perceived to exist, the idea that representation needs supporting and may be buttressed by the techniques of administrative law has value. Concepts of participatory democracy also play an important part in legitimating the concepts of 'governance' and 'policy networks' being developed as a framework of analysis by the Commission.[21]

Standard-setting has always been an important element in governance as conceived by the European Commission, and recently its interest in the technique has grown. This development follows the reports of the Committee of Independent Experts set up to advise the European Parliament on mal-administration within the Commission.[22] Dismayed by the apparent reluctance among the members of the Commission hierarchy to acknowledge their responsibilities, the Experts set out to establish standards of 'personal integrity and good conduct' as a framework inside which Commission public servants would operate. The hoped-for effect would be a more homogeneous administrative culture for the multicultural Commission. The starting point was the work of the Nolan Committee on Standards in Public Life, set up in 1994 by the United Kingdom Government to 'examine current concerns about standards of conduct of all holders of public office'. In its first report the Nolan Committee listed seven principles of public life seen as essential to all public office-holding. Alongside the personal qualities of selflessness, integrity, objectivity, honesty, and leadership, we find listed accountability and openness or transparency. Nolan defines accountability as meaning that '[h]olders of public office are accountable for their decisions and actions to the public and must subject themselves to what ever scrutiny is appropriate to their office'. Openness is said to require that '[h]olders of public office should be as open as possible about all the decisions and actions that they take. They

---

[20] See further P. Craig, 'Democracy and Rule-making within the EC: An Empirical and Normative Assessment', in P. Craig and C. Harlow (eds.), *Lawmaking in the European Union.* (Kluwer, 1998) and 'The Nature of the Community: Integration, Democracy, and Legitimacy', in P. Craig and G. de Búrca (eds.), *The Evolution of EU Law* (Oxford, Oxford University Press, 1999).

[21] European Commission, White Paper on European Governance (COM(2001)428 final), fully discussed in Chap. 7.

[22] Committee of Independent Experts, *First Report on Allegations Regarding Fraud, Mismanagement and Nepotism in the European Commission.* (Brussels, 15 Mar. 1999), and *Second Report on Reform of the Commission—Analysis of Current Practice and Proposals for Tackling Mismanagement, Irregularities and Fraud* (Brussels, 10 Sept. 1999). And see below, Chap. 3.

should give reasons for their decisions and restrict information only when the wider public interest clearly so demands'.[23]

The term 'transparency' seems to be a piece of market jargon which has, however, largely replaced the vocabulary of openness and freedom of information traditional in discussions of government and public law. The Nolan list of values links the two concepts of transparency and accountability, a common juxtaposition. Council of Europe programmes, for example, stress the need for a 'transparent and open' decision-making process. The European Ombudsman has also emphasized the need for 'democratic, *transparent* and accountable administration' in the EU.

Deirdre Curtin, probably the most powerful academic advocate of transparency amongst EU constitutionalists, treats transparency as a value in its own right, arguing that a 'public right to know' is a precondition for a mature system of democracy. Her approach links transparency and *citizenship* rather than transparency and *accountability*,[24] and reflects concern over the weakness of civil society at Union level. It can, however, be cogently argued that the lack of a strong civil society in the EU is not only a key factor in 'democracy deficit',[25] but also has an extremely negative impact on the arrangements for accountability. In this manner, political accountability is not to be confined to electoral accountability or inside representative institutions but extends also to a continual process of 'giving an account' to an informed and active civic society. In other words, public democratic accountability of this type forms the all-important framework of values inside which formal machinery for accountability operates most effectively. It also helps to form the sense of political and ethical responsibility for which the Nolan Committee argued. The knowledge of democratic accountability thus underlies all public-service accountability. The participatory democracy favoured by Curtin is, however, designed to control *policy outcomes*. It is therefore *prospective* in character and forms an element in participatory or deliberative democracy rather than offering only the *retrospective* satisfaction of an explanation after the event. Yet retrospectivity was earlier identified as the hallmark of accountability. When, however, Curtin insists that 'a right to public

[23] Lord Nolan, *First Report of the Committee on Standards in Public Life*, Cm 2850, (London, HMSO, 1995), 14.

[24] D. Curtin, 'Betwixt and Between: Democracy and Transparency in the Governance of the European Union' in J. Winter *et al.*, *Reforming the Treaty of European Union—The Legal Debate* (The Hague, Kluwer, 1996); D. Curtin, *Postnational Democracy, The European Union in Search of a Political Philosophy* (The Hague, Kluwer Law International, 1997) and D. Curtin, 'Democracy, Transparency and Political Participation' in V. Deckmyn and I. Thomson (eds.), *Openness and Transparency in the European Union* (Maastricht: EIPA, Deckmyn & Thomson, 1998).

[25] D. Chryssochoou, 'Europe's Could-be Demos: Recasting the Debate' (1996) 19 *W. European Politics* 787.

knowledge of government deliberations, albeit a qualified one, is ... necessary for effective democratic control',[26] it is 'fire-watching' rather than the retrospective 'fire-fighting' function to which she refers. Only occasionally does Curtin cross the line, and then hesitantly, to draw on accountability and scrutiny as justifications for transparency, as when she remarks that 'without an adequate flow of information even *ex post facto* accountability of the governors to the people is meaningless'.[27]

In contrast, Jacques Ziller has argued that transparency is a relative good, closely related to the model of government in which it operates.[28] Information regimes are highly functional, lending support to, and drawing support from, the systems of government which surround them. He presents European systems of government as falling into two distinct groups. The first, hierarchical model is that developed in France and Prussia during the nineteenth century (though Ziller accepts that today such regimes are normally modified by input from parliamentary institutions). Here official secrecy is the rule, access to government information being both exceptional and controlled. Secrecy operates to lend support to the hierarchical controls and the doctrines of political responsibility on which these systems rely for accountability. In Ziller's second, or 'Swedish', paradigm, open government is the paramount constitutional value. In the decentralized Swedish system, where local administration and government agencies possess a strong measure of autonomy, accountability is dependent on openness and public awareness, with the media assuming a crucial information function. In this decentralized system, transparency serves both a prospective, participatory, policy-making function and a significant retrospective, accountability role. Somewhat pessimistically, Ziller concludes that the two models of European administration are largely incompatible, and that attempts to meld them are likely to fail. This is not a view likely to recommend itself to the European Commission.

II RESPONSIBILITY, ACCOUNTABILITY, AND LIABILITY

The emphasis so far on Oliver's work should not suggest a British monopoly of accountability. The constitutional principles of the European Union have to be drawn from the common stock of the Member States' traditions. Her definition is of interest, however, because it seems to epitomize a moment of transition between classical theories of political responsibility and the moment when we begin to see responsibility transmuted or partially

---

[26] Curtin, 'Betwixt and Between', n. 24 above, 392.

[27] Curtin, 'Betwixt and Between', n. 24 above, 95.

[28] J. Ziller, 'European Models of Government: Towards a Patchwork with Missing Pieces' (2000) 54 *Parliamentary Affairs* 102.

replaced by the new terminology of 'accountability'.[29] Mulgan suggests, however, that he can find no exact equivalent in the European literature for the term 'accountability',[30] a finding which might suggest that the significant semantic transition from 'responsibility' to 'accountability' has not occurred or is incomplete in other European systems. If this were so, it would help to explain both the apparent lack of interest in the concept in institutional studies of the EU and the failure to come to grips with the problem of holding public bodies accountable at Union level. There is some support for this standpoint. Pierre Avril suggests[31] that Italian, Spanish, and French, all need to borrow the English word if they wish to indicate '*la responsabilité des gouvernants devant le peuple, au double sens de lui rendre compte et de tenir compte de lui*'. Here we find three terms used to replicate the cluster of ideas supposedly contained within Oliver's notion of public accountability: the classical '*responsabilité*'; the verb '*rendre compte*', used in the sense of 'account for', and '*tenir compte de*' in the sense of 'take into account'. Avril believes that it 'is not by chance' that the French language possesses no exact equivalent to accountability, and explains the different usages by reference to sharply differing attitudes to Parliament in the two neighbouring societies:[32]

Il faut se rappeler que le parlementisme française avait toujours pratiqué une conception tres particulière de la democratie, selon laquelle le role des électeurs se limitait strictement à la nomination des representants lesquels étaient entièrement libres de leur comportement car ils s'identifiaient au peuple qu'ils representatient et qui n'avait donc plus droit à la participation.

This passage falls back on the least demanding definition of democratic accountability in terms of the right to choose a government and is also tantamount to saying that the French parliament possesses no real scrutiny function, a question which arises in respect of other national parliaments, and is examined in some detail in Chapter 4. Classical English theory also sees the parliamentary representative as free-standing and autonomous, but this has proved no barrier to the imposition of ministerial responsibility. Surprisingly, however, other French authors take a similar stance. Christian Bidegaray calls responsibility 'an English invention', bound up with the character of the

---

[29] A few years earlier, a pioneering British study of regulation by lawyers had used the terms 'control' and 'accountability' interchangeably, suggesting that the transition was then incomplete: see R. Baldwin and C. McCrudden (eds.), *Regulation and Public Law* (London, Weidenfeld and Nicolson, 1987), 35–45. Compare N. Lewis, 'Regulating Non-Government Bodies: Privatization, Accountability, and the Public-Private Divide' in J. Jowell and D. Oliver (eds.), *The Changing Constitution* (2nd. edn., Oxford, Oxford University Press, 1989).

[30] N. 5 above.

[31] P. Avril, 'Les Fabriques des politiques' in N. Wahl and J.-L. Quermonne (eds.), *La France presidentielle*, (Paris, Presses de la FNSP, 1995), 65.

[32] Ibid.

British parliamentary system.[33] Olivier Béaud, on the other hand, equates '*responsabilité*' with the English term 'accountability', though he suggests that the implications of neither term are well understood in France.[34] In contrast, Philippe Segur is clear that the term '*responsabilité*' implies, and always has implied, '*l'obligation pour les gouvernants de répondre devant le Parlement des actes accomplis dans l'exercice de leurs fonctions selon une procedure determinée par la Constitution*'.[35] This is perhaps surprising in a country where the 1789 Declaration of the Rights of Man affirms that '*Le societé a le droit de demander compte à tout agent public de son administration*'. This affirmation did not, however, prevent the celebrated Law of 16–24 August 1790 from prohibiting 'judges of the ordinary courts' from 'interfering in any manner whatsoever' with the administration and from 'calling to account' administrators in respect of the exercise of official functions.[36] Other Latin countries find the same difficulty with translation. An Italian author, describing the changing nature of governmental responsibility to parliament and to the electorate in post-war Italy, draws a distinction between the terms 'responsibility' and 'accountability', but retains the English words.[37] In Dutch and Flemish again, the term '*verantwoordelijkheid*' (literally, responsibility) is used to indicate political responsibility of ministers to parliament. In the Netherlands, the concept of ministerial responsibility is strongly recognized.

Two deductions follow from this imperfect survey. The first is that the terminology of accountability is not in use everywhere and, when it is found, is often an English import. The second, is that some element of political responsibility is acknowledged to be an essential element of the relationship between governors and governed, and that parliaments play some part in the relationship, normally through a process in which an explanation is offered by the government to a representative assembly. The way in which that explanation is exacted, and the terms on which it is offered may, however, differ very greatly in different systems. This is a point to be borne in mind in later chapters when considering the role of national parliaments and the

[33] C. Bidegary, 'Le principe de responsabilité fondement de la democratie' in Special Issue, 'La Responsabilité des Gouvernants' (2000) 92, *Pouvoirs*, 7. And see C. Bidegary and C. Emeri, *La responsabilité politique* (Paris, Dalloz, 1998).

[34] O. Béaud, 'La responsabilité politique face à la concurrence d'autres formes de responsabilité des gouvernants' in Special Issue, 'La Responsabilité des Gouvernants', n. 33 above, 23.

[35] P. Segur, *La responsabilité politique* (Paris, PUF, 1997), 17. Segur cites in support the classic constitutional text of A. Esmein, *Elements de droit constituionnel français et comparé*. (Paris, Larose, 1899), 572.

[36] Note in this context that L. Neville Brown and J. Bell, *French Administrative Law* (4th edn., Oxford, Oxford University Press, 1993), 43 use the phrase 'call to account' to translate the historical French '*citer devant eux*'.

[37] A. Manzella, 'La transition institutionnelle' in S. Cassese (ed.), *Portrait de l'Italie actuelle* (Paris, La documentation française, 2001), 61.

European Parliament respectively in closing the accountability gap created by upward delegation of functions.

III LEGAL ACCOUNTABILITY?

In French, however, the word '*responsabilité*' carries a double sense of legal 'liability', terms which English tends to distinguish, except perhaps in the case of criminal responsibility. This raises an important and difficult point about the role of courts in securing accountability.

Béaud describes in France a popular desire to substitute legal for political responsibility.[38] Segur explains the trend as originating in popular distrust of a corporatist system of government, in which politicians and administrators are seen as interlocked and wholly supportive of each other.[39] In such a system, responsibility can be passed from politicians to public servants as and when convenient, a shuffling off of responsibility for which modern systems of governance have created and accentuated the many opportunities (for example, by the introduction of agencies and other semi-autonomous bodies). To secure true accountability, the introduction of a neutral third party (the judge) is perceived as necessary. This intervention may take place in several ways. Béaud in fact talks specifically of penal liability as appropriate to supply the element of blame, censure, and sanction for which the public looks. He instances the celebrated *affaire du sang contaminé*, where haemophiliacs were infected by routine blood transfusions with blood infected with the HIV virus. Here it was the *criminal* courts to which the public turned to enforce the accountability of the medical director and the French Prime Minister of the day, Laurent Fabius.[40] Though ultimately unsuccessful, the prosecution entailed a major innovation, the stripping from ministers of parliamentary privilege and immunity from the courts. A formal complaint was also lodged with the prosecution authorities asking for a criminal investigation to be opened against officials of the French state after deaths from Creutzfeldt-Jakob disease sparked off a panic over controls on French beef.[41] The obligation of President Chirac to account to criminal courts for improper use of public funds for private purposes became a *cause célèbre* and featured in a presidential election. Liability was at first imposed by a French court, though an appeal court reversed the decision.[42] According to Jean-Bernard

---

[38] Béaud, n. 34 above, 18.

[39] Segur, n. 35 above, 28.

[40] M. DeGoffre, 'La responsabilité penale du ministre pour fait d'autrui' [1998] *Revue de droit public* 433. And see O. Béaud, *Le sang contaminé. Essai critique sur la criminalisation de la responsabilité des gouvernants* (Paris, PUF, 1999).

[41] Reported in *The Times*, 7 Nov. 2000.

[42] *The Times*, 5 July 2001 and 11 Oct. 2001.

Auby, even in France, with its celebrated system of administrative justice charged with control of the public service, public servants are more afraid of the criminal court than the administrative judge.[43] Such developments are not confined to France. In Italy, where judicial independence is protected by the Constitution and judicial appointments are in the hands of an independent Council of the Judiciary, a similar trend is evident. It is widely believed that, given the phenomenon of political coalition, only the intervention of an apolitical judiciary can secure any measure of personal accountability. In the Italian Tangentopoli prosecutions, the revelation of widespread corruption in successive governments and the political classes led to the substitution of prosecutions for political responsibility. In Italy, however, the Chamber of Deputies refused to lift the immunity of the Socialist leader, Bettino Craxi.[44] A similar stance was taken when threats to prosecute Premier Berlusconi in respect of pecuniary impropriety were heard.

In countries with strong systems of public law, law stands at the centre of the constitutional system of accountability, and equal, or even greater, trust is placed in courts than parliaments. Constitutional courts play an active role in standard-setting and maintaining values. They also 'police the boundaries of the constitution', holding governments accountable within its frame. The post-war German constitution affords a good example.[45] As we shall see, these are all roles developed by the European Court of Justice. In France and countries where a French system of administrative law was adopted, account-ability is largely a function of the Council of State and not of civil courts. Whether, as in England, the power is exercised by what Dicey famously termed the 'ordinary' courts or, as in France, by special administrative courts, is largely immaterial to the present debate, though it may affect the degree of control actually exercised by courts. Where the emphasis lies in any system is largely explicable in terms of history and culture, though the relationship is always dynamic and liable to change over time.

Sometime in the nineteenth century the term 'control' lost its close link to financial audit and entered the standard vocabulary of administrative law. In modern legal systems, 'control' and 'liability' have been separated, the former being reserved for the public-law power to review the legality of

[43] J.-B. Auby, 'La bataille de San Romano, Refléxions sur les évolutions récentes du droit adminisrtif', *AJDA*. 20 Nov. 2001, at 912, 919.

[44] S. Waters, ' "Tangentopoli" and the Emergence of a New Political Order in Italy' (1994) 17 *W. European Politics* 169; D. Nelken, 'A Legal Revolution? The Judges and Tangentopoli' in S. Grundle and S. Parker (eds.), *The New Italian Republic: From the Fall of the Berlin Wall to Berlusconi*. (London, Routledge, 1996).

[45] K. von Beyme, 'The Genesis of Constitutional Review in Parliamentary Systems' in C. Landfried (ed.), *Constitutional Review and Legislation*. (Baden-Baden, Nomos, 1998). More generally on the role of constitutional courts see A. Stone Sweet, 'Constitutional Politics: The Reciprocal Impact of Lawmaking and Constitutional Adjudication', in Craig and Harlow (eds.), n. 20 above.

administrative action possessed by modern courts. Classic French administrative law speaks of *contrôle juridictionnel de l'administration*, where English law uses the less compelling term 'judicial review'. In Italian, the appropriate term is again '*controllo*', significantly used by Girolamo Strozzi[46] to describe the competence of the European Court of Justice. The same pattern is found in Belgium and the Netherlands, where 'control' is the term most prominent in public-law texts, used impartially to cover financial, political, and legal control.[47] '*Aansprakelijkheid*' and '*overheidsaansprakelijkheid*' both denote accountability, but are generally reserved for legal accountability for maladministration.[48] Whatever the terminology and whichever court has jurisdiction, we can notice in every European jurisdiction how control has developed rapidly during the last century, a tendency notably heightened through the development of EC law as a transnational legal order distinct from international law, with its own strong and distinctive court in the ECJ.

IV AUDIT, ACCOUNTABILITY, AND 'NEW PUBLIC MANAGEMENT'

Christopher Hood has made a semantic link between 'accountability' and 'comptrol', which he describes as 'deeply embedded in the European tradition of constitutional (limited) government and formal public accountability in financial affairs'.[49] His resort to this spelling, traceable to the medieval period, reflects the audit usage preserved in the ancient English office of Auditor and Comptroller-General, an officer of the House of Commons responsible for auditing the accounts of government departments and other public bodies. The usage is, however, replicated in the French term '*Cour des Comptes*' and the Italian use of the term '*controllo contabile*' to describe the powers of the '*Corte dei Conti*'.[50] The same usage is adopted by Giuseppe Cogliandro who, in an article devoted to 'the controls' of the

---

[46] G. Strozzi, 'L'Istituzioni dell'Unione Europea' in M. Chiti and G. Greco (eds.), *Trattato di Diritto Amministrativo Europeo* (Milan, Giuffré, 1997), Parte Generale, 132. P. Piva, 'An Introduction to Italian Public Law' (1995) 2 *European Public Law* 299, 300 translates control as 'regulate'.

[47] E.g., J. Dujardin and J.V. Lanotte, *Inleiding tot the publiek recht: Basisbegrippen* (Bruges, Die Keure, 1994); F. Stroink, *Algemee Bestuursrecht. Een inleiding* (Zwolle, WEJ Tjeenk Willink, 1996), uses the phrases '*toezicht op bestuursorganen*' and '*controle op het bestuur*'.

[48] W. Lambrechts, *Geschillen van bestuur* (Antwerp, Kluwer, 1998); H. Van Wijk and W. Konijnenbelt, *Hoofdstukken van administratief recht* ('s-Gravenhage, Vuga, 1984). I am grateful to Stijn Smismans of the EUI for help on this point.

[49] Hood, n. 14 above.

[50] Strozzi, n. 46 above, at 125–6.

European system of administration, writes almost exclusively of financial control and audit.[51]

Over the last two decades, the English-speaking world has witnessed a transformation of the traditional book-keeping function implicit in the terms 'audit' and 'comptrol', in which audit is seen primarily as a protection against corruption, waste, and the illegal disbursement of public funds. The introduction of the term 'value for money audit' signifies a wider and more rounded form of accountability which, as with regulation and rule-making, is at once prospective and retrospective. Value for money (VFM) audit permits auditors to step outside the numerical framework of traditional audit and to construct standards of 'quality' and 'performance' by which operators will be judged, as well as to monitor their effective implementation.[52] Briefly, 'VFM' audit substitutes the *quantifiable* criteria of financial accountability for *policy-oriented* standards of performance and effectiveness. These penetrate the policy-making process, surfacing as performance indicators. The British Citizens' Charter programme is, for example, replete with performance indicators, which range from 'accuracy targets' in the payment of welfare benefits to 'waiting time targets' for the health service and police.[53] The standards may themselves be derived from audit—as where a survey of mean performance of a given local authority service is conducted and used to establish performance indicators across the country or region and then, at a later stage, enforced through audit. In this way, public audit can rapidly evolve from a simple accounting function into a proactive system capable of being used as a transmission-belt for the key values of central management. As described by the leading theoretician,[54] the term audit today 'symbolises a cluster of values: independent validation, efficiency, rationality, visibility almost irrespective of the mechanics of the practice and, in the final analysis, the promise of control'. If it is true, as the author goes on to suggest, that 'these apparent virtues have come together to make audit a central part of the "reinvention of government"',[55] then Power's inclusive definition renders accountability and audit almost synonymous. Together with regulation, value for money audit has come to be seen as a central feature of the management revolution which has, in the last decade of the twentieth century, changed the way in which public services are administered throughout the English-speaking world,.

That the British governmental system has experienced a steep rise in regulation and audit as techniques of accountability is due to the radical

---

[51] G. Cogliandri, 'I Controlli', in Chiti and Greco, n. 46 above.

[52] See for an introduction J. Stewart and K. Walsh, 'Change in the Management of Public Service' (1992) 70 *Public Administration* 498, 505. And see Chap. 5, below.

[53] See N. Lewis, 'The Citizen's Charter and Next Steps: A New Way of Governing?' (1993) 64 *Political Quarterly* 316.

[54] M. Power, *The Audit Explosion*. (London, Demos, 1994), 17.

[55] Ibid.

and reforming government of Margaret Thatcher, who introduced into the public services of the United Kingdom a culture of accountability through financial responsibility and 'New Public Management'. NPM was born in the United States, a by-product of market economics and of public-choice theory. It allows state or public-service activities to be conceptualized in terms of market[56] and informs the expectations that citizens, described in the rhetoric of NPM as consumers, have of their public services. There is a close resemblance between Power's definition of audit and Christopher Hood's summary of the components of NPM.[57] Hood lists as important elements in NPM: hands-on professional management, explicit standards and measures of performance, rewards linked to measured performance, control and parsimony in the use of resources, disaggregation of public-sector systems and institutions, open competition and private-sector management styles. An 'audit society' has effectively been installed, and its regulatory and numerical values are fast outstripping the values of law and parliamentary democracy in providing standards of accountability. The United Kingdom, the only Member State to undergo a sustained period of right-wing government firmly committed to market ideology inside and outside government,[58] leads the field inside Europe in the new management ideology.

NPM is much concerned with accountability; indeed, this is probably how the phrase has come into common use in English. Vincent Wright, writing for a French audience,[59] found difficulty in finding a suitable vocabulary to express the management revolution within the public service. He spoke of '*la mise en place d'un système d'évaluation ex post quantifié et externe*' and talked of replacement of the classic British system by '*un état évaluateur*'. In an era of concern with the growing expense of the welfare state, few European governments have altogether escaped the embrace of NPM, while globalization of issues of public management and policy design has taken the process further, manifesting itself in international codes of practice, disseminated under the auspices of international bodies like the World Bank, OECD, or Council of Europe. Interest in standard-setting has then seeped back into management discourse within the EU, notably through the Report of the Independent Experts, perhaps a foreseeable tendency in an organization whose main administrative output is regulatory.

[56] See further Harlow and Rawlings, n. 18 above, 130–1.
[57] C. Hood, 'Public Management for All Seasons' (1991) 69 *Public Administration* 3.
[58] D. King, *The New Right, Politics, Markets and Citizenship* (Basingstoke, Macmillan, 1987). On the spread of NPM in Europe, see D. Farnham, S. Hodson, J. Barlow, and A. Hondeghem (eds.), *The New Public Managers in Europe: Public Servants in Transition* (Basingstoke, Macmillan, 1996). And see Chap. 3 below.
[59] V. Wright, 'Le cas britannique: le démantelement de l'administration traditionnnelle' in L. Rouban and J. Ziller (eds.), Special Issue, 'Les Administrations en Europe: D'une Modernisation à l'Autre' (1995) 75 *AJDA* 355, 361.

By managers, however, the concept of accountability is given a very different emphasis from that which it would receive amongst public lawyers or even politicians. Their type of managerial accountability is radically different from the political accountability considered earlier in this chapter; indeed, Hood has suggested that it depends on different values.[60] Where both political and legal responsibility are external in character, management accountability is hierarchical and internal to the organization,[61] though usually buttressed by the external accountability of audit. Again, political and legal responsibility are primarily retrospective (though the standard-setting functions of courts and legislatures have also been noted). Audit too started its life as largely retrospective, although it has now assumed an extensive standard-setting function through the policy-making possibilities of VFM audit. The modern managerial objective is, in short, total, 'before and after', supervisory control.

The public dimension of NPM accountability is conceived in terms of 'stakeholders'.[62] Internal stakeholders comprise staff and management; external stakeholders comprise sections of the public, such as taxpayers or customers. One way, albeit negative, of achieving accountability to external stakeholders is through complaints procedures, ombudsmen, and the ubiquitous citizens' charter, which tend to replace, in NPM thinking, formal dispute-resolution by and accountability to courts. Nevertheless, by prioritizing complaint, the stakeholder perspective tends to put the stress on legal accountability, setting in train a process of 'juridification', whereby law sets the framework for public bodies, while its interpretation also devolves ultimately on courts.[63] Alternatively, 'outwards' public accountability may be drawn more widely, owed to the public at large, and conceived in terms of a 'responsive' public service.[64] (The OECD, for example, has used responsiveness and accountability as synonymous terms.[65])

The relationship between these new conceptions of managerial accountability and the more traditional doctrines of political responsibility may in practice prove uneasy. Designed in part to establish political control of administration, they may in practice, through a process of agencification and quasi-privatization, end by facilitating a dilution of the classic political

---

[60] Hood, n. 57 above.

[61] P. Day and R. Klein, *Accountabilities; Five Public Services* (London, Tavistock, 1987), 26.

[62] D. Farnham and S. Horton, 'Public Managers and Private Managers; Towards a Professional Synthesis?' in D. Farnham *et al* (eds.), n. 58 above, 33.

[63] C. Scott, 'The Juridification of Regulatory Relations in the UK Utilities Sectors' in J. Black, P. Muchlinski, and P. Walker (eds.), *Commercial Regulation and Judicial Review* (Oxford, Hart Publishing, 1998).

[64] The message of the management classic: D. Osborne and T. Gaebler, *Reinventing Government* (New York, Addison Wesley, 1992).

[65] OECD, *Administration as Service: The Public as Client* (Paris, OECD, 1987).

doctrine. In the UK 'Next Steps Programme', for example, ministers were intended to retain responsibility for policy, while managers at the head of executive agencies would take on responsibility for execution or operation.[66] The justification for the supervisory role retained by ministers lay in their political responsibility to Parliament. But the separation of managerial from political responsibility created an opportunity for responsibility in the full sense of the word to be downloaded to managers, as politicians learned to distinguish 'responsibility' and 'accountability', with a view to evading the blame and censure referred to in the definitions of 'control' and 'accountability' cited earlier. In the United Kingdom, where the hiving off of many central government functions to agencies facilitated the slippage, the argument was seriously advanced that full ministerial responsibility, carrying the sanction of censure and resignation, should arise only where the *personal involvement* of a minister could be shown; accountability, on the other hand, would indicate no more than a ministerial obligation to 'give an account' of the department's performance to Parliament and the public, an altogether weaker meaning— weaker, incidentally, than that implied by the French phrase '*rendre compte*'. This novel meaning was firmly rejected by a Select Committee of the UK House of Commons.[67] A similar dilution of traditional forms of political responsibility is discernible in the response of the Santer Commission to review by the Independent Experts. It too sought to distinguish political from administrative responsibility, retaining only a *collective* Commission responsibility for policy- and decision-making and downloading to Direct-ors-General the responsibility for implementation of policies, maladminis-tration, and lesser administrative errors. As with the House of Commons, this unworkable separation of functions did not go unchallenged by the Experts. Asserting that 'it should not be stretched too far', the Experts insisted that Commissioners must 'continuously seek to be informed about the acts and omissions of the directorates-general for which they bear responsi-bility.'[68]

Severance of political responsibility from administrative accountability is a serious hazard of modern government, part and parcel of a tendency to pass responsibility from politicians to public servants. Attractive as this is to politicians, it may ironically be equally attractive to managers and adminis-trators, because it seems to support the idea of agency or managerial auton-omy. New conceptions of managerial accountability associated with audit and NPM are then brought into play to fill the gap left by the decline of

---

[66] C. Harlow, 'Next Steps Agencies and Problems of Accountability' (1999) 4 *Rivista trimestrale di diritto publico* 1086.

[67] Public Service Committee, 'Ministerial Accountability and Responsibility', HC 813 (1995/6), para. 170. See also A. Tomkins, *The Constitution After Scott* (Oxford, OUP, 1998), 59–63.

[68] Committee of Independent Experts, *First Report*, n. 22 above, para. 9.3.4.

political responsibility. In practice, however, the political accountability deficit is not so easy to fill—hence the tendency, noted earlier in this chapter, for the public to press for criminal sanctions and enforcement through the legal process. Heightened managerial accountability may also bring into play a further ratchet effect, whereby policy-making is so tightly controlled that it becomes impossible for the policy-maker effectively to carry out its regulatory and policy-making functions. This is a serious difficulty with the complex procedural standards introduced and expensively monitored by courts (see Chapter 6).

V CONCLUSIONS: ACCOUNTABILITY AND THE EU

This chapter has tried to examine the notion of accountability and place it tentatively within a European context. It is perhaps not surprising to find that the term has until recently possessed little resonance in the literature of European studies. Accountability has evolved its current catch-all meaning primarily within the English-speaking world, where its use has become so common in the discourse of government and public administration that it is sometimes hard to remember that in several European languages no exact equivalent or translation is available.

Academics have generally approached the problems of governance in the EU either through institutional analysis or through theoretical analyses of the transnational system of governance.[69] A significant secondary focus has been the 'democratic deficit' and problems of legitimacy.[70] The well-known article by Shirley Williams,[71] which inaugurated a British debate on the 'democratic deficit', gives prominence to the term 'accountability' in the title but is almost entirely concerned with the performance of the European Parliament and the leaching of power from national parliaments. In her conclusion, Williams has in mind primarily accountability through traditional representative parliamentary institutions, though she also insists that the decision-making institutions of the EU 'must become truly accountable, not to Europe's governments or her bureaucrats, but to her people'.[72] Eight

[69] E.g., M. Jachtenfuchs, 'Theoretical Perspectives on European Governance' (1995) 1 *European Law Journal* 115; A. Stone, 'What is a Supranational Constitution? An Essay in International Relations Theory' (1994) 3 *The Review of Politics* 441; S. Hix, 'The Study of the European Community: The Challenge to Comparative Politics' (1994) 17 *W. European Politics* 1.

[70] G. de Búrca, 'The Quest for Legitimacy in the European Union' (1996) 59 *MLR* 349; G. Majone, 'Europe's "Democracy Deficit": The Question of Standards' (1998) 4 *European Law Journal* 5.

[71] S. Williams, 'Sovereignty and Accountability in the European Community' (1990) 61 *Political Quarterly* 299.

[72] Ibid., at 317.

years on, Christopher Lord described accountability as one of the four elements which go to make up democracy's 'irreducible core'. Political equality and popular control demand 'responsive rule', requiring that 'political leaders and power relations be *authorised* by the people; that the continuous flow of decisions should be made in a manner that is *representative* of public needs and values; and that rulers should be *accountable* to the people, who should be the ultimate judges of their performance'.[73] Lord sees effective democratic accountability in terms of four elements; first, *electoral accountability*, which legitimates and provides authorization; second, the continuous *parliamentary accountability* of political leaders to a representative assembly; third, *administrative accountability*, defined much in terms of the classic British system of ministerial responsibility; and finally *judicial* or *legal accountability*. Lord's broad categorization, with its emphasis on political accountability, could provide a basis for a common understanding of the concept in most of the Member States. Certainly, high priority is everywhere given to doctrines of political responsibility, with a corresponding emphasis on control by courts.

These forms of political accountability are typically external, though it has always been recognized that administrations or bureaucracies are subject to hierarchical control. Borrowing from the private sector, public administration theory in the English-speaking world is today heavily influenced by ideas of public choice based on market theory.[74] Market-led managerial systems of accountability have been borrowed from the profession of accountancy and from private-sector management and inserted into the public service. To these ideas we owe the type of managerial controls today associated with the label of 'New Public Management', honed and developed by the institutions entrusted with audit, to which discipline we probably owe the earliest use of the term 'accountability'. Within the discipline of public administration, there has been a willingness to push the concept of accountability deeper, using it to penetrate the hidden corners of administrative systems and to supply deficiencies in classical political doctrine. The elite of the EU, political, administrative, and intellectual, has perhaps been slow to recognize this transfer of allegiance, at least until the notorious fall of the Santer Commission placed the new management techniques squarely on the political agenda. It is, as we shall see in later chapters, difficult to supply the deficit in political accountability at EU level through audit and new public-management techniques because of the existing management deficit within the EU. Despite this, accountability and NPM are ideas with a growing resonance both in the EU and its Member States.

[73] C. Lord, *Democracy in the European Union* (Sheffield, Academic Press, 1998), 15.
[74] N. Lewis, *Choice and the Legal Order, Rising above Politics* (London, Butterworths, 1996).

2

Some Accident Black Spots

I ARCHITECTURE AND ACCOUNTABILITY

Juliet Lodge has described the European Union as a polity which 'does have a system of governance. But the polity does not yet conform to any model of liberal democratic, representative government. It is merely assumed that democratic principles should guide it'.[1] She is by no means alone in expressing this view. Simon Hix also characterizes the Community as a democratic political system in terms of the formal frameworks developed by political scientists for definition.[2] It is democratic, Hix maintains, because it possesses:

- A stable and clearly-defined set of rules for collective decision-making and rules governing relations between and within these institutions;
- A civic society, allowing citizens and social groups to achieve objectives through the political system;
- A significant impact on resource allocation and the distribution of social goods and values;
- Continuous interaction or 'feedback' between the political outputs, leading to change and innovation.

Possessing all these elements, the EU is a political system, though not a state.

An alternative and respectable approach to European governance is that the EU, even if not yet 'a state', is developing towards statehood or, at the very least, proto-statehood. Again it is assumed that a European state would

---

[1] J. Lodge, 'The European Parliament' in S. Andersen and K. Eliassen (eds.), *The European Union: How Democratic Is It?* (London, Sage, 1996), 200.

[2] S. Hix, *The Political System of the European Union* (Basingstoke, Macmillan, 1999), 2. See also S. Hix, 'The Study of the European Community: The Challenge to Comparative Politics' (1994) 17 *W. European Politics* 1; A. Stone Sweet, 'What is a Supranational Constitution? An Essay in International Relations Theory' (1994) 3 *The Review of Politics* 441.

necessarily possess, within the parameters of the Treaties, the characteristics of a model of liberal-democratic, representative government.[3] The two reports of the Committee of Independent Experts discussed in detail in Chapter 3 were shaped within such an assumption. They seek broadly to replicate the arrangements for accountability commonly found in modern representative democracies, loosely based on separation of powers doctrine and premised on parliamentary accountability. The Experts did not give much consideration to the crucial question whether the European Parliament was a sufficiently empowered and robust institution to carry the weight of a classical system of political accountability; probably they preferred to assume that it was.

In this type of analysis, the point of departure for accountability often lies in classical doctrines of institutional checks and balances associated with the doctrine of separation of powers.[4] The Treaties install a set of institutional balances peculiar to the EU and its needs, developed by the Court of Justice on the one hand to inhibit the EU from exceeding its lawful competence, and on the other to inhibit the EU institutions from encroaching on each other's prerogatives. To quote the ECJ in a leading case,[5] institutional balance is 'a system for distributing powers among the different Community institutions, assigning to each institution its own role in the institutional structure of the Community and the accomplishment of the tasks entrusted to the Community'.

The problem with reliance on separation of powers or institutional balance as a mechanism for ensuring accountability is that the efficacy of the mechanism is dependent on the model of governance inside which it is operating. Jacques Ziller has identified at least three styles of governance within the existing Member States[6] and enlargement will surely bring others. Ziller himself favours a model of loose decentralization, grouped around relatively autonomous agencies, a style of governance emanating from Sweden. To develop the EU in this direction would, as argued in the previous chapter,[7] necessitate a much stronger principle of transparency on which new forms of accountability could be based—though whether civil society is sufficiently developed at Union level to take the weight of public accountability remains doubtful. Alternatively, forms of institutional balance less closely related to the institutional arrangements and balances of a nation state might be installed. This is in fact the line taken by Colin Scott in the seminal article

---

[3] Further discussed in Chap. 7 below.
[4] G. Tsebelis and G. Garrett, 'The Institutional Foundation of Intergovernmentalism and Supranationalism in the European Union' (2000) 55 *International Organizations* 357.
[5] Case C–70/88, *European Parliament* v. *Council* [1990] ECR I–2041.
[6] J. Ziller, 'European Models of Government: Towards a Patchwork with Missing Pieces' (2001) 54 *Parliamentary Affairs* 102.
[7] Above, 12–13.

already cited[8] which addresses the problems of accountability in the modern regulatory state.

The classical machinery for accountability, Scott argues, is most relevant and effective within the parameters of a relatively centralized nation state—perhaps always an ideal-type. Once the ideal-type has been left behind, classical machinery for accountability can break down. In addition to the classical principle of democratic accountability, defined by Scott to mean that 'all public bodies act in ways which correspond with the core juridical value of legality, thus correspond with the democratic will',[9] Scott introduces two further models. The first of these he calls the *interdependence* model, in which the actors are 'dependent on each other in their actions because of the dispersal of key resources of authority (formal and informal), information, expertise, and capacity to bestow legitimacy such that each of the principal actors has constantly to account for at least some of its actions to others within the space, as a precondition for action'.[10] Such a model could perhaps be applicable to the notorious Comitology network,[11] designed to permit the Council to retain a measure of control over the Commission in its exercise of delegated powers of regulation. It could be applicable too, in conjunction with 'network theories' of policy-making,[12] to specific areas of EU policy, such as environmental policy-making. Scott's alternative is the '*redundancy model*' of accountability, which he sees as applicable to situations governed by the 'horizontal' mechanisms of market or contract, such as competition and public–procurement law, and also to regulatory agencies, where 'overlapping (and ostensibly superfluous) accountability mechanisms reduce the centrality of any one of them'.[13] (This could be another way of saying that none of the mechanisms is effective.) The redundancy model is seen by Scott as a feature of many EU expenditure programmes, notably the structural funding programme, where redundancy in this sense 'is built into the accountability mechanisms deliberately by EU decision makers, by requiring joint funding, and therefore ensuring that both domestic and EU audit institutions necessarily take an interest in single expenditure programmes within member states'.[14] The very real problems with this structure are examined in Chapter 5.

If Scott's analysis is taken as a starting point, it could perhaps provide a key to problems of accountability which derive directly from the EU's anarchic

---

[8] C. Scott, 'Accountability in the Regulatory State' (2000) 27 *Journal of Law and Society* 38.
[9] Ibid., at 43.
[10] Ibid., at 50.
[11] See below, 67–71.
[12] See below, 180–1.
[13] Scott, n. 8 above, 52.
[14] Ibid., at 54.

structure, and some aspects of the architecture which either cause particular problems of accountability or are specifically designed with autonomy in mind are in fact addressed in the remainder of this chapter. Chapter 3 focuses more closely on the Commission, as the central executive agency of the EU. The brief account here focuses narrowly on accountability and does not attempt an in-depth analysis of any institution or policy area.

II THE COUNCIL: PREROGATIVE AND IMMUNITY

The Treaties which govern the European Communities and Union are not, as those who press for a written constitution for Europe well understand, a constitution, nor even a substitute for a constitution. They retain the characteristics of Treaties as instruments of international law. The Treaties are fluid and dynamic and have, in this respect, served the EU well. The Treaty-making process is, however, neither widely consultative nor especially transparent, deficiencies which are beginning to be seen as threatening its legitimacy.[15]

Proposals for amendment may come from any Member State or from the Commission, and are submitted to the Council, which consults the European Parliament and, in case of changes in the European monetary area, the European Central Bank (ECB) (TEC Article 48). The Council may then authorize the President to summon 'a conference of representatives of the governments of the Member States' or IGC. This gathering is not a typical constitutional convention (if such a thing can be said to exist), though it can be defended on the ground that regular and more representative constitutional conventions are not a real possibility; their legitimacy rests partly on rarity, and to summon them repeatedly would undercut their value. The fact remains, however, that the IGC is an inter-*governmental* conference, situating the modalities of treaty change in the realm of international affairs. This is significant. Similarly significant is the origin of the EU in the realm and discipline of international affairs. Responsibility for foreign affairs is classically an executive function, and even in modern constitutions is a matter often left to the head of state and government. The fact that modifications to the EU constitution are seen as treaty change diminishes the expectation of popular consultation; it also may significantly limit the control exercised by national parliaments.[16]

The procedures could, of course, be changed, and change is beginning to be discussed. The Convention which drafted the European Charter of Fundamental Rights was differently composed. It consisted of one Commission

---

[15] G. de Búrca, 'The Quest for Legitimacy in the European Union' (1996) 59 *MLR* 349.
[16] Below, Chap 4.

member, fifteen representatives of national governments, thirty representatives of the European Parliament, and sixteen from national parliaments, and a similar model is being used to draft the European Constitution. At present, Members of the European Parliament are allowed to attend IGCs, but only as observers, but a body more like the Conventions could easily be convened to consider, draft, or even approve Treaty amendments. The inclusion of parliamentary representatives might be seen as lending legitimacy to the amendment process, although it must be borne in mind that accountability and legitimacy are not identical concepts. The addition of a few parliamentarians would act as a fig-leaf to cover problems of legitimacy but would hardly operate to provide any great measure of accountability. And, in any case, since the control of national governments over the Treaties would be diminished by such changes, nothing more confining than a consultative procedure is likely to emerge.

The Treaties do contain one important provision for democratic accountability, in that changes need to be ratified by 'all the Member States in accordance with their constitutional requirements' (TEC Article 48). In the majority of cases, this provision is implemented through parliamentary approval or through a referendum; both are standard mechanisms for democratic accountability. Referenda have certainly brought occasional surprises, in the celebrated case of the Danish referenda after the Maastricht Treaty,[17] or in the case of Ireland after Nice, suggesting that representative government does not always have its finger on the popular pulse. But popular control through a referendum is normally restricted to a straight yes or no, and is no substitute for participation at the drafting stage, while parliamentary control over treaty-making may in practice be very limited.

The random process of treaty amendment is at least partially responsible for an institutional structure best described as irregular, warranting the label bestowed by a disenchanted observer of a Europe of 'bits and pieces'.[18] The so-called 'pillar structure' of the TEU had the effect of introducing a complex division between EC and EU affairs: the formal, EC structure, which governed the general competences, contrasted with the second-pillar common foreign and security policy and the Third Pillar, largely covering immigration and asylum. The inevitable consequence was diminished national responsibility and accountability for policy and rule-making in the Second and Third Pillars. This was intentional; TEU Title V operated to *reduce* national accountability by imposing commitment to co-operation and joint action in foreign policy which would not be subject to national scrutiny

---

[17] See P. Svensson, 'The Danish Yes to Maastricht and the EC Referendum of May 1993' (1982) 17 *Scandinavian Political Studies* 69.

[18] D. Curtin, 'The Constitutional Structure of the Union: A Europe of Bits and Pieces' (1993) 30 *CML Rev.* 17.

nor approvals.[19] TEU Article 27 seeks, on the other hand, to provide an element of consistent administration, providing that the Commission is to be 'fully associated' with work carried out in the fields of common foreign and security policy. What the Second and Third Pillars had in common was lessened input from two of the most important Community institutions, the European Commission and Parliament.

It may be that the Treaty of Amsterdam lessened coherence, by introducing provisions for 'closer co-operation' whereby groups of eight or more Member States wishing to move at a speed faster than that at which it is possible to mobilize the whole Council are authorized by TEU Article 43 to move ahead, and to make use of the Treaty institutions, procedures, and mechanisms in so doing.[20] This procedure, controversial because it introduced the possibility of a 'Europe of many speeds', in which the big players could move ahead to the detriment of weaker members, will be regulated more closely by the Treaty of Nice with a view to allaying the suspicion of the smaller Member States.[21] Whatever we think of these various provisions— and opinions naturally vary—they are hardly a recipe for transparency or simplicity. What may happen is suggested by the Euro Group, a group of European finance ministers, set up outside the Treaty with a view to excluding those governments which have not joined up from discussing management of the euro. Because it has no legal base in the Treaty, the Euro Group has no legal powers, nor does it yet possess a separate administration or secretariat (though one has been projected) but operates through national administrations. Its decisions, from which significantly the Commission is formally excluded, can be implemented by Ecofin; equally they could be implemented at national level through co-operative decisions. The Euro Group has been gaining steadily in influence and is rumoured to be seriously interested in harmonization of tax and social welfare policies. We can thus compare its evolution with that of the Schengen group in pre-Third Pillar matters, the only difference being that the Euro Group has not yet progressed so far.[22] This is an example of the way in which complex methods of policy-making, starting from informal inter-governmental co-operation, ending

---

[19] See House of Lords, *Scrutiny of the Inter-Governmental Pillars of the European Union*, HL 124 (1992/3) and generally M. Cremona, 'External Relations and External Competence: The Emergence of an Integrated Policy' in P. Craig and G. de Búrca (eds.), *The Evolution of EU Law* (Oxford, Oxford University Press, 1998).

[20] C.-D. Ehlermann, 'Differentiation, Flexibility, Closer Co-operation: The New Provisions of the Amsterdam Treaty' (1998) 4 *European Law Journal* 246. Closer co-operation is in principle limited to exceptional circumstances.

[21] X. Yataganas, 'The Treaty of Nice: The Sharing of Power and the Institutional Balance in the European Union—A Continental Perspective' (2001) 7 *European Law Journal* 242, 279–81.

[22] See D. Wyatt and A. Dashwood, *Wyatt and Dashwood's* European Community Law (4th edn., London, Sweet and Maxwell, 2000).

for the present with 'closer co-operation', have been allowed to blur the procedural formality of the Treaties. The pillar structure is involved. The law-making procedures are Byzantine, with more than twenty ways to make law at Union level (see next section below). The number and variety of committees and working groups which can be set up to consider and formulate policy options are, quite simply, staggering (see section IV below). It undercuts transparency to the despair of the ordinary citizen and, with opacity, accountability is lost.

III THE COUNCIL AND LAW-MAKING

Recognition of weaknesses in EU law-making, both qualitative and procedural, goes back well before the Edinburgh Council in 1993, arising probably from the rush to complete the Single Market.[23] Criticism of quality, important because badly drafted legislative instruments can constitute a powerful impediment to transparency, has always been taken seriously by the Commission, which has pushed the IGC to take radical, corrective action. On many occasions the Commission has asked to go further than the IGC would go for procedural changes. Indeed, it could be said that before every IGC a chorus of demands is heard for further simplification of the complex law-making procedures, while afterwards it is said that much has been done but much remains to be done. Whether it is possible to simplify rule-making procedures in the modern age of regulation is in any case a difficult question; the complexity of the subject matter suggests otherwise.

Rule-making in the EU, as with other transnational bodies, is made more complex by the fact that it partakes of many of the characteristics of diplomacy. A multiplicity of parties, conscious of their own interests, is involved. Their needs must all be reflected in a final, consensual text. The text is promulgated in eleven languages, behind which lurks the conceptual vocabulary of several different legal systems. These are not the ingredients of good drafting. That is, however, no excuse for the complexity of the rule-making *procedures*. Alan Dashwood, an EC lawyer with a long and authoritative experience of EU law-making, concluded after the Nice IGC that 'a high price is paid in the coin of democratic accountability for a process of making EU law that is unintelligible except to Brussels professionals'.[24] His is not a

---

[23] E.g, Resolution of 11/12 Dec. 1992; Council Resolution of 8 June 1993 [1993] OJ C166/1 and *Report of Independent Experts on Legislative and Administrative Simplification*, Com. Sec(95)1379 (2 Aug. 1995). See now Commission White Paper on Governanu COM(2001) 428 pp. 20–23; Communications from the Commission European Governance. Better Lawmaking COM(2002) 275 final and for action plans COM(2002) 276–278.

[24] A. Dashwood, 'The Constitution of the European Union after Nice: Law-making Procedures' (2001) 26 *EL Rev.* 215, 232 and 'Community Legislative Procedures in the Era of the Treaty on European Union' (1994) *19 EL Rev.* 343.

lone voice. Even if linguistic and political difficulties are conceded, much is due also to problematic institutional relationships. Rivalry between the Council and EP is especially problematic[25] but the complex pillar structure, on which the EU embarked at Maastricht, also creates significant political problems.

The Council of Ministers, originating in the world of international affairs, brought the methods of diplomacy to management of the Community. It was considered secretive and inaccessible, in contrast to the Commission, which gained a reputation for informality and accessibility. Maastricht—and probably the accession of Member States with more open systems of parliamentary democracy[26]—helped to change the agenda: the European Council set new guidelines for greater transparency and Council proceedings have gradually become less secretive. True, the Council does not operate like a parliament and has not gone so far as the EP in facilitating public access to information. There are still no full minutes, but since the Edinburgh Council in 1992, the Council of Ministers has published the record of votes. It now provides briefings and press releases after every meeting, and policy debates on future work programmes may also be made public via the accessible and user-friendly Europa website. In contrast to the Council, the EP is directly elected and has always seen the European public as its constituency; the Council is a body composed of Member State representatives and necessarily has an eye to national governments (an inter-governmentalist approach). In the terminology of accountability it would be fair to say that there is a tendency for the EP to see itself as representing democratic accountability in a wide sense, while the Council, straddling two systems, has its basis in collective and individual ministerial responsibility, owed in principle to national parliaments whose scrutiny it is in practice happy to avoid.

IV COMMITTEES AND CORRIDORS

Although the Council is inter-governmental, it is of course a permanent institution, with its own services and advisers. The inter-governmental character of the EU has brought with it (as we shall see in the next chapter) a predilection for committees,[27] though committees are in any event an inevitable feature of modern, regulatory government, originating in the need for 'joined-up government'. In nation states, committees link national and regional government; the EU adds a further level. Committees are corridors linking the EU architecture; they link national and regional capitals

[25] See Chap. 4 below.
[26] Ziller, n. 6 above; D. Curtin and H. Mejers, 'The Principle of Open Government in Schengen and the European Union: Democratic Retrogression?' (1995) 32 *CML Rev.* 390.
[27] See E. Vos, 'The Rise of Committees' (1997) 3 *European Law Journal* 210.

to Brussels; they service the Presidency, crucial whenever this post falls to one of the smaller Member States; and help to link otherwise unco-ordinated Council formations. In the next chapter, we shall see them supplementing the limited expertise of the Commission, providing expert participation in policy development and drafting, and linking the public services of the Member States.[28] Committees create a dilemma for governmental account- ability; on the one hand, they are a major factor in the development of participatory modes of government, an important element in accountability; on the other, they can be seen as adding greatly to complexity and hampering transparency.

At the apex of the Council committees stands the COREPER, a formal body recognized in the Treaties (TEC Article 207) and composed of senior officials from Member State foreign ministries. Anecdotal accounts of the methods of senior members of COREPER suggest that these remain very much those of old-style diplomacy. Meetings are private and negotiations confidential. One observer talks of 'dense norms of interaction, thick trust, and culture of compromise found in COREPER', describing the atmosphere of an 'exclusive male club with an accent on classical diplomacy'.[29] This may or may not be an accurate picture of the way in which COREPER and its committees operate today, when COREPER is increasingly part of a Euro- pean bureaucracy. Lewis suggests, however, that these attributes are not unique but characterize the EU decision-making system.[30] Several factors go to make up a shared culture common to all who work on EU affairs, including judges and EC lawyers. There is a sense of participation in the making of a unique and important enterprise. Equally, the geographical isolation of the EU institutions, removed from Europe's great capitals and spread between the lesser cities of Brussels, Luxembourg, and Strasbourg, facilitates a degree of autonomy and insulation. Over time, this has come to constitute a European elite seen by those who participate as essential to effective decision-making. If this is not a picture of *democratic* decision- making, it is one that certainly finds an echo, and is a cause of complaint, in many national systems, especially in the areas of security, defence, and foreign affairs. The difference is that, in representative democracy, some version of political responsibility to parliament is normally in place. The ambiguous institutional structure of the European Council and Council of Ministers makes this difficult, if not impossible.

[28] G. Schafer, 'Linking Member State and European Administrations—The Role of Committees and Comitology' in M. Andenas and A. Turk (eds.), *Delegated Legislation and the Role of Committees in the EC* (London, Kluwer Law International, 2000).

[29] A description cited by J. Lewis, 'The Methods of Community in EU Decision-making and Administrative Rivalry in the Council's Infrastructure' (2000) 7 *Journal of European Public Policy* 261, 262, and 265.

[30] Ibid.

In considering COREPER's contribution to Council proceedings, we must remember that after the Single European Act in 1986 rapid implementation of the Single Market was demanded. A huge volume of directives (around 300) was identified as necessary for this purpose, and a procedure had to be devised to allow these to pass rapidly into law. COREPER acts essentially as a filter, passing to the ministers as 'A points' matters on which agreement has been reached. It would be exceptional for these to be reopened in council meetings, and it has in any case been calculated that about 20 per cent of all decisions actually reach the Council, the remainder being taken by the Commission or by committees somewhere in the system.[31] The negative side of this filtration process is that decisions have in effect—though not, of course, legally—been passed to a corps of invisible and unaccountable public servants.

COREPER is also the apex of a network of feeder committees, which often take the real decisions; around 10–15 per cent of decisions reach COREPER itself.[32] COREPER I deals with technical matters, including the Single Market, while COREPER II handles 'political' questions, such as finance and external affairs; underneath, we find the important Political Committee, the Economic and Finance Committee, and the Article 36 (previously the K4) Justice and Home Affairs Committee, responsible for policy-making in the Third Pillar, both of which COREPER theoretically oversees. A level down, we find a web of sub-committees and working groups. Highly variable in number, the latter have been described as 'one of the EU's great unsolved mysteries'.[33] It is not possible to provide a detailed picture because of the lack of empirical academic studies. What characterizes working groups, however, is their shifting population. For the most part they are made up of national civil servants, clustered around a small core of permanent Commission representatives. National officials participate at an early stage in policy-making, their contribution being to warn, inform, and 'add insights' concerning national policy and legislation.

Why is this important? Surely it is almost unavoidable in any modern system of regulatory government, where parliaments have long ceased to be the only law-maker and routinely delegate rule-making responsibilities to bureaucrats? It is widely felt that access to the labyrinth of committees that

[31] M. van Schendelen, 'The Council Decides: Does the Council Decide?' (1996) 34 *Journal of Common Market Studies* 37.

[32] W. Wessels, 'The EC Council: The Community's Decision-making Center' in S Hoffmann and O. Keohane (eds.), *The New European Community. Decision-making and Institutional Chance.* (Boulder, Colo., Westview, 1991), 140.

[33] F. Hayes Renshaw and H. Wallace, *The Council of Ministers* (Basingstoke, Macmillan, 1997). At 97, they estimate around 50 permanent working groups and 50–150 *ad hoc* groups at any one time, but M. Westlake, *The Council of the European Union* (London, Cartermill, 1995), 312, gives the much higher figure of 250.

service modern governments is essential if the policy and law-making process is to be truly accessible to the public, open, and accountable. Committees, like bureaucracies or well-disciplined cabinets, are prone to develop a corporate ethos, which often sharply diverges from that of the politicians theoretically responsible to the public for policy-making. EU committees foster networking between their members, creating a hidden advice and information network, and building an informal support group for proposals at national level, a process of input and output known as *engrenage*.[34] This creates a powerful, alternative power structure within the decision-making process, whereby policy-making takes place behind closed doors, and is conducted as a bargaining process between non-elected national civil servants, not necessarily subject to appropriate political control at national level. All that is officially published about the working groups is the number of person-days that they consume, at the last count a rapidly rising figure.[35] Consequently, fears of lobbying and interest-group law-making, already a matter of concern in EU affairs, are heightened. The 'Nolan values', an important accountability yardstick, are then imperilled.

In their authoritative study of the Council, Fiona Hayes Renshaw and Helen Wallace conclude that 'turning the spotlight on the [COREPER] would probably reduce its effectiveness, to the detriment of the Council and the EU as a whole'.[36] They do not seem unduly worried over lack of transparency and accountability. Surely it is important that the vast majority of Community decisions, both formal and informal, are being taken by politically unaccountable decision-makers? Deirdre Curtin and Hendrik Meijers describe 'legislative knowledge' as 'the knowledge most fundamental to democracy', and draw attention to the extent to which the Council legislative process falls short of standards of openness obtaining in national parliaments.[37] To its credit, the Commission is aware of the problem, and is introducing reforms to bring the Comitology, for which it is responsible, into the open so that the public can see how it functions. Similarly, there ought to be control over the policy-making activities of permanent Brussels representatives. We cannot afford to accept a system of which it can plausibly be said that 'administrative élites have designed the EU system to give themselves powerful executive and legislative powers, beyond the control of national

---

[34] J. Beyers and G. Dierickx, 'The Working Groups of the Council of the European Union: Supranational or Intergovernmental Negotiations?' (1998) 3 *Journal of Common Market Studies* 289; D. Rometsch and W. Wessels, 'The Commission and the Council of the Union', in G. Edwards and D. Spence (eds.), *The European Commission* (2nd edn., London, Cartermill Publishing, 1994).

[35] Hayes Renshaw and Wallace, n. 33 above, 98. Between 1968 and 1994, the number doubled from 1,253 to 2,580 working days.

[36] Ibid., at 84.

[37] Curtin and Mejers, n. 26 above, 392.

parliaments',[38] nor should we accept a system in which national policy-makers can use the European card to trump national legislatures and dictate the domestic agenda, avoiding domestic political accountability for unpopular decisions.[39] We ought therefore to be demanding that the Council and COREPER parallel recent efforts by the Commission to bring their Comitology out into the open. Greater transparency in Council policy- and rule-making would go some way to closing the accountability gap opened by transfer of functions to the EU level.

V THE COUNCIL AND TRANSPARENCY

Curtin's whole-hearted commitment to democratic openness has not so far been fully recognized by any of the EU institutions, though there is a greater interest in the European Parliament. The EP stands to benefit from openness more than the Council, which stands to lose its policy immunity at national level. An interesting thread runs through the debate on access to information, however: the extent to which it has been propelled by a small group of Member States, particularly the Netherlands, Denmark, Sweden, and Finland. These Member States have consistently brought pressure to bear from within the Council and have also lent support to many of the challenges to decisions refusing access to documentation brought before the Community Courts This debate has assumed all the characteristics of political campaigning at national level, with the difference that some of the protagonists in the struggle are states.

In terms of Ziller's argument over the nature of European administration and its consequential impact on information regimes,[40] what we are currently seeing is a series of disjointed attempts at the fusion of incompatible regimes, the protagonists being those Member States which most strongly represent the two models of European government. Neither group can afford entirely to abandon or withdraw too far from its point of departure in openness or official secrecy for fear of the potential negative impact on domestic political systems; in Sweden and Finland, where the constitution strongly underscores the notion of citizens' rights, the problem is compounded. A split Council can achieve consensus only with difficulty and often with resort to ambiguous language, leaving the battle to be resumed in institutions outside the Council and between inter-governmental conferences. The institutions have also taken up different positions, based partly on their differing attitudes, partly

---

[38] Hix, n. 2 above, 31.

[39] See M. Smith, 'The Commission Made Me Do It: The European Commission as a Strategic Asset in Domestic Politics' in N. Nugent (ed.), *At the Heart of the Union* (Basingstoke, Macmillan, 1997).

[40] Chap. 1 above, 13.

on the balance of power between the Member States representatives of which the institutions are composed.[41] The positions of the EP and Council have already been outlined, though the power struggles within and between each over a period of time should not be over-simplified or under-estimated. The Commission, possessing a reputation for informal openness and accessibility, has been scrupulous in transcribing the policy preferences of the Council, which tend to promote confidentiality. It can in any event argue that its hands are tied: the majority of the exceptions inserted in the joint Code of Conduct governing access to Commission and Council documents which followed the Maastricht Treaty are couched in *mandatory* terms.[42] The Courts have taken a consistent, if limited, line on openness, reflecting the mandate to protect individual interests through procedural due process, which is perhaps their greatest contribution to accountability. Like the Commission, the Community Courts have to seek to resolve the contradiction between the various statements and Declarations emanating from Council and Parliament, seeking on their face to promote transparency in all its forms, and the highly restrictive formulae of the Codes of Conduct. In practice, this function has fallen largely to the Court of First Instance.

At Maastricht, the Council opened the way to treating transparency, a term by then high on national political agendas, as an element in the development of European democracy and a 'right of citizenship'. In the crucial Declaration 17 on Democracy, Transparency, and Subsidiarity annexed to the TEU, the Council linked transparency firmly to democratic government, declaring that 'transparency of the decision-making process strengthens the democratic nature of the institutions and the public's confidence in the administration'. In the Commission response to the Declaration, we find a similar emphasis on citizenship rights:[43]

The Commission views this declaration as an important element of the Community's policy on transparency of the institutions. Improved access to information will be a means of bringing the public closer to the institutions and of stimulating a more informed and involved debate on policy matters. It will also be a means of increasing the public's confidence in the Community.

Proponents of open government, however, normally attach great importance to the style in which measures permitting access to information

---

[41] In theoretical terms, a contest between intergovernmentalist and new institutionalist theories of European governance is occurring: see D. F. Puchala, 'Institutionalism, Intergovernmentalism and European Integration' (1999) 37 *Journal of Common Market Studies* 317.

[42] Code of Conduct Concerning Public Access to Council and Commission Documents (93/730/EC) [1993] OJ L340/43, as amended by the Council [1996] OJ L325. The Code was adopted by the Commission in Decision 94/90 [1994] OJ L46/55. For the EP, see [1997] OJ L263/26.

[43] Public Access to the Institutions' Documents (93/C 156/05) [1993] OJ C156/5.

are drafted.[44] They favour an opening statement, establishing a *right* of access, subject to a tightly drafted list of exceptions. Although the joint Codes of Conduct promulgated by the Council and Commission opened with the assurance that 'the public will have the widest possible access to documents held by the Commission and the Council', this tone of openness was not borne out by the text. This contained a list of *mandatory* exceptions to disclosure so extensive as to change the balance: from positive rights with negative exceptions to a text which treats access as the exception. The Code exceptions were wide enough to cover:

- the protection of the public interest (exemplified by public security, international relations, monetary stability, court proceedings, inspections, and investigations);
- the protection of the individual and of privacy;
- the protection of industrial and commercial secrecy;
- the protection of the Union's financial interests; and
- the protection of confidentiality as requested by the natural or legal persons that supplied the information or as required by the legislation of the Member State that supplied the information.

After all this, the institutions had a *discretion* to refuse access in order to protect an institution's interest in the confidentiality of its proceedings.

That this formulation was dangerously restrictive was understood immediately by the Netherlands, a Member State which has consistently pushed the issue of openness in the governance of the Community. The Netherlands challenged the legal basis of the Code of Conduct before the ECJ[45] with the argument that the Code, designed to implement Declaration 17, which 'vests in individuals the *right* to participate in the activity of the Council also at the preparatory and investigatory stages', is based on a democratic 'right to know'. It could therefore never have as its legal base TEC Article 207, which deals with the powers of the institutions to settle their own rules of procedure. This reasoning was taken up in an intervention by the European Parliament, in which it was argued that 'the principle of openness of the legislative process and access to legislative documents entailed thereby constitute essential requirements of democracy and therefore cannot be treated as organisational matters purely internal to the institution'. Thus the institutions, by proceeding through internal codes of conduct, a mode of legislative procedure which notably excludes input from the EP, were subverting the democratic processes of the Union and resiling from the principle of openness as a democratic right. The ECJ, though apparently with some

---

[44] P. Birkinshaw, 'Freedom of Information and Open Government: The European Community/Union Dimension' (1997) 14 *Government Information Quarterly* 27.
[45] Case C–58/94, *Netherlands* v. *Council* [1996] ECR I–2169.

reluctance, felt it necessary to support the position taken by the Council, backed by the Commission and France. It ruled that provision for access to documents was a matter of institutional procedure and laid the responsibility to act firmly on legislative shoulders; any further action to delineate a more general right of access to public information, the Court insisted, would have to await the intervention of the legislature. Traces of a rights-based approach are visible in the Advocate-General's Opinion, more sympathetic to the case presented by the Netherlands than the final judgment. Tesauro A. G. spoke of the right of access to information as 'the democratic principle, which constitutes one of the cornerstones of the Community edifice' and even went so far as to suggest that it is increasingly seen as 'clearly a *fundamental civil* right'.[46]

Five years later, it is not much easier to assess the legislators' ambiguous contribution.[47] On the one hand, certain declarations by the Council, together with a new regulation which replaces the Codes,[48] enhance the commitment to transparency and appear to move the EU steadily, if slowly, towards the destination of a citizen 'right to know'. The new text opens with a lavish declaration of commitment to openness, this time linking the two values of transparency and accountability:

Openness enables citizens to participate more closely in the decision-making process and guarantees that the administration enjoys greater legitimacy and is more effective and *more accountable vis-à-vis the citizens in a democratic system*.

Too wide a right of access would, however, seriously undermine the narrowly drawn legislation of some Member States, notably the United Kingdom and France. This has produced ambiguous articles to deal with the right of Member States to lay down the conditions under which they pass information to the Commission. The unfavourable reaction of the EP to a Council draft is visible in the final text of the Regulation, which has benefited from many amendments making access easier and limiting exceptions. Emanating from the European Parliament, these were introduced during the co-decision procedure. But the text still fails overall to measure up to the high standards of transparency affirmed by the opening declaration. It retains the basic principle of the mandatory exceptions, the target of the CFI,

---

[46] Compare paras. 34–36 (ECJ) with para. 16 of the Opinion at 2180. See also Case T–83/96, *Van der Wal* v. *Commission* [1998] ECR II–545, where ECHR Art. 6(1) is cited, noted by S. Kadelbach (2001) 38 *CML Rev.* 179–94 and Davis (2000) 25 *EL Rev.* 303. And see Cases C–174, 189/98P *Netherlands and Van der Wal* v. *Commission* [2000] ECR I–0001.

[47] D. Curtin, 'Citizens' Fundamental Right of Access to EU Information: An Evolving Digital Passepartout?' (2000) 37 *CML Rev.* 7; I. Harden, 'Citizenship and Information' (2001) 7 *European Public Law* 165.

[48] Regulation EC 1049/2001 of the European Parliament and the Council of 30 May 2001 regarding public access to European Parliament, Council and Commission Documents [2001] OJ L145/43.

though it does refine the long list, regrouping them under specific heads. It also includes proportionality tests of public interest in respect of certain of the exceptions. It will, however, necessarily fall once more to the Community Courts and European Ombudsman to police institutional practice and whittle away at the list, as they have in the latest cases continued to do.[49] This is by any standards a slow and expensive road to openness. We need too to note how a security classification was introduced furtively by the Council, apparently at the request of NATO, and without adequate consultation with the European Parliament.[50]

Recent case law of the Community Courts is pushing the EU towards openness. In the case of the Swedish journalists,[51] the CFI imposed a rigorous test of proportionality on the institutions in the exercise of their discretion not to disclose documents. Again, when the Finnish MEP for the Green Party, Mrs Heidi Hautala, asked the Council for a policy statement made in the framework of the Common Foreign and Security Policy (Title V) dealing with arms exports, she was refused access by the Council in reliance on the public-interest exception of international relations in the Code of Conduct. The CFI required the Council officials to examine the documents with a view to partial disclosure or 'redaction'.[52] The Council argued that a right of access to *documents* was narrower than a right of information. This point is now settled at the insistence of the European Parliament by the new Regulation, which specifically covers *information* and not, as in the Codes of Conduct, *documents*. In court, the Council described Declaration No 17 as a political statement without legal effect, an argument which, though technically true, sits uncomfortably alongside its political professions. It fell to A. G. Léger in the ECJ to explain the crucial place of transparency in the scheme of things. Referring (perhaps optimistically) to the 'consistency in the political will of the Member States', the Opinion pulls together the three threads of transparency, accountability,

---

[49] Case T–174/95, *Svenska Journalistförbundet* v. *Council* [1998] ECR II–2289; Case T–C-353/99P, *Council* v. *Hautala* [1999] ECR II–2489 and 6 December 2001, (ECJ); Case T–204/99, *Mattila* v. *Council,* 12 July 2001; Cases C–174, 189/98P *Netherlands and Van der Wal* v. *Commission* [2000] ECR I–0001; Case T–188/97, *Rothmans* v. *Commission* [1999] ECR II–2463; Case T–20/99, *Denkavit Nederland* v. *Commission* [2000] ECR II–3011; Case T–111/00, *British American Tobacco International (Investments) Ltd* v. *Commission,* 10 Oct. 2001.

[50] Council Decision of 14 Aug. 2000 amending Decision 93/731/EC on public access to Council documents and Council Decision 2000/23/EC on the improvement of information on the Council's legislative activities and the public register of Council documents [2001] OJ L212/9.

[51] Case T–174/95, *Svenska Journalistförbundet* v. *Council* [1998] ECR II–2289.

[52] Case C-353/99P, *Council* v. *Hautala* [1999] ECR II–2489 and 6 December 2001, (ECJ).

and participation by civil society in a balanced system of democratic government, noting:[53]

the emergence of a right closely related to the foundations of the Community. As Advocate General Tesauro observed in his Opinion in *Netherlands v Council*, the openness of the public authorities' action is closely linked with the democratic nature of the institutions. The fact that citizens are aware of what the administration is doing is a guarantee that it will operate properly. Supervision by those who confer legitimacy on the public authorities encourages them to be effective in adhering to their initial will and can thereby inspire their confidence, which is a guarantee of public content as well as the proper functioning of the democratic system. At the highest level of that system, providing the public with information is also the surest method of involving them in the management of public affairs.

VI THE COUNCIL AND 'THIRD-PILLAR' MATTERS

The term 'Third Pillar' is a metaphor, used to cover the provisions on co-operation in the fields of justice and home affairs added to the Treaties by TEU Title VI, Articles K–K9, though now replaced. The innocuous title sheltered a swathe of sensitive home affairs and security matters, which broadly comprised: asylum policy; border controls; immigration policy; relations with third-country nationals and their residence rights throughout the EU; ways and means to combat illegality in these fields; anti-drug and drug-addiction policy; judicial co-operation; customs co-operation; and, last but never least, police co-operation. These are all matters of central political importance, on which national parliaments would expect to have a voice. The history of national co-operation in many of these areas is a long one, which dates back at least to the Trevi group, set up as early as 1976 to work on terrorism and towards co-ordinated policing.[54] A long period of unaccountable, executive policy-making, conducted through *ad hoc* groups, working groups, and committees, followed. The format was deliberately one of informal, intergovernmental co-operation, designed to exclude the Community institutions, the pretext being the absence of EC competence in the area. The Trevi experiments were followed up by an Ad Hoc Group on Interpol and a Working Group on a European Drugs Unit, the outcome being two agencies, in both cases working in an area where the Community had no clear competence. Similar techniques were used to foster co-operation in the fields of asylum and immigration. France and Germany joined up to the Schengen agreement on open borders in 1985, as did Italy in 1990. Working groups

---

[53] Opinion, point 52.
[54] See S. Collinson, *Migration, Visa and Asylum Policies in Europe* (London, HMSO, 1995).

were set in place to draft co-ordinated measures; at these, the Commission had observer status. The drafts were said to be a 'laboratory of what the Twelve (the EC) will have to implement by the end of 1992',[55] yet input into the text of the rules from democratically elected sources was almost entirely lacking. Similarly, the Dublin Convention on asylum applications,[56] a document with dramatic effect on the rights of third-country nationals, was a product merely of the Schengen group.

The engine of third-pillar policy-making has for some years been a rotating committee, previously known as the K4 (now Article 36) Committee and composed of one official per Member State plus a Commission representative. Like that of the Council of Ministers, its composition changes according to the matter under discussion. The changing membership means that it may at one meeting be composed of entirely different officials from the next. As policy-maker, it lacks the driving force of a national government and also the driving force of the Commission. It faces in several directions at once: technically a committee advisory to the Council, it is more or less in the hands of national civil servants. As it is technically a Community body, responsibility to national governments has been lost, and it has to be remembered in this context that officials, who operate policies, are not always in line with their ministers. Finally, ministers can evade the detailed scrutiny of national parliaments: 'The Community Made Me Do It'. In the United Kingdom, for example, ministers in promoting immigration legislation often present texts agreed by the Council or Article 36 Committee, relying on the common action to justify and legitimate both text and policy.[57]

The problems of acquiring sufficient information about third-pillar matters to challenge the development of Community policies was demonstrated in an interesting experiment conducted by the Swedish Journalists' Union, designed to test the degree of openness and accountability under national law against the third-pillar regime. The SJU applied under Swedish law for documents used by the Justice Council, obtaining around 80 per cent; under EC law, the Council secretariat was prepared to release just 20 per cent.[58] As noted, the CFI annulled this decision as

---

[55] F. Webber, 'European Conventions on Immigration and Asylum' in T. Bunyan (ed.), *Statewatching the New Europe, a Handbook on the European State* (Nottingham, Statewatch, 1993), 143.

[56] The Dublin Convention determining the state responsible for examining applications for asylum lodged in one of the Member States of the European Communities (15 June 1990).

[57] E. Guild, 'The Constitutional Consequences of Lawmaking in the Third Pillar of the European Union' in P. Craig and C. Harlow (eds.), *Lawmaking in the European Union* (London, Kluwer Law International, 1998), 75–8; D. Kostakopolou, 'Is There an Alternative to "Schengenland"?' (1998) 46 *Political Studies* 886.

[58] Note, however, I. Österdahl, 'EU Law and Swedish Law on Public Access to Documents' in M. Andenas and N. Jarsborg (eds.), *Anglo-Swedish Studies in Law* (Uppsala, Iustus

'disproportionate', as it did in the similar case brought by Mrs Hautala, MEP. Something similar occurred in the later case of *Kuijer*,[59] where a researcher in asylum issues requested documents relating to the Centre of Information, Discussion, and Exchange on Asylum, a Council advisory body, and was refused on the ground of potential damage to international relations. Yet information supplied by Denmark showed that much of the material in the refused reports was not particularly sensitive. In these cases, the CFI has made the running in moving the institutions of the EU towards acknowledging a civic right to access information.

More recently, the European Ombudsman (EO) has entered the field, following a complaint by an NGO engaged in a democratic audit of third-pillar activity. For over two years the EO strove for a friendly solution, pointing out that it was a 'principle of good administrative behaviour' for a public authority to maintain a register of documents and that the prohibition on publication of the requested information was not mandatory, which left it open to the Council to cede gracefully. Finally, the EO wrested from the Council the grudging concession that at least a list of 'instruments adopted' would in future be provided on the Internet.[60] After prolonged negotiation, a register was set up and the promise implemented to the EO's satisfaction in 1999. In a second complaint[61] from the same NGO that the Council had refused access to Minutes of the Article 36 Committee, on the ground that the request was a 'repeat application' as defined by the Code and also related to multiple documents, the EO made a 'critical remark',[62] challenging the Council's negative interpretation of these terms. Although the EO was prepared to accept that the Council was motivated by a 'legitimate concern to safeguard the efficiency of its administration', the true motivation is perhaps more clearly revealed in an earlier response from the Council, querying the complainant's motives. The Council's representatives claimed that '[t]he complainant uses a systematic technique to obtain access to all Council JHA documents. That technique consists of initially requesting the agendas of all Council bodies dealing with JHA matters and subsequently requesting all the

---

Förlag, 1999), 258, states that 'an ironic side-effect of the Swedish right of access to official documents may be that people in Sweden will have greater access to documents originating from the EU lawmaking process than to documents originating from the national legislative process'.

[59] Case T–188/98, *Aldo Kuijer* v. *Council*, 6 Apr. 2000.

[60] Complaint 1055/25 Statewatch against the Council (25. Nov. 1996), *Annual Report for 1998*, 256–9; *Annual Report of 1999*, 232–3.

[61] Complaint 1053/25/STATEWATCH/United Kingdom/IJH against the Council, *Annual Report for 1996*, 167–82. For implementation, see *Annual Report for 1999*, n. 60 above, 232–5.

[62] This is a technical term indicating that the EO will not make a finding of maladministration but is nonetheless not entirely satisfied with the administrators' conduct of an affair.

documents included on those agendas.' Surely that is the essence of a public 'right to know'?

We have then in the Third Pillar precisely the type of transnational problem that the Community was set up to regulate, even if it lay outside the original, economic ambit of that body. We can now begin to discern that the Community institutions, though still in many instances defective, were developed precisely as an antidote to the sort of secret, transnational govern-ance which characterizes policy-making in the areas of Justice and Home Affairs. This was, in any event, the argument put forward by migrants' and civil liberties groups in the period before the Maastricht Treaty. Even though it was a compromise, the TEU did not *reduce* accountability; to the contrary, it was the culmination of a steady fight by campaigning groups and a section of the Council to bring policy-making under control.[63] At Amsterdam again, migrants' groups consistently opposed the introduction of new areas of Community competence 'without the correspondingly forceful democratic and judicial controls which apply to other areas of Community law and which generally apply at the national level'.[64] They sought the help of an alliance of smaller Member States, notably the Netherlands, in the Council, hoping for full transfer of competence to Community level, with political account-ability to the European Parliament, legal control by the ECJ, and a more transparent and more accountable policy-making process with the co-oper-ation of the Commission. But this was not the package agreed at Amster-dam.[65] TEC Article 67 retained for the time being the old-fashioned consultation procedure for ex-third-pillar matters, which in general the EP would like to see replaced, as it is the least favourable to the EP of EU law-making procedures.[66] At Amsterdam, the Council was cautious. The two most relevant committees of the European Parliament, the Committee on Civil Liberties and Human Rights, and Legal Affairs Committee, which despite lack of technical competence have stubbornly monitored the area, are thought to be far too liberal for the taste of some Council members and national officials.[67] Possibly for similar reasons, the jurisdiction of the ECJ in Title IV matters was curtailed, although we should not leave out of account 'the well known tendency of the Court, never formally expressed, to interpret the EC Treaty and other treaties so as to award itself the maximum possible

[63] E. Guild, *European Community Law from a Migrant's Perspective* (The Hague, Kluwer Law International, 1999), 233.

[64] Migration Policy Group and others, 'Guarding Standards—Shaping the Agenda', June 1999; See JUSTICE, *The Democratic Deficit, Democratic Accountability and the European Union* (London, JUSTICE, 1996).

[65] See K. Hailbronner, 'European Immigration and Asylum Law under the Amsterdam Treaty' (1998) 35 *CML Rev.* 1047.

[66] But see Art. 67(2), requiring transition to co-decision after 5 years. And see Declaration 5 of the Nice Treaty, which envisages transition in 2004.

[67] Guild, n. 57 above, 73.

jurisdiction over the effect, legality, and uniform interpretation of EC acts'.[68] And late in 2001, the EP adopted a resolution demanding that the Commission submit, by the end of the year, a proposal for comprehensive reform of instruments of police and judicial co-operation, including a revision of the Europol Convention, to bring the whole area into line 'with highest standards and methods of democratic control of police forces of the Member States.'[69] The reform should aim to bring the instruments within the scope of the EC Treaty.

In terms of democracy and accountability, what has been going on is a secretive and sub-standard law-making process, in some ways facilitated by the existence of the EU, in others perhaps impeded. It could be construed as a game plan or new kind of 'forum shopping', in which governments use global structures to evade democratic controls at national level by seeking the most favourable transnational venue at which to introduce disputed policies.[70] Common action may be used to modify national policies or even international commitments without the impediment of keen debate in national fora.[71] The recent Council Common Position on terrorism, bitterly contested by civil liberties groups throughout Europe, is an example of such a usage.[72] At stage 1, some European governments agree to and set up working parties to develop areas of mutual interest. Documents are drafted and promulgated, perhaps as soft law, perhaps as conventions to which the partners adhere. The second stage is to test the policies by putting them into practice at a point when they are still relatively flexible. They may finally be brought within the competence of the Community, as occurred at Amsterdam, when a wide new area of competence, which brought the *acquis* of the Schengen Convention within the capacious boundaries of the European Community, was domesticated under the rubric of 'an area of freedom, security and justice'. But this should not be allowed to disguise the fact that the Schengen *acquis*, now binding on the Member States except in respect of negotiated opt-outs, was actually drafted by an *ad hoc* group of representatives of six of the Member States behind closed doors, and the process of incorporation was described by the House of Lords, well-furnished with an expert legal

---

[68] S. Peers, 'Who's Judging the Watchmen? The Judicial System of the "Area of Freedom, Security and Justice"' (1998) 18 *Yearbook of European Law* 338. And see E. Guild and S Peers, 'Deference or Defiance? The Court of Justice's Jurisdiction in Immigration and Asylum' in E. Guild and C. Harlow (eds.), *Implementing Amsterdam, Immigration and Asylum Rights in EC Law* (Oxford, Hart Publishing, 2000).

[69] European Parliament, 13 Nov. 2001, Rapporteur, M. Turco.

[70] See V. Guiraudon, 'European Integration and Migration Policy' (2000) 38 *Journal of Common Market Studies* 251.

[71] G. Goodwin Gill, 'The Individual Refugee, the 1951 Convention and the Treaty of Amsterdam' in Guild and Harlow (eds.), n. 68 above, at 156–9.

[72] Council Common Position of 27 Dec. 2001 on combating terrorism (2001/930CFSP).

membership, as one in which Member States had signed up to a protocol of which no one knew the content.[73]

Largely unnoticed, Tampere marked a further step towards a common policy on migration, based on policies drawn up by a High Level Working Group responsible to the Council, whose mandate was unhesitatingly renewed.[74] 'Experts' have been working behind the scenes for some years on the co-ordination of criminal justice systems in the *corpus iuris* project. Again, the House of Lords Select Committee on the European Union has twice evaluated progress on this project,[75] concluding that it is both irrelevant and infeasible. The House was especially critical of the underhand way in which the proposals were being brought forward, believing that the stability of national criminal justice systems could be endangered. It was unhesitatingly endorsed, however, by the Tampere European Council. Jörg Monar has described this evolutionary process as a 'laboratory method', in which small-scale experiments (Stage 1) facilitate, and may in the end be used to legitimate, the substitution of a single Europe-wide policy for national policies agreed by national parliaments. In terms of accountability, the costs are high: we are left with deficits in both parliamentary and judicial control.[76] The deficit is greater where the chosen medium for implementation is, as with Europol and Eurojust, a trans-national agency.

The Council has shown some awareness of the problems facing it in the fields of transparency and democratic accountability, as a report prepared for the Council prior to the IGC at Amsterdam shows.[77] This identified three main lines of opinion within the Council, two of which relate strongly to accountability. A first group of Member States apparently stressed *transparency:* the Council was not sufficiently open to the public when working as a legislative body. A second group blamed *complexity:* it was too difficult for citizens to link outputs to institutions, processes, and Treaty provisions, in short to know 'who does what' in European policy-making, and where the blame lay for error. This echoes a constant theme in reports from the EP, self-appointed defender of democracy and chief rival to the Council.[78] The EP blames the complex 'pillar' structure, which allows Member State

[73] House of Lords, 'Defining the Schengen Acquis', HL 87 (1997/8). See also 'Incorporating the Schengen Acquis into the European Union', HL 139 (1997/8); 'Schengen and the United Kingdom's Border Controls', HL 37 (1998/9).

[74] Tampere European Council, Presidency Conclusions, 15 and 16 Oct. 1999, Doc 200/99, para. A.I.2.

[75] 'Mutual Assistance in Criminal Matters', HL 135 (1997/8); 'Prospects for the Tampere Special European Council', HL 69 (1998/9).

[76] J. Monar, 'The Dynamics of Justice and Home Affairs: Laboratories, Driving Factors and Costs' (2001) 39 *Journal of Common Market Studies* 747, 760.

[77] European Council, *Reflection Group Report* (Brussels, 1995).

[78] Of a series of EP committee reports too numerous to cite, see especially European Parliament, *Report on the Co-decision Procedure after Amsterdam* (Brussels, 1998); *Report on the*

governments to evade the formal Treaty processes, resorting to the age-old instruments of diplomacy: informal networking and back-stairs negotiation. The institutions of representative government are similarly threatened by the multiplicity of legislative processes, many dominated by an unaccountable Comitology.[79]

This line of criticism from the Council places the Commission in the ambivalent position of the 'servant with two masters', accountable to both the Council and European Parliament, whose views frequently diverge.[80] Some think that the Commission should be *more* accountable to the Council, a view which sees the Commission as the Union's supervisory agent and primary point of reference for accountability. Another view is that the Commission should cut down on its activities, being content to delegate more generously. This would mean effectively to *divest* itself of accountability. This dilemma lies at the heart of the European enterprise: set up as regulator, responsible to the Member States through their Council, the Commission has long outrun its masters' intentions.

VII MARKET ACCOUNTABILITY: THE EUROPEAN BANKING SYSTEM

Thus far, the discussion has been largely directed at democratic and public-law forms of accountability, leaving little room for Scott's alternative models. The clearest example of reliance by the Community on 'horizontal' methods of accountability is that of the European monetary system. In the elite world of banking, were, somewhat surprisingly, given the onward march of popular democracy, the overriding goal of price stability has made it acceptable to de-politicize the money-supply process and establish fiscal autonomy.[81] Fiscal autonomy means that, in a move to control inflation, a central objective in a majority of modern economies, banks are given a measure of independence and autonomy and freed from political interference, with a mandate to attend to price control and discourage inflation. The introduction of a European monetary area by the Maastricht Treaty on European Union, with the goal of replacing a number of national currencies with a single European coinage, without the introduction of fiscal instability and insecurity, was heavily

---

Moderation of Procedures for the Exercise of Implementing Powers—Comitology (Brussels, 1998); *On the Decision-making Process in the Council in an enlarged Europe* (Brussels, 1999).

[79] Below, 67–71.

[80] Theorized by A. Moravscik, 'Preferences and Power in the European Community: A Liberal Intergovernmentalist Approach' (1993) 31 *Journal of Common Market Studies* 473.

[81] M. Friedman, 'Should there be an Independent Monetary Authority?' in L.Yeager (ed.), *In Search of a Monetary Constitution* (1992).

dependent on confidence in the new banking system. As the German Bundesbank, national bank of the major economic player, had gained and guarded its fiscal autonomy jealously, it was probably inevitable also that this situation would be paralleled at European level. The creation of the European Central Bank (ECB) and European System of Central Banks (ESCB) was a deliberate move in the direction of autonomy, and in taking this line the Community was in any case only following a marked global trend towards autonomy. The mission of the European Central Banking System (ESCB) is stated in the Treaties as being 'to act in accordance with the principle of an open market economy with free competition, favouring an efficient allocation of resources' (TEC Article 105(1)) and the autonomy of the European Central Bank (ECB) is entrenched there by virtue of the fact that its statute is set out in a protocol, changes to which require Treaty amendment.[82] For better or worse, the closed appointment system of the ESCB is a paradigm 'Old Boys' Network', conducted by a banking elite. As with the European Commission, there is a stark prohibition (TEC Article 108) on taking instructions from the EU institutions or national governments. Similarly, governments of Member States pledge themselves in the Treaty 'not to seek to influence the members of the decision-making bodies of the ECB or of the national central banks in the performance of their tasks' (TEC Article 108).

How and to what extent is the European banking system to be made accountable? Here we find a marked difference of opinion between the bankers and expert advisers and academics. Turning first to the former, we find that the concern of the bankers is primarily with 'performance accountability'. This means no more than that performance in maintaining price stability in the medium term should be used by the public to judge the success of the Eurosystem. Otmar Issing, a Member of the ECB's Executive Council, has defended a high degree of autonomy on the basis of 'market accountability', saying:[83]

Precisely because the ECB has been assigned a clear and narrow task, it is democratically legitimate and economically sensible to grant it independence from the regular political process. And ultimately, precisely for this reason, its accountability can and should be based primarily, if not exclusively, on its observable record in fulfilling its mandate.

Issing goes on to distinguish accountability from transparency, believing the two should not be seen as synonymous. Like many lawyers, he defines accountability narrowly in terms of legality, or conformity with a clearly

---

[82] TEC Art. 107(4). Parts of the Statute may be amended by qualified majority, but only after consulting the ECB and EP (TEC Art. 107(5)).

[83] O. Issing, 'The Eurosystem: Transparent and Accountable or "Willem in Euroland"' (1999) 37 *Journal of Common Market Studies* 503, 517.

defined statutory mandate, on which it would be possible to challenge the ECB before the Community Courts. Otherwise, accountability relates to the market, and '[t]he issue of *accountability* for the ECB's performance with respect to its clearly defined mandate needs to be logically separated from concerns over the *transparency* of the policy-making process itself (as opposed to the outcomes of this process)'. Issing believes that 'the key to credibility and transparency is not to promise more than one can deliver'.[84] It does not need to be said that this definition of transparency is unusually narrow. Openness is confined to publicizing the Bank's monetary policy, a market panacea supposed to permit success or failure to be evaluated by the public. What the public could do in these circumstances is not very clear.

This highly attenuated form of accountability is not enough to satisfy Willem Buiter, a member of the Bank of England's new Monetary Policy Committee, who believes that decision-making by technocrats is acceptable and viable only if the institution to which these decisions are delegated is accountable to the public at large and to its elected representatives.[85] Buiter, who shows considerable hostility to the 'completely non-transparent' German Bundesbank, sees its failings replicated in the 'lack of openness, transparency and accountability written into the statutes of the ECB and reinforced by its operating procedures'.[86] He believes that the principle of 'performance accountability' is wholly insufficient to give the banking system credibility. Real transparency means opening up of the decision-making process; publication of individual voting records, minutes, and ECB inflation forecasts are necessary for banking legitimacy in the eyes of the public. This view conforms more closely to the management and audit accountability which is a condition of New Public Management (NPM), in which transparency is an essential precondition of accountability; it is also more in line with Anglo-American market theories of accountability.

Rosa Maria Lastra wavers between the two opinions. On the one hand, political accountability is a 'must'; in a democracy, she sees 'no real case for a central bank which is totally independent from government; there must be a two-way flow of cooperation and consultation'.[87] 'Accountable independence' is Lastra's stated goal, and this depends upon a 'binding legal and institutional framework' which specifies 'the different ways in which central banks can be held accountable for their actions'. Accountability will depend largely on transparency, but the central bank must be under an obligation to 'explain and justify' to a court, to the legislature, and to public

[84] Ibid., at 506.
[85] W. Buiter, 'Alice in Euroland' (1999) 37 *Journal of Common Market Studies* 181, 187.
[86] Ibid., 185.
[87] R. M. Lastra, 'European Monetary Union and Central Bank Independence' in M. Andenas, L. Gormley, C. Hadjiemmanuil, and I. Harden (eds.), *European Economic and Monetary Union: The Institutional Framework* (London, Kluwer, 1997), 300.

opinion. As this framework is presently supplied by, and entrenched in, the EC Treaty, however, it gives a guarantee of virtual autonomy, and Lastra describes the ECB as only 'somewhat accountable' to parliaments.[88] But since she believes that national parliaments have long lost control of government budgets and that 'parliamentary control and approval of a government's budget can be more of a formality than a real check',[89] the new arrangements are broadly welcome; a banking system formally immune from accountability is at least also immune to governmental manipulation.

Christos Hadjiemmanuil is less complacent when he talks of a 'double loss' of political control over 'decisions of the utmost importance to a significant proportion of Europeans'. In addition to the vertical loss of control by national communities in favour of a distant centre, there is also a horizontal transfer of power to an unaccountable ECB.[90] Jacob de Haan and Laurence Gormley also believe that 'monetary policy ultimately must be controlled by democratically elected politicians'[91] and argue that the democratic accountability of the ECB is poorly organized. On the one hand, the ECB is not truly accountable, as its mandate can only be changed through the notoriously difficult process of Treaty amendment, requiring unanimity; on the other hand, it is not sufficiently independent. The experience of making appointments to the Commission, more especially the presidency, suggests that the ECB will not be immune from political pressure and interference—a guess substantiated by the circumstances surrounding the appointment of Wim Duisenberg, reputedly the outcome of a Council bargain between France and the Netherlands.

Sverker Gustavsson asks the rhetorical question whether EMU represents an *irrevocable* surrender of democratic accountability in the area of monetary policy?[92] The answer famously given by the German Constitutional Court was that the surrender was *provisional only*. At every step to further congruence, Member States, through the Council of Ministers, remained in charge, while change also required the consent of national parliaments.[93] But, as Gustavvson points out, this analysis is unrealistic, ignoring the degree of autonomy deliberately accorded to the European banking system, which

---

[88] Ibid.

[89] Ibid., at 301.

[90] C. Hadjiemmanuil, 'Democracy, Supranationality and Central Bank Independence' in J. Kleinemann (ed.), *Central Bank Independence: The Economic Foundations, the Constitutional Implications and Democratic Accountability*,

[91] J. de Haan and L. Gormley, 'Independence and Accountability of the European Central Bank' in Andenas *et al.* (eds.), n. 87 above, 352.

[92] S. Gustavvson, 'Reconciling Suprastatism and Accountability: A View from Sweden' in C. Hoskyns and M. Newman (eds.), *Democratizing the European Union, Issues for the Twenty-first Century* (Manchester, Manchester University Press, 2000).

[93] See the 'Maastricht decision', Bundesverfassungsgericht, 2nd chamber (Senat), Cases BvR 2134/92 and 2 BvR 2159/92, 12 Oct. 1993, BVerfGE 89, 155.

renders control by the Council very difficult; morever, only minimal control is in practice exercised by national parliaments over their government's actions in Council. Nor has any parliament 'ever dared to defy the provisionally established suprastatal order'. So from this point of view, the move at Maastricht from single market to monetary union could prove historically critical, risking the 'introduction of fiscal federalism without a corresponding growth in the powers of the European Parliament'. This Gustavvson sees as 'a far worse constitutional predicament' than that involved in the present level of regulatory and deregulatory co-operation. Buiter predicts the slightly different outcome[94] of a slide over time towards political accountability because the European Parliament will not be content to be wholly excluded from monetary policy-making. It will use its limited powers of audit and to be consulted over appointments to 'sharpen its teeth' on its oversight function, exacting political responsibility as a further lever to extend its widening competence and powers. What will then have resulted from EMU is an unintended transfer, not only of economic policy-making but of political accountability from national to Community level. Thus a considerable weight of academic opinion supports Buiter's views in believing market accountability to be untenable.

The idea that areas of economic life as important as banking and fiscal regulation can be left to 'market accountability' of the type endorsed by Issing, involves three dangerous fictions. The first is that the market is capable of imposing anything more than notional accountability; this is, indeed, implicitly recognized by Issing. Even in consumer transactions, the paradigm private-law activity, the dissatisfied consumer is left effectively without any accountability other than to withdraw his custom; government has had to intervene, notably through EC law, to regulate consumer transactions. Secondly, the idea of the ECB as a 'market', from which dissatisfied governments can withdraw their custom, is frankly ridiculous. The third fiction is that, in the modern era, banking remains a 'private' function; whatever the situation may have been in the days of John Locke, management of the economy is seen today as a central governmental responsibility. In public-law terms, the ECB is a quasi-autonomous agency, with in practice a questionable degree of latitude. This should be enough to put public lawyers on guard; they should be asking for new—or, rather, for the reinstatement of old—accountability mechanisms.[95] Historically, the power of parliaments rests in the ancient power to grant 'supply' and they cannot afford to lose control over finance, the economy, or taxation. If Lastra's belief that parliamentary control and approval of these functions is not 'a real check', or if Buiter is

[94] Buiter, n. 85 above, 183.
[95] The arguments were long ago advanced by A. Shonfield, *Modern Capitalism* (Royal Institute of International Affairs, Oxford: Oxford University Press, 1965), but the later article by M. Freedland, 'Government by Contract and Public Law' [1994] *PL* 86 is also instructive.

wrong to predict that the European Parliament will 'sharpen its teeth', then parliaments need to do something about this, otherwise serious changes in the balance of power between government and parliaments are under way, under the guise of fiscal autonomy. If, on the other hand, Buiter's prophecy is right, then we need to think seriously about this slippage of power, perhaps ultimately of competence, from national governments to the EU. These are very important issues, on which there ought to be not only public account-ability but, more importantly, open public debate.

VIII CONCLUSIONS

The Conclusions of the Tampere Council state that the area of freedom, security, and justice must be based 'on the principles of transparency and democratic control. We must develop an open dialogue with civil society on the aims and principles of this area in order to strengthen citizens' acceptance and support'.[96] As a general principle this is no doubt admirable, even if it raises questions of how an 'open dialogue with civil society' is to be con-ducted, if civil society is not minded to have one? But what this brief survey of potential trouble-spots has shown is the number of problems which need to be dealt with before EU policy-making can begin to be described as transpar-ent and subject to democratic control. The architecture of the EU was not originally constructed with openness or accountability in mind, nor was the EU modelled on a parliamentary democracy. Its embryonic assembly was purely consultative, and the short history of the European Parliament has been one of clawing power back from the other institutions. In Chapter 4, we shall ask how far it has been successful.

[96] Conclusions of the Tampere European Council (15 and 16 Oct. 1999), para. 7.

3

The Power House

I A COMMISSION AT BAY

Accountability was placed squarely on to the political agenda of the Commission in the winter of 1999, when it was rocked by a political scandal. A vote of censure was tabled against the College of Commissioners in the European Parliament and, although the vote of censure was unsuccessful, the President, Jacques Santer, and his Commissioners resigned as a body on 15 March 1999. This unprecedented event was widely publicized in the media and saluted as marking the dawn of a new era in European political life.

The affair involved multiple allegations of fraud and mismanagement. These stretched back before Santer's appointment, to a point in 1995 when the European Court of Auditors had refused to certify the Commission's annual accounts on the ground that nearly £3 billion ecu could not be accounted for. The Commission's slow and inadequate response to these allegations of mismanagement led the EP to freeze 10 per cent of the Commissioners' salaries. In 1998, there was further concern when the Commission's anti-fraud unit (UCLAF) announced that at least 600,000 ecu from the Commission's humanitarian budget for 1993–5 (the ECHO programme) was missing. UCLAF blamed the delay in discovering this irregularity in part on the Commission's failure to keep the Court of Auditors (ECA) fully informed. A leak from the Commission's internal audit unit later in the year, alleging nepotism in the award of Commission contracts and Commissioners' complicity in fraud, increased the suspicion and feelings of dissatisfaction.

On 14 January 1999, the EP adopted a Resolution on improving the financial management of the European Commission. At the same time, it called for a Committee of Independent Experts (*Comité des Sages*) to be established, to report to Commission and Parliament jointly,[1] with a mandate 'to examine the way in which the Commission detects and deals

---

[1] The Committee published two reports, interim and final: Committee of Independent Experts, *First Report on Allegations of Fraud, Mismanagement and Nepotism in the European Commission*, 15 Mar. 1999 (hereafter IR) and *Second Report on the Reform of the Commission*,

with fraud, mismanagement and nepotism, including a fundamental review of Commission practices in the awarding of all financial contracts'.[2] This preliminary mandate was later filled out by a Conference of the Presidents of the EP to include the question of responsibility. The Experts were to consider 'to what extent the Commission, as a body, or Commissioners individually, bear specific responsibility for the recent examples of fraud, mismanagement or nepotism raised in Parliamentary discussions, or in the allegations which have arisen in those discussions'.[3] This formula was later widened by the Committee to take in 'reprehensible acts committed by the Commission's administrative services', taking into account 'the conduct of the administration in the cases under review'.[4]

The Committee was composed of five distinguished 'experts', of whom three were auditors and two lawyers, with a noticeable absence of management or public-administration expertise.[5] It is interesting to speculate why the EP did not rely on the offices of its European Ombudsman (EO), in whose remit maladministration directly falls, or at least include him among the experts. Such a choice would have enhanced accountability, by demonstrating the capabilities of the permanent investigatory machinery available to the European Parliament,[6] at the same time enhancing the profile of the EO. The Experts, on the other hand, saw themselves as 'neither a Community institution nor a Community agency [and] certainly not a Community court'. They had no formal investigative power, and authority was vested in them 'by virtue solely of an agreement between the Commission and Parliament that (i) all relevant documentation the Committee wished to look at would be made available and (ii) that the staff of the institutions would be exempted from all secrecy obligations imposed on them by Staff Regulations'—quite a concession! In short, the Committee was no more than a temporary advisory committee 'operating by consent and drawing its authority from the resolution of Parliament and the commitment of both Parliament and the Commission to support its work and to recognise its findings'.[7]

In three of the cases investigated in depth—the ECHO programme of humanitarian aid, the Leonardo programme of subsidy for vocational

---

Analysis of Current Practice and Proposals for Tackling Mismanagement, Irregularities and Fraud, 10 Sept. 1999 (hereafter FR).

[2] IR, n. 1 above, para. 1.

[3] Point 6 of Note from the EP Conference of Presidents, 27 Jan. 1999.

[4] IR, n. 1 above, para. 1.1.5.

[5] The Chairman, Mr André Middelhoek (Holland), and Mr Pierre Lelong (France) were both former Presidents of the European Court of Auditors. Mrs Inga-Britt Ahlenius was a Swedish auditor. Of the two lawyers, Mr Juan Carrillo Salçedo (Spain) was a distinguished human rights lawyer and Mr Walter van Gerven (Belgium) a previous Advocate-General of the European Court of Justice.

[6] The EO reports to the Petitions Committee of the European Parliament.

[7] IR, n. 1 above, paras. 1.2.1–1.2.3.

training, and the MED programme of grants to Mediterranean countries affected by the Gulf War—the Experts identified instances of 'mismanagement in detecting or dealing with fraud, mismanagement or nepotism perpetrated by the administrative services of the Commission and by third parties working for the Commission'.[8] A number of officials, notably the head of the Tourism Unit, found guilty of fraud, nepotism, and misuse of Community funds, were heavily censured. The MED programme in particular gave evidence of maladministration. It was said to be 'marked by improvisation, haste and, indeed, incompetence, with grave consequences: irregular delegation of powers, failure to comply with competitive tendering rules, and, above all, manifest conflicts of interest caused by the Commission services themselves'.[9] There was a 'loss of control by the political authorities over the Administration that they are supposedly running. This loss of control implies at the outset a heavy responsibility for both the Commissioners individually and the Commission as a whole'.[10] In their terse and celebrated conclusion, the Experts spoke of 'a growing reluctance among the members of the hierarchy to acknowledge their responsibility. It is becoming difficult to find anyone who has even the slightest sense of responsibility'.[11]

Publication of the Interim Report on 15 March 1999 occasioned the unprecedented resignation not merely of individual Commissioners but of the Commission as a College, though, later, a few Commissioners were to return as members of the Prodi Commission.[12] Inside the European Parliament, the resignations were greeted as a resounding political victory. MEPs rejoiced that the EP had come of age, that the 'democratic deficit' seemed to have melted away in the night. The media had an unprecedented field day. The incident seemed to confirm the worst suspicions of the European public, hostile in an uninformed way to the 'Brussels bureaucracy', about the wide powers of the Commission and its apparent lack of accountability.

In its Interim Report, the Committee of Independent Experts had proceeded largely on the basis of political *responsibility*, individual and collective; indeed, in the concluding paragraph,[13] the word 'responsibility' (in the French version, '*responsabilité*') occurs six times. The analysis closely parallels the classic British doctrine of ministerial responsibility to Parliament: individual and collective responsibility are distinguished, as are political and administrative responsibility. 'Accountability', on the other hand, makes

---

[8] Ibid., paras. 2.3.1–2.4.13. And see, for a fuller account, Chap. 5, p. 121.

[9] IR, n. 1 above, para. 3.8.4.

[10] Ibid., para. 9.2.2.

[11] Ibid., para. 9.4.25.

[12] M. Santer himself added a familiar political twist to the story by resurfacing as a Luxembourg MEP, elected under a list system. In that capacity, he is now a delegate to the Constitutional Convention.

[13] IR, n. 1 above, para. 9.4.25.

only a cursory appearance in the Interim Report, as do the terms '*comptable*'
and '*comptabilité*', in the French version, in the sense of 'book-keeping' or
'accountancy', the usual translation in the English text. Towards the end of the
conclusions, however, the Experts make an important statement of
principle:[14]

The principles of *openness, transparency and accountability*... are at the heart of
democracy and are the very instruments allowing it to function properly. Openness
and transparency imply that the decision-making process, at all levels, is as accessible
and accountable as possible to the general public. It means that the reasons for
decisions taken, are known and that those taking decisions assume responsibility for
them and are ready to accept the personal consequences when such decisions are
subsequently shown to be wrong.

In its second report, the Committee of Experts moved further in the same
direction. The general approach of this report, which ranges widely and is, for
such a body, exceptionally detailed in its recommendations, is to provide a
package of remedies against maladministration. The Experts revisited the
question of political responsibility on which they had focused in the Interim
Report, patterning their model of political responsibility on that of a democratic nation state. In consequence, much space had to be devoted to analysis
of the relationships between the Commissioners, their *cabinets*, and permanent civil servants, with a view to establishing lines of accountability, collective
and individual. Not surprisingly, since the institutional structure differs in
many ways from that of the traditional nation state in which doctrines of
political responsibility have evolved, the discussion was somewhat inconclu-
sive. A key role was, however, allocated by the Experts to the EU's 'democratic institutions', of which the European Parliament, described as
paramount, was the only one with which the Experts dealt, ignoring for the
most part the competing claims of the Council and national parliaments. The
Experts were, in other words, convinced by the two-tier, horizontal division
of powers in the EU, whereby EU institutions play in one team and national
institutions in another. As Chapter 4 will show, this division is a major
obstacle to accountability in EU affairs. Without much consideration of
what this would mean in practice, the Experts however insisted that the
Commission would have to 'account both positively (giving account) and
negatively (being held to account)' to the EP.[15]

It was left to the incoming President, Romano Prodi, to bring the threads
together in a speech to the European Parliament on 4 May 1999. Defining
the role of Commissioner, Signor Prodi said:[16]

---

[14] Ibid., para. 9.3.3 (emphasis added).   [15] FR, n. 1 above, para. 7.1.5.
[16] **http://europa.eu.int/comm/commissioners/prodi/speeches/130499en.htm**.

I am firmly convinced that increasing the *efficiency and accountability* of the Commission in future largely depends on greatly reducing the grey areas which currently tend to blur demarcation lines of autonomy and responsibility between those performing more political tasks and those more involved with administration.

He went on to make the link with efficiency and transparency, promising, '[o]nce we have increased the Commission team's capacity to provide political direction, we will be able to set about increasing the *transparency, efficiency and accountability* of their departments, as required by the Treaty of Amsterdam and demanded by European public opinion'. Accountability had arrived squarely on the Commission political agenda. Not only did the speech link accountability to efficiency but it spoke also of the need to set in place demarcation lines 'of autonomy and responsibility' between those within the Commission who performed *political* tasks and those responsible for administration. There were clear pointers to the dual set of controls familiar in nation states: on the one hand, political control associated with doctrines of ministerial responsibility to a parliament; on the other, the hierarchical controls associated with bureaucracy.

II THE COMMISSION: ACCOUNTABLE? AND TO WHOM?

The object of starting with this short case study is *not* to present the Commission as dysfunctional. The Commission is clearly not dysfunctional, as evidenced by its record of achievement over many years. Nonetheless, as the case study indicated, its structure is not designed with accountability in mind. Its origins lie in a period when the EEC was the conception of an elite and elite governance was central to the conception of European integration.[17] The perception of the Commission was of an elite. Its obligations would be to the *Community*, and independence was bestowed upon it to assure autonomy from the machinery of the first-tier nation states. The Commission was to be:

the 'bonding element' within the supranational institutional structure of the European Union. It would drive forward the motor of integration, recommending policies for action, administering the Treaties and acting as a watchdog of the 'Community' interest. It was intended to be a technocratic and elite body, rather than a political entity.[18]

---

[17] D. Dinan, *Ever Closer Union? An Introduction to the European Community* (Basingstoke, Macmillan, 1994), chap. 1 and the sources there cited. For a more theoretical perspective see P. Craig, 'The Nature of the Community: Integration, Democracy, and Legitimacy' in P. Craig and G. de Búrca (eds.), *The Evolution of EU Law* (Oxford, Oxford University Press, 1999).

[18] J. Shaw, *Law of the European Union* (3rd edn., Basingstoke, Palgrave, 2000), 110.

It must also be remembered that the Commission was established at a time before a representative parliament, to which, in orthodox fashion, it might be seen to be accountable, was in being. The principle of accountability can hardly be spelled out of the Treaties, which have been described as 'terse' on this point, though also ambiguous.[19] The Treaties are emphatic about the Commission's 'independence', even if they admit of the possibility of a vote of censure in the EP (TEC Article 201). TEC Article 213 emphasizes the *apolitical character* of the Commission, insisting that the Commissioners shall 'be completely independent in the performance of their duties', neither seeking nor taking instructions 'from any government or from any other body'. Although Simon Hix describes the Commission in terms of 'cabinet government',[20] based on collective responsibility, autonomy in the performance of its duties seemingly placed the Commission in a different position *vis-à-vis* political accountability to governments in every Member State, since the legitimacy of the College was not based on the normal democratic accountability of suffrage. In this respect, it could be argued that the Commission more closely resembles, and was intended to resemble, the quasi-autonomous executive agency with which Majone associates the Community. This analysis was, however, apparently not considered, or perhaps simply not accepted by the Independent Experts.

The characteristic of elite or regulatory independence was reflected in the mode of appointment, which mitigates against accountability. The Commission today consists of twenty members, a number considered by some to be high, and which after Nice remains under consideration in the light of enlargement. Control over the College of Commissioners has not been rendered easier by the fact that Commissioners have always been appointed by Member States rather than by the President, although all appointments have now been made subject to parliamentary ratification (TEC Article 214)—a power of which the EP has made good use. The Treaty of Amsterdam improved the accountability position by giving the President a right of veto over Member State appointments, and President Prodi, in the wake of the Santer affair, extended his authority by engineering an informal agreement whereby individual Commissioners would resign if asked by the President to do so. The Nice Treaty formalized this position and allows the President with the consent of the College to appoint Vice-Presidents (TEC Article 217); otherwise appointment is for a fixed term of five years, subject to provision for compulsory retirement and other exceptional circumstances (TEC Articles 215, 216), when the ECJ has to be invoked. These changes, invoking the external authority of Court and Parliament and

---

[19] A. Tomkins, 'Responsibility and Resignation in the European Commission' (1999) 62 *MLR* 744, 757.

[20] S. Hix, *The Political System of the European Union* (Basingstoke, Macmillan, 1999), 32.

reinforcing the authority of the President, move the procedures for appointment, organization, and dismissal in the direction of political and managerial responsibility.

Today's Commissioners are for the most part career politicians and have held senior posts in national or regional governments; between 1967 and 1995, only 21 per cent of Commissioners had held no elected office prior to appointment, while nearly 70 per cent had held ministerial office.[21] They are therefore likely to be well conversant with doctrines of ministerial responsibility, although their understanding and experience of the doctrine and, for that matter, of the duties and obligations of office may differ widely. Investigation of the Santer Commission showed, for example, the extent to which standards of conduct or rules about political appointments might vary from one Member State to another. Commissioners tend, despite the terms of TEC Article 213(2), to possess and keep links with national political parties, which inevitably colour their view of their own and the Commission's functions. Unlike the ministers of a national government, the Commissioners do not devise, share, and defend any common political agenda, so that the glue, which is the strongest factor in the collective cabinet responsibility used by the Independent Experts as their prototype, is likely to be absent. This makes the Commission look more like a coalition; in the worst case, a weak coalition comparable to those of Italy, where unstable coalition has been the order of the day.[22] As in France, relationships between Commissioners and functionaries are conducted by *cabinets*, which form the link between the political and bureaucratic Commission. It has been suggested that these relationships are often uncomfortable,[23] not unexpected, as the minister/functionary relationship is often a tense one in national civil services.

Initially, it was envisaged that the corporate and collective spirit would be greater than the intergovernmentalist tendencies of its members would permit of the Council and, to a certain extent, this distinction seems pertinent. As many commentators record, however, the collegial spirit is in practice often undercut by intergovernmentalist tendencies inside the Commission bureaucracy. The Commission is organized in Directorates (DGs) headed by permanent Directors-General. Failure to meld the different cultures of which the Commission bureaucracy is compounded and which have proved hard to

---

[21] Ibid, 35 and Table 2.3, at 36. E. Page and L. Wouters, 'Bureaucratic Politics and Political Leadership in Brussels' (1994) 72 *Public Administration* 445 show that, of the 1993 Commission, 58% had previously held ministerial office and 80% had a background in politics, with 35% from the civil service.

[22] P. Pasquino, 'Les transformations du système politique (1992–2000)' in S. Cassese (ed.), *Portrait de l'Italie actuelle* (Paris, La documentation française, 2001).

[23] T. Christiansen, 'Tensions of European Governance: Politicised Bureaucracy and Multiple Accountability in the European Commission' (1997) 4 *Journal of European Public Policy* 73, 80.

unify, has impeded the internal cohesion of the Commission bureaucracy. One of the ingredients for Weberian bureaucracy, submission to strong hierarchical control, has been partly missing, so that the hierarchical controls particularly associated with accountability in centralized national civil services may be weak.[24] In considering the capacity of the College of Commissioners to exercise political leadership and control inside the Commission, we ought to bear in mind that an uneasy balance of power is not unusual in national systems of government, where rapid changes of ministry weaken the hand of the politicians. Without a long experience of Brussels, however, Commissioners may tend to be more in the hands of their permanent civil service than in national or regional government, where the political context and culture are shared. The relative autonomy of the Commission may also be a problem, bringing freedom from the investigative parliamentary committees and probing ombudsman inquiries to which national government is subject and which helps to tie political and bureaucratic actors together in the face of a common enemy.

Simon Hix sees partisan, though not necessarily party-political, attitudes as present in the body of civil servants who make up the Commission bureaucracy; particular DGs may possess strong cultures and even ideologies. Hix feels able, for example, to single out Employment and Social Policy as possessing a 'highly corporatist culture', while telecommunications is 'more pluralist and focused on technical expertise and ideas'.[25] This is not unusual; similar observations are often made about ministries in a national civil service. What is, however, different is that, in the transnational Commission, policy areas can come to be dominated by particular nationalities, a specialization which can undercut the supposedly neutral character of the Commission, at least if 'policy' and 'political' are equated.[26] Environment is, for example, an area associated with strong leaders capable of articulating, and anxious to promote, green policies.[27] It is not, of course, being suggested that this is improper or undesirable; it is, on the contrary, precisely the type of commitment or 'responsibility' for which the Independent Experts looked. Nor is there anything unusual; a vast body of research directed at the subject confirms that this is the usual way for bureaucracies to operate and bureaucrats to

[24] This emerges clearly from the reports and working papers of the Commission, e.g., European Commission, *Reforming the Commission*, COM(2000)200, discussed in the final chap.
[25] S. Hix, n. 20 above, 37. See to the same effect M. Cini, 'Administrative Culture in the European Commission: The Cases of Competition and Environment' in N. Nugent (ed.), *At the Heart of the Union: Studies of the European Commission* (London, Macmillan, 1997).
[26] See the report prepared for the Commission: *Approche anthropologique de la commission européenne* (Brussels, European Commission, 1993).
[27] D. Chalmers, 'Inhabitants in the Field of EC Environmental Law' in Craig and de Búrca (eds.), n. 17 above, 662–71.

behave.[28] What does mark out the Commission is its transnational make-up, and the fact that it is drawn from national administrations with variant traditions, with the cultures of which it is deeply imbued.[29] The danger of factionalism is accentuated by the habit of seconding staff from national civil services, useful as a learning process but inevitably a factor mitigating against 'independence' in the Treaty sense. It is also stirred up by the quota system, according to which jobs must broadly reflect national representation. This practice, long outlawed by the ECJ,[30] has not entirely disappeared. All these factors, when taken together with strong unions and a complex and legalistic staff code which culminates in a right of appeal to the Court of First Instance,[31] make disciplinary action difficult. These deficiencies emerged clearly as an important element in the irregularities which precipitated the fall of the Santer Commission. Leslie Metcalfe has diagnosed a serious managerial deficit, suggesting that the Commission possesses 'many of the characteristic weaknesses of traditional national civil services with the added complication of a multinational staff recruited from all the member states'.[32] This would point to an input of the techniques associated with 'New Public Management'. Some moves in this direction have been instigated and, under the supervision of Vice-president Neil Kinnock, are already under way.[33]

III THE COMMISSION'S CHANGING FUNCTIONS

The functions for which the Commission should in principle be accountable are set out in TEC Article 211, which provides that, 'in order to ensure the proper functioning and development of the common market', the Commission shall:

[28] For an introduction to the literature in the context of the Community, see E. Page, 'Administering Europe' in J. Hayward and E. Page (eds.), *Governing the New Europe* (Cambridge, Polity Press, 1995).

[29] On divergent administrative traditions see J. Burnham and M. Maor, 'Converging Administrative Systems: Recruitment and Training in European Union Member States' (1995) 2 *Journal of European Public Policy* 185; W. Kickert, *Public Management and Administrative Reform in Western Europe* (London, Edward Elgar, 1997). See also I. Bellier, 'Une culture de la Commission Européenne? De la rencontre des cultures et du multilinguisme des fonctionnaires' in Y. Mény *et al. Politiques Publiques en Europe* (Paris, Harmattan, 1995).

[30] Case 15/63, *Lassalle* v. *Parliament* [1964] ECR 31; Joined Cases 81–88/74, *Marenco* v. *Commission* [1975] ECR 1247.

[31] Regulation 259/68 [1968] JO L56/1 laying down the Staff Regulations of Officials and the Conditions of Employment of Other Servants of the European Communities. For judicial competence, see TEC Arts. 225 and 236 and Declaration 16 of the Nice Treaty.

[32] L. Metcalfe, 'The European Commission as a Network Organisation' (1996) 26 *Publius: The Journal of Federalism* 43, 52.

[33] See Chap. 7, 187–9.

- ensure that the provisions of this Treaty and the measures taken by the institutions pursuant thereto are applied;
- formulate recommendations or deliver opinions on matters dealt with in this Treaty, if it expressly so provides or if the Commission considers it necessary;
- have its own power of decision and participate in the shaping of measures taken by the Council and by the European Parliament in the manner provided for in this Treaty;
- exercise the powers conferred on it by the Council for the implementation of the rules laid down by the latter.

Simon Hix describes the Commission as the 'core executive' of the Community.[34] Although its duties could be said to depart, in their blend of policy-making, rule-making, and implementation, from the classical sense of the term 'executive', they are entirely consonant with the functions of a modern civil service in a national system, most of which have long deviated from a triadic separation of functions, but which manage to co-exist reasonably happily with doctrines of ministerial responsibility. On the other hand, the Commission functions are equally compatible with our alternative analysis of the Commission as a particular form of regulatory agency,[35] again with an entirely normal mix of rule-making, policy-making, and executive functions. This analysis could be said to be more in line both with the Commission's stated independence and autonomy and with Jean Monnet's initial vision of the Commission as an apolitical, functionalist bureaucracy, designed to protect the collective interest of European citizens. Because the agency model suggests a greater degree of autonomy and less external oversight, many who work in the Commission, especially in the field of competition, would probably, for this reason, prefer the second version.

Because it is not in the business of service delivery nor, except in certain limited areas such as competition policy, of 'direct administration', most of the Commission's energies are devoted to policy-making and regulation, a sharp contrast with both national and regional administrations. The Commission does not, in New Public Management (NPM) jargon, have a direct relationship with 'customers' or hear their reactions. Again atypically, the EU administration is not conducted through executive agencies, although in its latest White Paper the Commission's fears of 'agencification' seem to be lessening.[36] The Commission is consequently heavily dependent on the administrations of Member States and their regions in respect of service delivery and enforcement. (Its very particular enforcement functions are

---

[34] S. Hix, n. 20 above, 32.
[35] M. Everson, 'Administering Europe' (1998) 36 *Journal of Common Market Studies* 195.
[36] European Commission, White Paper on European Governance, COM(2001)428 final, 23–4.

addressed in a later section.) To paraphrase the famous aphorism of Osborne and Gaebler,[37] the Commission is a body which 'steers' and does not 'row'. Its role has been defined as that of 'policy entrepreneur', tapping into outside expert groups, advisory bodies, and networks in the exercise of its policy-making functions,[38] a work pattern consonant with the 'policy network' theory analyses noted in Chapter 1. This is a work pattern leading to a web of advisory committees and working groups, often appointed on a transitory basis, for which the Commission is theoretically responsible. As these begin to act as policy-makers in their own right, acquiring an autonomy and consequential immunity from accountability which legally is not theirs, they have attracted criticism of lack of accountability and transparency. In principle, it is the Commission which acts as agent in ensuring accountability; in practice, although Commission representatives participate in and work with policy networks, it is by no means clear that the Commission can supervise them. Arguably indeed, inability to secure full financial and managerial accountability from its many collaborators led to the downfall of the Santer Commission. Leslie Metcalfe has argued that the Commission's failure to define its role in terms of 'organiser of networks' and put its definition firmly into practice underlies many of its internal management deficiencies.[39]

The steady increase in the functions of the Commission has been noted by many commentators.[40] In the half-century during which the Commission has presided with some success over the affairs of the EU, its functions have changed radically. Not only have its duties greatly expanded with the increasing power and influence of the EU, but they have also changed in character: from rule-making and market regulation to administrator of grants and, in the most recent phase, adviser on foreign affairs, defence, justice, and immigration. The enforcement functions have also expanded dramatically and, as we shall see, more is expected of the Commission in this field. Yet the Council, which has not hesitated to load the Commission with new functions, has notably failed to provide the extra staff and funding which would make the load bearable. The increasing disequilibrium is summarized by Metcalfe:[41]

[37] D. Osborne and T. Gaebler, *Reinventing Government* (New York, Addison Wesley, 1992).

[38] B. Laffan, 'From Policy Entrepreneur to Policy Manager: The Challenge Facing the EC' (1997) 4 *Journal of European Public Policy* 422, 423.

[39] Metcalfe, n. 32 above.

[40] E.g., J. Ziller, 'De la nature de l'administration européenne' (2000) 95 *Revue française d'administration publique* 357, 361.

[41] Metcalfe, n. 32 above, 46. See to the same effect N. Nugent, 'The Leadership Capacity of the EC' (1995) 2 *Journal of European Public Policy* 603; T. Christiansen, 'A Maturing Bureaucracy? The Role of the Commission in the Policy Process' in J. Richardson (ed.), *European Union: Power and Policymaking* (London, Routledge, 1996).

The Commission itself has not been overhauled since its creation, despite major changes in its operating environment. It was designed in the 1950s for a relatively homogenous group of six countries embarking on a limited programme of economic integration in a period of rapid economic growth. Essentially, the same organisation is now expected to serve the needs of fifteen more diverse countries engaged in an advanced process of integration in far less favourable economic circumstances.

The consequence has been to make the Commission increasingly dependent on staff seconded for short periods from national civil services and on short-term contracts concluded with the many 'experts' who cluster around the Commission in Brussels. By the end of the 1990s, this trend was creating problems of which President Santer was well aware and, to his credit, sought to address. These emerged first in reports from the European Court of Auditors to surface with high visibility in the reports of the Committee of Independent Experts, which attracted wide publicity. President Prodi sees the answer as lying in a Commission which does less but does it well. Thus the current agenda for reform, discussed in the final chapter, aims at the twin goals of a more efficient and effective Commission and, in parallel, a more transparent and accountable Commission.

IV THE COMMISSION AND RULE-MAKING

Regulation in the narrow sense of rule-making has become a standard governmental function and tool of regulatory governance,[42] and executive rule-making power is in line with national practice everywhere. In Anglo-American theory the regulatory power is described as 'delegated', a term which marks the relationship as one of principal/agent and accountability. In other systems, a regulatory power may be explicitly recognized as an inherent executive function, as it is in Article 37 of the French Constitution; accountability is then more limited. In common with many national executives, the European Commission possesses important rule-making powers, but is unique in possessing the sole power to initiate policy and regulation under TEC Article 211. This suggests a wider remit and more significant policy-making functions than those allowed in principle to national civil services, a difference which makes it again more like a regulatory agency.

The term 'implementation' in TEC Article 211 carries a specialized meaning, the reference being to the regulatory powers granted to the Commission to 'implement' general EC regulations, for which the Council bears responsibility. Primarily directed towards the single market, these implemen-

---

[42] R. Baldwin, *Rules and Government* (Oxford, Clarendon, 1995); C. Hood and C. Scott, 'Bureaucratic Regulation and New Public Management in the United Kingdom: Mirror-Image Developments?' (1996) 23 *Journal of Law and Society* 321.

tation powers have nonetheless been widely used in other policy areas, e.g., agriculture and overseas aid. At the first stage, these are powers of policy-making, compatible with the Commission power of legislative initiative. This stage usually involves a co-ordinating function of searching for solutions acceptable across the EU. The Commission has to be sure that policy is acceptable to Member States, a necessity which has stimulated the practice of transnational committees; the relationships of the Commission with national administrations through the practice of regular secondment are also helpful. A further factor in the development of committee governance, and its use in the law-making process, lies in the increasing technicality of the regulation. Law and regulation are no longer composed of broad general principles, expressed in language easily comprehensible to the public; they have come instead to consist of detailed lists: for example, of product-safety standards, or methods of regulating emission of gases into the environment, comprehensible only to the scientists and producers by whom they are formulated. Technicality is a special feature of EU regulation[43] and justifies the wide use of specialists, but the problem of technicality is heightened in the EU context by the need to produce equivalence in many languages.

The policy-making stage may terminate with legislative proposals or alternatively end in informal rules or 'soft law', which often play a significant role in policy development.[44] Soft law is objectionable to many lawyers because it evades the democratic controls of parliamentary scrutiny; more-over, it is not, as formal EU acts are, squarely founded on a legal base in the Treaties. This may sometimes mean that control by courts is also evaded. The Commission's response to public concern has been to promote demo-cratic self-management in the rulemaking and standard-setting processes, delegating wherever possible to the 'social partners' or manufacturing groups, such as CELEC.[45] Rules agreed in this way can then be implemented by the Commission—in terms of accountability a procedure to be criticized. Cur-rently, the Commission is also interested in 'the open method of governance'

[43] S. Weatherill, 'Compulsory Notification of Draft Technical Regulations: The Contri-bution of Directive 83/189 to the Management of the Internal Market' (1996) 16 *Yearbook of European Law* 129.

[44] F. Snyder, 'Soft Law and Institutional Practice in the European Community' in S. Martin (ed.), *The Construction of Europe, Essays in Honour of Emile Nöel* (Dordrecht, Kluwer, 1994), 197; M. Smith, 'Autonomy by the Rules: The European Commission and the Development of State Aid Policy' (1998) 36 *Journal of Common Market Studies* 55; G. della Cananea, 'From Judges to Legislators? The Codification of EC Administrative Procedures in the Field of State Aids' (1995) 5 *Rivista Italiana di Diritto Pubblico Comuni-tario* 967.

[45] Commission standardization in the EC: Communication from Commission to Council and the European Parliament, COM(91)521 final. Some of the processes are discussed in essays in P. Craig and C. Harlow (eds.), *Lawmaking in the European Union* (London, Kluwer International, 1998).

and in wide use of framework legislation,[46] modes of governance which might return responsibility to the Member States. The novel forms of law-making are seen as more accountable, in that the rules are made either by those directly interested—a dubious means of public accountability, raising the spectre of self-interested lobby groups—or by representatives of civil society, even though these are not directly elected, and are difficult to identify or choose. The latter problem is a theme running through many of the ideas in the Commission White Paper on Governance. The scope of Commission relationships with members of advisory committees and the role which the latter play in national governance are already problematic, as the opportunities for informal contact and influence between Commission staff and national civil servants or experts are much harder to regulate or control.

A more far-reaching reform of EU rule-making would be the introduction of an 'evidence-based' legislative process, meaning that no new measure should be undertaken unless there is a clear balance of relevant evidence in favour of it. Suggested by Frank Vibert,[47] this idea aims unashamedly at de-regulation. Vibert demands as a mandatory precondition to *all* rule-making a cost-benefit analysis of every legislative proposal, in which the costs of action are weighed against the risks, a complex process resembling environmental impact assessment, or the 'bench-marking' demanded as a condition of social legislation by feminists and other interest groups. Based in rational-choice theory, the idea seeks to make regulators more accountable for their choices, judged by the standards and performance indicators of rational choice. In so doing the theory fundamentally misconstrues the political process. Political and, more especially, legislative policy-making is not based on rational choice; it is the outcome of processes of interest-representation, lobbying, bargaining, compromise, and concession. These are processes not readily amenable to explanation or accountability through the managerial standards of NPM and audit. Legislators do not set themselves performance indicators by which to judge the success or failure of legislation, though policy-makers and those who implement the legislation may do so. EU technical rules and standards are kept under review by the Commission and by Member States and the expert Comitology committees are well placed to monitor and advise.

---

[46] White Paper on Governance, n. 36 above. See for comment D. Hodson and I. Maher, 'The Open Method as a New Mode of Governance' (2001) 39 *Journal of Common Market Studies* 719; D. Wincott, 'The Commission and the Reform of Governance in the European Union' (2001) 39 *Journal of Common Market Studies* 897.

[47] F. Vibert, *Governance in the European Union—From Ideology to Evidence* (London, European Policy Forum, January, 2001).

V GOVERNANCE BY EXPERTS: THE COMITOLOGY

In the exercise of regulatory powers of implementation, the Council has chosen to restrain the Commission by setting in place a network of management and regulatory committees, which represent the interests of Member States in the Commission's work of implementation. These are the committees to which the term 'Comitology' technically refers. Installed by a formal Council decision,[48] their legality was tested in court by the EP, concerned that legislative accountability would be undercut.[49] The Comitology, as with all committees, has assumed a life of its own. This has made it the target of heavy criticism from academic observers, on the dual grounds of lack of transparency and accountability. Briefly, both management and regulatory committees can prevent the Commission from proceeding with a measure without their approval,[50] requiring a re-submission; thus the choice may dramatically affect the regulatory outcome, upsetting the 'institutional balance' between the EU institutions. This lends substance to the suspicion of the EP, which sees the Comitology as undercutting its role, and lending to Commission implementing measures the full authority of the Council, while concealing the fact that the Council has often never been consulted.[51] The British House of Lords, in the course of a very thorough scrutiny by a Select Committee of the new Comitology decision,[52] recommended that the role of the European Parliament should be enhanced and management and regulatory committee procedures simplified, as ultimately they have been.

The relationship between the Commission and its committees is made more complex by limitations on its powers to delegate. As already indicated, all modern governments work in practice through abundant delegations of rule-making and policy-making functions to agencies and

[48] Council Decision 87/373/EEC of 13 July 1987 laying down the procedures for the exercise of implementing powers conferred on the Commission, now replaced by Council Decision of 28 June 1999 laying down procedures for the exercise of implementing powers conferred on the Commission [1999] OJ L184/23.

[49] Case 302/87, *Parliament* v. *Council (Comitology)* [1988] ECR 5615.

[50] On the subtleties of the variant procedures see E. Vos, 'EU Committees: the Evolution of Unforeseen Institutional Actors in European Product Regulation' in C. Joerges and E. Vos (eds.), *EU Committees: Social Regulation, Law and Politics* (Oxford, Hart Publishing, 1999), 24–6. The procedures were modified and replaced by Council Decision of 28 June 1999.

[51] K. St. C. Bradley, 'Institutional Aspects of Comitology: Scenes from the Cutting Room Floor' in ibid.

[52] House of Lords, 'Delegation of Powers to the Commission: Reforming Comitology', 3rd Report of the Select Committee on the European Communities, HL 23 (1998/9) Conclusion 16. In 'European Monetary Union and Political Union', 27th Report of the Select Committee on the European Communities, HL 88 (1989/90), the Select Committee recommended that *all* 'delegated legislation'—the terminology is British—should be laid before the EP.

committees, a practice which invariably produces problems of accountability. The purpose of delegation will be defeated by too tight a rein on agents, but wide latitude for delegates allows too much play in the accountability principles. The attitude of the Community Courts has been rather strict in this regard. In the early *Meroni* case,[53] decided in respect of the Coal and Steel Community, before the tentacles of the Commission had spread through fifteen Member States, the ECJ virtually outlawed such practices by holding that broad discretionary powers could not be delegated. The effect was to hold the Commission legally accountable for illegality and maladministration on the part of its agents. This did not inhibit the Commission many years later from adopting a 'now you see it, now you don't' approach by arguing[54] that a Comitology management committee was 'entirely distinct from and independent of the Commission' and thus excluded from the ambit of the Code of Conduct on access to Community documents. The CFI ruled rather boldly that Comitology committees are *not* entirely separate from the Commission, which presides over their meetings and provides secretarial and administrative support, so that, in consequence, access to their papers is governed by the Commission's code of practice on access.

Until recently, even basic facts about the operation of the Comitology, such as who staffs the Committees and what is spent on them, was unknown.[55] Membership, a closely guarded secret, is now published on the Commission's website. In 1994, the EP froze the appropriations until supplied with hard information about the Comitology's operation.[56] The secrecy surrounding it means that it has emerged as a threat to representative democracy, seen as replacing accountable, democratic policy-making with a model of interest representation. Suspicion that the Comitology is an extended model of interest representation disguised behind a screen of supposedly impartial expertise has led to an argument that agencies be substituted for committees at the centre of the policy networks.[57] This is probably part of a wider disenchantment with the European law-making process, very widely seen as a naked interest-group model, characterized by unre-

[53] Case 9/56, *Meroni* v. *High Authority* [1957/8] ECR 133. See also Case 25/70, *Koster* [1970] ECR 1161; Case 23/75, *Rey Soda* [1975] ECR 1279. And see K. Lenaerts, 'Regulating the Regulatory Process: "Delegation of Powers" in the EC' (1993) 18 *EL Rev.* 23.

[54] Case T–188/97, *Rothmans* v. *Commission* [1999] ECR II–2463.

[55] G. Buitendijk and M. van Schendelen, 'Brussels Advisory Committees: A Channel for Influence?' (1995) 20 *EL Rev.* 37; R. H. Pedler and G. F. Schafer (eds.), *Shaping European Law and Policy. The Role of Committees and Comitology in the Political Process* (Maastricht, European Institute of Public Administration, 1996).

[56] K. St C. Bradley, 'The European Parliament and Comitology: On the Road to Nowhere?' (1997) 3 *European Law Journal* 230, 242.

[57] But see M. Shapiro, 'The Problems of Independent Agencies in the United States and European Union' (1997) 4 *Journal of European Public Policy* 276.

strained lobbying by powerful, commercial enterprises,[58] even if the Commission at least has a Code of Conduct to govern its relationship with lobby groups.[59] Because they frequently emanate from lawyers, reform proposals often turn on greater procedural protection for interested parties, usually taking the form of an American-style Administrative Procedures Act.[60] But this solution would graft a 'notice-and-comment' procedure on to the existing Comitology procedure, making this solution yet more cumbersome than it already is; the USA, after all, does not possess a Comitology. It would also heighten the problem of interest groups.

The EP's Special Committee of Inquiry into the BSE crisis, set up to investigate the way in which the Commission had handled the import of beef products from the United Kingdom, was probably the first occasion on which the internal workings of the Comitology were exposed. The Report suggests the relative impotence of non-specialists when faced with scientific advisers. The Report concerned the Scientific Veterinary Committee, a Commission advisory committee representative of national interests; and the Standing Veterinary Committee,[61] a Comitology management committee, supposedly objective in its composition and opinions. It revealed failures at several levels in the operation of these committees. First, it transpired that the Animal Health section of the Scientific Veterinary Committee was chaired and dominated by British experts; consequently, it was argued, its thinking 'reflected' that of the British Ministry of Agriculture (though given the fact that only British veterinary experts admitted to widespread infection of stock with BSE, then reputedly unknown in other Member States, this is perhaps more understandable than at first sight it might seem). The alleged bias could have been heightened by the fact that advisory committees use a block-vote system based on national size. The role of transparency in accountability is highlighted when we learn that, because the Commission did not publish the

[58] D. Coen, 'The European Business Interest and the Nation State: Large Firm Lobbying in the European Union and Member States' (1998) 18 *Journal of Public Policy* 75; S. Mazey and J. Richardson (eds.), *The European Lobbying Process* (Oxford, Oxford University Press, 1993); D. Obradovic, 'Policy Legitimacy and the European Union' (1996) 34 *Journal of Common Market Studies* 191 presents a balanced, theoretical picture.

[59] European Commission, 'An Open and Structured Dialogue Between the Commission and Special Interest Groups', SEC(92)2272 (1992). And see now the White Paper on Governance, n. 36 above.

[60] R. Dehousse, 'Towards a Regulation of Transitional Governance? Citizen's Rights and the Reform of Comitology Procedures' in C. Joerges and E. Vos (eds.), *EU Committees: Social Regulation, Law and Politics* (Oxford, Hart Publishing, 1999).

[61] Set up respectively by Commission Decision 81/651/EEC establishing a Scientific Veterinary Committee [1981] OJ L233/32 and Council Decision 68/361/EEC setting up a Standing Veterinary Committee [1969] OJ L255/23, as amended by Council Decision 81/447/EEC [1981] OJ L186/22.

opinions of dissenting members, the potential for bias had not been obvious. After the worst of the BSE crisis was over, it was decided to download inspectorial functions by moving the EU's veterinary inspection service out of the agriculture DG, transferring the unit to Ireland. The Commission had suggested an agency, somewhat cynically, in the light of what had been discovered, pleading the need for transparency and account- ability. The proposal was, however, ultimately vetoed by the European Parliament.[62]

Deficiencies of Comitology legislative procedure also emerged from the BSE inquiry. Under pressure from the UK, the Commission had decided to lift the embargo on bovine semen and other ancillary beef products. The relevant management committee, the Standing Veterinary Committee, split in such a way as to deprive the Commission of the requisite qualified majority, with the result that it was obliged to refer the decision back to the Council. In Council too attempts to gain a qualified majority failed. The procedure then left the Commission free, under the governing procedure set out in the Comitology decision, *to adopt its original proposal.* This it duly did, totally undermining the requirement of qualified majority. Notably, no procedural change to close this loophole was included in the recently revised Comitology decision.

Partly in response to concerns raised by these revelations, changes to the way in which the Commission handles Comitology appointments have been introduced. These try to embody the ethical standards for public life re- quested by the Committee of Independent Experts. It has been conceded that the committees shall be more independent. A Scientific Steering Committee for consumer products and safety has been set up.[63] General criteria for appointments have been established and published by the Commission, and provision made for declarations of interest. The SSC will decide its own agenda and, for the first time, membership. Subject to the ever-present need for commercial confidentiality, minutes and all opinions will be published. Whether these changes will render the committees more accountable, by more firmly identifying the locus of decision-taking, or less accountable by lending them the cloak of impenetrable scientific legitimacy, remains to be seen. The provisions seem, however, to presage new policies on expert advice contained in the recent Commission White Paper on European Governance. This not only provides for the publication of guidelines on 'collection and use of expert advice in the Commission to provide for the

---

[62] G. Chambers, 'The BSE Crisis and the European Parliament' in Joerges and Vos (eds.), n. 60 above. And see Chap. 4.

[63] Commission Decision 97/579/EC setting up Scientific Committees in the field of consumer health and safety [1997] OJ L237/18; E. Vos, 'EU Committees: the Evolution of Unforeseen Institutional Actors in European Product Regulation' in Joerges and Vos (eds.), n. 60 above, 39.

accountability, plurality and integrity of the expertise used' but also for publication of the advice given. Hans Schepel, however, views impenetrability as an inevitable side-effect of globalization, which installs scientific expertise as the 'dominant model of denationalised decision-making' and provokes demands for 'public institutionalisation and designs for legal process which would ensure accountability'.[64] This rather pessimistic approach suggests that accountability is out of reach.

VI COMMISSION ENFORCEMENT: REQUEST OR COMMAND?

A novel feature of the Community system lay in the decision to vest a generalized enforcement power in the Commission. This is contained in TEC Article 226, which vests the right to invoke the infringement procedure in the Commission (though TEC Article 227 affords a similar opportunity to Member States). A three-stage procedure is envisaged:[65]

- at Stage 1 (administrative) the Commission, apprised of a failure by a Member State to fulfil a Treaty obligation, sends a letter of 'formal notice' demanding an explanation;
- at Stage 2 (administrative) a 'reasoned opinion' follows, in which the Commission states a time-limit for rectification;
- at Stage 3 (judicial) the Commission 'may bring the matter before the Court'.

For the limited purposes of this book, which is not primarily concerned with the 'effectiveness' of EC law, Article 226 can be seen as setting the scene for a dual accountability. On the one hand, we have the accountability of the Member State to its European partners, their obligation to comply with legislation being derived from the duty of loyalty established by TEC Article 10. This necessarily involves enforcement, possibly even sanction and fine. On the other hand, there is a growing potential accountability of the Commission for the use of its powers.

Francis Snyder distinguishes seven types of effectiveness (though several of his categories may overlap). They include:[66]

---

[64] H. Schepel, 'Legal Pluralism in the European Union' in P. Fitzpatrick and J. Bergeron (eds.), *Europe's Other: European Law Between Modernity and Postmodernity* (Aldershot, Ashgate, 1998), 56.

[65] A. Gil Ibañez, *The Administrative Supervision and Enforcement of EC Law, Powers, Procedures and Limits* (Oxford, Hart Publishing, 1999), 12–17.

[66] F. Snyder, 'The Effectiveness of European Community Law: Institutions, Processes, Tools and Techniques' (1993) 56 *MLR* 19, 25–6.

- The enactment of Community policy into Community law;
- Provision for the direct application of Community regulations by Member States;
- The transposition of directives into Member States' law;
- Implementation by national civil services;
- The use of Community law by economic actors;
- Recourse to national courts under the doctrine of 'direct effect';
- Enforcement of Community law by national courts.

If either of the last two elements is missing, we should speak of a gap in the legal accountability which Lord described as an essential facet of democratic accountability.[67]

The primary concern of the Commission has always been with transposition, which theoretically ought not to be too problematic; many directives now oblige Member States to make a report on implementation to the Commission, which should make transposition relatively easy to police.[68] There is in fact a high level of implementation and notification: over 90 per cent in every Member State, though this falls short of the Commission target of 98.5 per cent. The ratio of Court referrals to letters of formal notice is also consistently low.

We ought therefore to be able to deduce that Member States are fulfilling their obligations adequately. However, this is not necessarily the end of the story, since 'transposition' and 'enforcement' are not necessarily one and the same thing. It is the stage of actual *implementation* which is most problematic for the Commission, which does not have at its disposal recourse to national courts. Nor does the Commission have at its disposal a general inspectorate, nor indeed any general inspectorial function, probably because this would trench on national administrations.[69] The Commission has to rely largely on national administrations and agencies for implementation and these vary both in powers and efficiency. This is a pressing problem for environmental protection and, in 1991, the British Government called for an environmental inspectorate to monitor compliance with EC environmental legislation;[70] later, however, when the European Environmental Agency was established,[71] the Council omitted to endow it with an inspectorate or even with enforcement powers. Until such time as the EU follows the pattern of modern governance by setting up a network of true regulatory agencies, this

---

[67] Above, 24.

[68] See further Gil Ibanez, n. 65 above, 65–70.

[69] A handful of powers to set up inspectorates does exist under particular programmes, notably in the areas of food production and animal welfare: see ibid., 72–84.

[70] R. Macrory, 'The Enforcement of Community Environmental Laws: Some Critical Issues' (1992) 29 *CML Rev.* 362.

[71] Regulation 1210/90 on the establishment of the European Environmental Agency and the European environment and information network [1990] OJ L120/1.

puts the Commission in a weak position *vis-à-vis* Member States. It also helps to explain three phenomena noticed by students of the enforcement processes: (i) a heavy reliance on negotiation as an enforcement technique; (ii) the long-standing alliance between the ECJ and Commission; (iii) the apparent preference of Court and Commission for an army of 'citizen enforcers', active both in complaining to the Commission and in enforcing EC law in national courts.[72]

The wide discretionary powers defended by the Commission and ceded by the Court are justifiable in terms of the Commission's regulatory/enforcement function. A regulator needs to be free to prefer long-term to short-term goals,[73] a fact normally recognized by allowing strong discretion to regulators. Heavy reliance on negotiation to secure compliance is also in line with 'best practice' among regulators.[74] It should not be assumed that every failure to comply is deliberate or even conscious; there are many reasons for Member States' failures to report or transpose, ranging from difficulty with the increasingly complex *acquis communautaire* at the time of accession, to constitutional difficulties in cases where implementation rests with provincial authorities unwilling to implement or incapable of implementing. Not all of these seem to demand legal accountability. Arguably, too, over-use of judicial proceedings blunts the edge of the sanction, while delay is a significant factor. According to the Commission's Scoreboard,[75] 'cases that go to the ECJ take many years to get settled; in about 80% of cases, the Court does not hand down its judgement until three years after the case is opened'. Legal enforcement procedures, in short, are not always as effective as might be imagined.

One serious gap in Article 226 procedures which left the ECJ without means to enforce its judgments must be mentioned. This was filled by a Treaty amendment introduced at Maastricht, which permits the Commission, in the event of non-compliance with a Court ruling in infringement proceedings, to apply to the Court for a fine, or penalty payment, to be imposed (TEC Article 228). The penalty is designed to have a deterrent effect.[76] Yet the first case brought under the new dispensation suggests that even fines may prove illusory. Greece failed to take the necessary steps to implement the EC Waste Directives in respect of a site at Chania in Crete operated by a regional authority and used for the disposal of toxic and

---

[72] See 156–7 for the doctrine of direct effect and the enforcement of EC law by individuals.

[73] For a study of the Commission's possible objectives, see M. Mendrinou, 'Non-compliance and the European Commission's Role in Integration' (1996) 3 *Journal of European Public Policy* 1.

[74] S. Shavell, 'The Optimal Structure of Law Enforcement' [1993] *Journal of Law and Economics* 270; Baldwin, n. 42 above, 143–64.

[75] European Commission, Single Market Scoreboard (24 July 2001).

[76] Guidelines have now been issued by the Commission laying down an appropriate scale of payment, which is to reflect the duration of the infringement, its degree of seriousness, and the Member State's ability to pay: see Memorandum 96/C 242/07.

dangerous waste. The ECJ ruled, in infringement proceedings brought by
the Commission, that Greece was in breach of its obligations.[77] Five years
later, as no remedial action had been taken, the Commission returned to
the Court asking for a penalty payment. Taking into account the Commission guidelines and paying special attention to the question of urgency,
the ECJ on 4 July 2000 duly imposed a penalty payment of 20,000
euros daily.[78] On 22 December 2000, when Greece began payment under
threat that the Commission would otherwise withhold aid payments, nothing
had so far been done. On 1 March 2001, when the European Parliament's
Environment Committee met in Brussels, it was reported that Greece, which
by now owed 4.20 million euros, had paid off 2.98 million. The offending
dump of toxic waste remained operative until July 2001, when Greece finally
complied with the judgments—in all, a ten-year period of illegality.

The way in which the Commission has used its Article 226 powers,
combined with the low degree of judicial control, has brought a series
of complaints to the European Ombudsman from members of the public,
typically from environmental groups aggrieved by the failure of the Commission to bring infringement proceedings, though also from individuals.
The EO responded by inviting the Commission to tidy up its procedures,
with particular regard to making them more transparent and accessible to
complainants.[79] The Commission responded positively, introducing and
publicizing a new procedure.[80] Here we see how a new machinery for
accountability can be used in an unexpected way to turn the provision against
its operators. This is also a paradigm example of the trade-offs which have
sometimes to be made between accountability and regulation, though it is by
no means clear that the intervention of the EO will help to get the balance
right. It may make the procedure less effective, by swamping the Commission
in trivial complaints. It may, on the other hand, contribute to the Commission's accountability to the general public, by making it clear when the
Commission may intervene to help them and making it easier for them to
invoke its help.

[77] Case C–45/91, *Commission* v. *Greece* [1992] ECR I–2509.

[78] Case C–387/97, *Commission* v. *Greece* [2000] ECR I–5047. See M. Theodossiou, 'An
Analysis of the Recent Response of the Community to Non-compliance with Court of Justice
Judgments: Article 228(2) EC' (2002) 25 *EL Rev.* 41.

[79] The early cases are discussed by R. Rawlings, 'Engaged Elites: Citizen Action and Institutional Attitudes in Commission Enforcement' (2000) 6 *European Law Journal* 4. See now
complaint 715/98/IJH against the European Commission, EO, *Annual Report for 2000*, 39.

[80] European Commission, 'Improvement of the Commission's working methods in relation to infringement proceedings' SEC(1998)1733. The White Paper on Governance promises Guidelines on infringement procedure.

VII EUROPEAN AGENCIES?

An alternative way forward would be to combine rule-making and enforcement powers in specific policy areas and make extensive use of regulatory agencies, as most modern systems of government do. Within the EU, this is true of both Sweden and the United Kingdom, though the models they use are dissimilar. Until recently, the Community presented a very different picture, almost devoid of agencies. A stopper had been put on the creation of agencies by the *Meroni* decision.[81] Of the ten agencies in being in 1998, a majority possessed only information-gathering functions.[82] Such agencies, which lack both the regulatory and executive powers typical of British and American agencies, pose little threat to either transparency or accountability, their central function being to create a focal point at the centre of a policy network, enabling information to be collected, passed on to the Commission, and accessed by those interested. According to the first Director of the European Environment Agency, his agency is 'a new type of network administration', its mission being the provision of 'timely, targeted and reliable information to policy making agents and the public'.[83] There is no suggestion here that it should involve itself directly in the policy-making; its role is to supersede *for informational purposes* the complex network of in-accessible committees and other entities responsible for environmental policy-making, of which complaints are often heard, making it more access-ible to NGOs and the public.

Recently, as an aspect of concern over the imperfect enforcement of EU law, agencies have begun to accrue regulatory and executive functions. The European Agency for the Evaluation of Medicinal Products is, for example, described by Edoardo Chiti as based on a preventive control and a mechanism of supervision over authorized medicines.[84] It offers the oppor-tunity of a single European licence to market, operating through 'close cooperation between national competent authorities and the agency'. The agency has a Management Board representative of the Member States, the Commission, and the EP, which elects an executive director. National authorities and agencies are also involved in the network, used for inspection and supervisory purposes. Only technically are the decisions accredited to

---

[81] Case 9/56, *Meroni* v. *High Authority* [1957–8] ECR 133.
[82] A. Kreher (ed.), *The EC Agencies Between Community Institutions and Constituents: Autonomy, Control and Accountability* (Florence, EUI, 1997).
[83] D. Jimenez-Beltran, 'The European Environment Agency' in ibid., 59–60.
[84] E. Chiti, 'The Emergence of a Community Administration: The Case of Agencies' (2000) 37 *CML Rev.* 309, 320 (emphasis added).

the Commission. Overtly, the agency takes transparency seriously, if by that
we mean access to consultation papers and an Internet address. It has also
learned to take financial accountability seriously, after the EP in 1996
blocked its budget allocation, pending agreement on financial regulation
and audit.[85] But note the way in which the agency operates, through two
committees for Proprietary Medicinal Products and Veterinary Medicinal
Products composed of two members nominated by each Member State *both
of which antedate the establishment of the agency*. A feeling of *déjà vu* cannot be
avoided.

The proposal for a European Food Authority (EFA), part of the reorganization which followed the inquiry into the handling of BSE (above), contains the nucleus of something more powerful. The proposals contained in
the Commission White Paper[86] were largely informational, following the
pattern of the Environmental Agency: the EFA would have responsibilities
for monitoring, information gathering, risk assessment, provision and dis-
semination of scientific advice and information. One of the tasks of the EFA
would however be to operate the Rapid Alert System, which would provide
for the banning of unsafe and food products on a trans-European basis. These
were the functions incorporated into the final legislation.[87] The Select
Committee of the House of Lords, on the other hand, although it broadly
welcomed the proposal, wanted the EFA to possess clear policy-making
functions, supporting the Commission in negotiations with comparable
international agencies.[88] There is a distinct undertone in this report from
the British legislature in favour of an *independent* agency, while the Commission in its evidence to the House of Lords showed a distinct bias towards a
committee structure.[89] Perhaps this is why the legislation does not provide any
clear and appropriate accountability structure, despite the obvious problems
of agency accountability elsewhere in the world.

Agencies may sometimes be set up by the Council in areas where there
is no clear EU competence but where Member States wish for a measure
of joint policy-making. In this case, the agency, as with the flexible procedures criticized in the last chapter, is designed deliberately to evade political
accountability. Several existing agencies have this flavour, such as the Euro-

[85] See F. Sauer, 'The European Agency for the Evaluation of Medicinal Products and
European Pharmaceutical Approvals: Efficiency, Transparency and Accountability', in
Kreher, n. 82 above.
[86] European Commission, White Paper on Food Safety in the European Union, 5761/00
(COM(99)719), 12 Jan. 2000.
[87] Regulation 178/2002/EC of the European Parliament and of the Council laying down
the general principles and requirements of food law, establishing the European Food Safety
Authority and laying down procedures in matters of food safety [2002] OJ L31/1.
[88] House of Lords, Select Committee on the European Communities, 'A European Food
Agency', HL 66 (1999/2000).
[89] Ibid., paras. 75–78.

pean Drugs Agency[90] or Europol, mentioned in TEU Articles 29 and 30 but actually set up by a convention.[91] Europol exists for the exchange of information and to foster co-operation between the competent authorities in the Member States in preventing and combating terrorism, unlawful drug-trafficking, and other serious forms of international crime. It operates through a management board composed of Member State representatives and appoints its own Director and Financial Controller. Member States second personnel to both agencies. Europol's extensive IT capability is large enough to extend to personal data, and a common information system in parallel to the Schengen Information System was envisaged and is now becoming operative. Since Tampere, Europol has been authorized to 'receive operational data' and to request Member States to 'initiate, conduct or co-ordinate investigations or to create joint investigative teams in certain areas of crime'.[92] Eurojust, a sister agency first referred to in the Tampere Conclusions, was designed to enhance co-operation in the investigation and prosecution of organized crime. Although it was not formally established until Laeken,[93] due to disagreement over its competence and mandate, a 'provisional co-operation unit', seen as its precursor, was already active, as part of a wider project to harmonize criminal justice systems. These may be agencies on the way to executive status.

There are signs in the new White Paper on European Governance that greater use may be made of regulatory agencies in future. The Commission has agreed to define criteria, which set out an 'effective system of supervision and control'. But here we find a sharp contrast to the case of Europol and Eurojust, which lack clarity of structure and legal basis, and have been allowed to grow haphazardly, without proper oversight or regulation. In other cases, the Commission remains cautious, agreeing only to consider new agencies on a case-to-case basis and confining their decision-making powers to cases where it would not have to 'arbitrate between conflicting public interests, exercise political discretion or carry out conflicting economic assessments'. Everything points to the fact that the Commission is by no

[90] G. Estievenart, 'L'Observatoire europeen des drogues et des toxicomanies' in Kreher, n. 82 above.

[91] Council Act of 26 July 1995 made operational at Amsterdam and supported by an EP resolution (17 May 1995), asking that operational power be made available for the 'fight against serious cross border crime'.

[92] Tampere European Council, Presidency Conclusions, 15 and 16 Oct. 1999, Doc 200/99, para. C.I.3.

[93] Laeken European Council, Presidency's conclusions on justice and home affairs (17 Dec. 2001), paras. 37–45; 'EUROJUST—Helping the EU's legal systems to combat cross-border crime', Brussels, 14–15 Dec. 2001. See M. Delmas Marty, 'Guest Editorial: Combating Fraud—Necessity, Legitimacy and Feasibility of the Corpus Iuris' (2000) 37 *CML Rev.* 247; V. Mitsilegal, 'Defining Organised Crime in the European Union' (2001) 26 *EL Rev.* 565.

means ready to relinquish its grip over the policy-making process, and hence prefers a committee structure. Thus it is unlikely that the Community will move from a committee-based system of policy and rule-making towards an agency model. And committees and agencies in any event have in common their capacity for de-politicizing decision-making and immunizing it from political challenge.[94]

VIII CONCLUSIONS

Sparked off by the investigation of the Committee of Independent Experts, there has been a growing realization of a need for accountability of the Commission as the principal executive agency of the EU. The conventional terms in which the debate has been so far carried on are perhaps surprising. It has been suggested, for example, that the College of Commissioners should bear collective responsibility and should account externally to the European Parliament. At least in principle, the European Parliament has emerged as the body most heavily charged with the duty of exacting accountability. The desirability of greater transparency in several areas of operation has been clearly recognized, though not necessarily introduced. The need for increased managerial capacity of the Commission and for hierarchical accountability of the Commission bureaucracy has been agreed in principle, and some steps taken towards these objectives. This is all so far fairly orthodox, and sits comfortably within a statal framework of government.

However, there is little sign in what we have so far observed of radical alternatives. In the Comitology network, for example, where the actors can be seen as 'dependent on each other in their actions because of the dispersal of key resources of authority (formal and informal), information, expertise',[95] there is nothing to suggest that Scott's *interdependence* model is operative; indeed, a superficial survey suggests that it is not. Inside agencies, as in the networks developing around them, Member States and their institutions, including national agencies, pool information and expertise, but there is nothing to show that they have to account to each other for their actions, though this may be only because, to date, they have so few actions to account for. There are, in short, apparently no accountability schemes devised or promoted expressly for a transnational system of governance.

---

[94] M. Shapiro, 'The Problems of Independent Agencies in the United States and European Union' (1997) 4 *Journal of European Public Policy* 276.
[95] C. Scott, 'Accountability in the Regulatory State' (2000) 27 *Journal of Law and Society* 38.

4

A Plethora of Parliaments?

I MIND THE GAP?

Juliet Lodge has described the way in which we have failed to deal with, or perhaps even to notice:[1]

the extent to which the European Parliament has not won powers forfeited to national governments by national parliaments: neither can exercise effective control over either what national governments do in the EU or what the EU executive does. National governments were responsible for this situation and deliberately engineered a situation whereby the national parliaments were denied effective controls over national executives. This made it easier for national governments, working within the Council, to escape national as well as European parliamentary scrutiny and control.... National parliaments failed to engineer an effective scrutiny, monitoring or control role for themselves *vis-à-vis* national Ministers and governments. They also failed, until 1990, to engage in constructive dialogue—and more importantly, in continuing, regular, communication—with the European Parliament. Given that European Parliamentary scrutiny and control were negligible and deficient, the overall effect was to increase the democratic deficit. For a long time, however, electoral pre-occupations meant that it was assumed that the democracy deficit would be erased merely by the fact of the EP having been directly elected.

This passage represents more than a mere yearning for a strong, though mythical, Parliament, which 'once upon a time' had everything under control.[2] In reading it, we do not need to think in terms of 'strong' national parliaments, capable of enforcing accountability in national systems, were suddenly drained of power by undemocratic European institutions upon entry into the European Community. We know that parliaments everywhere have found increasing difficulty in holding governments accountable as governments have grown steadily more presidential in their ambitions

---

[1] J. Lodge, 'The European Parliament' in S. Andersen and K. Eliassen (eds.), *The European Union: How Democratic Is It?* (London, Sage, 1996), 188.

[2] See, e.g., R. Dehousse, 'Constitutional Reform in the European Community. Are there Alternatives to the Majoritarian Avenue?' (1995) 18 *W. European Politics* 118.

and more global in reach. In this respect, the European Parliament could be seen as exceptional in its ability to notch up an appreciable increase in power since 1979. What Lodge pinpoints is the scope afforded by multi-level governance for creating new, or exacerbating old, accountability deficits. When competence is transferred to the EU, especially in policy areas falling outside the single market, a double shift may occur. First, an issue of internal, domestic politics is moved into the less accountable area of foreign policy; secondly, accountability may be diminished because the rambling and inchoate structures of the EU lend themselves—as we saw in Chapter 2—to unaccountable governance. Policy-making is conducted through working groups, committees, and other informal methods of inter-state co-operation. This shifts power from politicians, at least nominally responsible, to functionaries who are neither elected nor accountable. Lodge also warns against the easy assumption that a shift in policy-making to Union level will automatically entail an expanded competence for the European Parliament, the mistake made by migrants' groups before Amsterdam. As we have seen, there are many ways for the Council to evade EP scrutiny and control, one of the simplest being reversion to the old-style, consultation procedure which minimizes the input of the EP.

The recent anti-terrorism initiative of the European Council, which led to proposals for a European arrest warrant, is a strong illustration of Lodge's point. The extraordinary European Council meeting in Luxembourg authorized an initiative by the Justice and Home Affairs Council (JHA) in the area of freedom, justice, and security where the parliamentary mandate has been recognized by the European Council as particularly strong. The exact terms were 'to *draw up* a common list of presumed terrorists'.[3] The JHA, however, issued a draft decision in which it *published* a list of terrorist groups and individuals.[4] The Article 36 Committee, acting on the basis of 'a broad consensus', with strong support from the European Council, used written procedure, thus avoiding debate at ministerial level. Not surprisingly, the EP reacted very strongly to both moves. It reproved the Council for using the written procedure and took an equally strong line over the draft decision for a European arrest warrant,[5] sending back sufficient amendments on consultation to warrant a further consultation by the Council before a common position could be agreed. In parallel, the draft was under consider-

---

[3] Conclusions and Plan of Action of the Extraordinary European Council meeting on 21 Sept. 2001, SN 140/01, 2.2.
[4] Commission Proposal for a Council Framework Decision on the European Arrest Warrant and the Surrender procedures between Member States (Brussels, 25 Sept. 2001).
[5] Proposal for a Council framework decision on the European arrest warrant and the surrender procedures between the Member States, Brussels (25 Sept. 2001) COM(2001)522 final/2, 2001/0215 (CNS). For the consultation, see Justice and Legal Affairs Committee A5-0397/2001 (rapporteur, Graham Watson).

ation by national parliaments, five of which had seen fit to impose a 'parliamentary reserve'. In the course of debate in Standing Committee, complaints were heard from members of the House of Commons Scrutiny Committee that no up-to-date draft of the proposed text was available. They were working with a French version of the draft, which might have been already superseded, sent on a person-to-person basis by a *Deputé* of the *Assemblée Nationale.* The Committee complained also that their call for a debate on the floor of the House, in view of the great importance of the issue, had been rejected.[6] The two-tiered attack brought more concessions on this occasion than either tier could have achieved alone, but a concerted campaign, which was almost certainly feasible, could probably have achieved still more.

Although Lodge places the blame for what is happening primarily on national *governments,* she does not absolve national *parliaments.* Partly because the purely consultative role of the Assembly in the initial stages suggested that political responsibility would remain at national level, many national parliaments did not initially recognize any need to play a part in the governing process of the Community. Parliaments had assented, if only by implication, to the exciting new project of European integration. In consequence, parliaments and governments locked up to form a single pro-Community elite. In Member States where little opposition to European integration manifested itself, the parliament might see its function primarily as affording 'regime support' for the national government at Community level; in other cases, elite support for the integration process led to a practice of self-abnegation, inspired by the belief that the insertion of the national parliaments into Community policy-making would be 'detrimental to the development of the European Parliament'.[7]

As the European Assembly gradually metamorphosed into a European Parliament, a breakdown of respective responsibilities was assumed, essentially in terms of two-tier democracy: a split along a horizontal line. It was for national parliaments to control the input of their own governments into the EU, while control of the EU institutions and of the collective activities of the Council would be left to the European Parliament. This division was tenable only so long as net gains were perceived from European integration, not offset by the effect of the integration process on national sovereignty and the powers of the national parliaments. In other words, so long as parliaments remained oblivious to the accountability gap. Maurice van Schendelen has attributed the surprisingly complacent performance of the Dutch Tweede Kamer in European matters, a sharp contrast to its attitude in domestic politics, to this

---

[6] 10th Report of the House of Commons Select Committee on European Scrutiny, HC 152 (2001/2002).

[7] V. Herman and R. van Schendelen, *The European Parliament and the National Parliaments*, (Farnborough, Saxon House, 1975), 267.

view of European affairs.[8] The Tweede Kamer moved to take back its
traditional scrutiny function only after it began to see the Netherlands as a
net loser or 'baby state' within the EU, when 'satisfaction with its own passive
position' rapidly changed to an impatient desire to become actively involved.
The Tweede Kamer took six months to ratify Maastricht, holding a public
hearing and publishing critical reports. There has been an equally significant
change of attitude to the European Parliament:[9]

In regard to the *EP and the Dutch delegation in particular*, the Second Chamber has
changed from patronage-like intimacy to critical estrangement. It still believes that
the EU has a democratic deficit, but no longer that this is part of only the EP's
balance-sheet; part of it lies in its own Chamber.

Growing suspicion of the EP by national parliaments was to prove damaging
to both tiers.

Before moving to consider the growing power of the EP and the way in
which the national parliaments are learning to deal with it, it is important to
recognize that talk of a *two-tier* division of parliamentary functions is misleading. The well-known phenomenon of the 'hollowing out' of the state[10]
has meant that, at the same time as functions are being transferred, deliberately or otherwise, outside the nation state, there has been a growth in
regional politics. Several of the Member State constitutions are rigorously
federal, while others have a strong regional flavour. The constitutional
arrangements of the Federal German Republic reflect its title, and the constitution provides strong protection for the Länder. In its celebrated *Maastricht*
decision,[11] the Bundesverfassungsgericht or German Federal Constitutional
Court made two important points. First, in a passage strongly supportive of
the role of national parliaments, it said:

In the federation of states formed by the European Union, democratic legitimisation
necessarily comes about through the feedback of the European institutions' actions
into the parliaments of the Member States; in addition...there is provision of
democratic legitimisation through the European Parliament... *Excessive weight of
functions and powers within the responsibility of the European federation of states would
effectively weaken democracy at national level, so that the parliaments of the Member*

---

[8] M. Van Schendelen, 'The Netherlands: From Founding Father to Mounding Baby', in
Special Issue, 'National Parliaments and the European Union' (1995) 1 *Journal of Legislative
Studies* 60, 70.
[9] Ibid. (emphasis added).
[10] P. Muller and V. Wright, 'Reshaping the State in Western Europe: The Limits to
Retreat' (1994) 17 *W. European Politics* 6; R. Munch, 'Between Nation-State, Regionalism
and World Society: The European Integration Process' (1996) 34 *Journal of Common Market
Studies* 379.
[11] Bundesverfassungsgericht, 2nd chamber (Senat) Cases BvR 2134/92 and 2 BvR 2159/
92 (12 Oct. 1993) BVerfGE 89, 155 or, in English, *Brunner* v. *The European Union Treaty*
[1994] 1 CMLR 57 (emphasis added).

States could no longer provide the legitimisation for the sovereign power exercised by the Union.

But the Bundesverfassungsgericht also insisted that Germany must remain a *federal* state. In 1995, the Court went further, in ruling directly on the *Länder's* right of participation in EU affairs.[12] An obligation was said to be imposed upon the Federation to act as trustee (*Sachwalter*) in respect of the Länder, protecting their interests whenever the EU took action in areas which lay within their competence. Yet this internal division of powers is reflected neither in Protocol 30 on the application of the principles of subsidiarity and proportionality attached to the TEU at Maastricht, which is framed strictly in terms of *national* and *transnational* responsibilities, nor in Declaration No 23 on the future of the Union, made at Nice. Calling for a 'deeper and wider debate' on the future of the EU, the Declaration talks of 'co-operation' with the EP, but otherwise of 'wide-ranging discussions with all the interested parties', including representatives of national parliaments and 'all those reflecting public opinion'. This formulation is significant both in the gradation of rank from the EP to national parliaments and in the omission of regional parliaments and assemblies. The order of deference is picked up in, and becomes central to, the argumentation of the Commission's White Paper on Governance.[13]

Austria too is a highly decentralized state, where power is devolved to ten *Bundesländer*, which have to be consulted on all matters within their competence, and whose opinions bind the federal government. This has been said to leave the Austrian Nationsrat on occasion as 'little more than a rubber stamp'.[14] Austria, with the advantage of late entry, is experimenting with a mandate system in respect of European affairs, which can protect its internal division of powers. The Government has to consult both Houses of the Nationsrat over EU policies, as well as the Länder in matters within their competence. In all directly applicable matters, Opinions of the Nationsrat bind the federal Government, which must report outcomes and can be subjected to a vote of censure (Article 23 of the Austrian Constitution). All Austrian nominations to significant EU offices also require approval from the Nationsrat. These procedures are in an experimental stage and have not yet been severely tested, though the issue might have arisen rather starkly at the point when punitive action against Austria was contemplated under TEU Article 7, in respect of the allegedly xenophobic opinions of Jörg Haider, at the time a provincial governor. As Austrian government representatives indicated in public statements, this could have raised the question of

---

[12] Decision of 22 Mar. 1995 [1995] *Europäische Zeitschrift für Wirtschaftsrecht* 437.

[13] Below, Chap. 7.

[14] J. Fitzmaurice, 'National Parliamentary Control of EU Policy in the Three New Member States' (1996) 19 *W. European Politics* 88, 90.

accountability for democratically elected regional representatives to a national government and parliament.[15]

In the Italian system of regional government, regions possess many of the legal powers necessary for the implementation of EU law, although the state has a monopoly of power in European affairs. A position can easily arise in which EC law is not implemented, opening the Italian state to infringement proceedings under TEC Article 226. To avoid this situation, a co-ordination committee has been created. Italian regions have also been permitted to establish Brussels offices, a practice becoming common throughout the EU. Accordingly, 'the state-as-a-unit paradigm which has long influenced EU policy making (the state is a single body speaking with one voice, that of the Ministry of Foreign Affairs) has been abandoned'.[16] This type of regional pluralism, which operates to complicate the already complex architecture of the European Union, may undermine the efforts of national parliaments to keep European affairs under parliamentary control.

Efforts made by the Commission, responsible for regional policies, to augment its own, direct relations with regions are not necessarily helpful.[17] In addition to the most recent set of ideas, expressed in the White Paper on Governance, suggestions have been made for expanding the powers of the Committee of the Regions—a body already struggling forcefully for 'parliamentary' status within the EU. Support from national parliaments, on whom such a development would undoubtedly rebound, is not notably forthcoming. There is a very real danger that fragmentation of the power of parliaments will simply reduce their authority within the EU to the profit of other, less representative actors, and that decrease in the authority of parliamentary bodies will diminish their ability to exact accountability. In such a case, Colin Scott's redundancy model of accountability, according to which the 'overlapping (and ostensibly superfluous) accountability mechanisms reduce the centrality of any one of them'[18] might become applicable to parliamentary accountability, the form of democratic accountability to which greatest weight is attached by the public as well as theorists. Ironically, we could be seeing a variant of classical versions of 'democratic deficit theory', in which democratic deficit is brought about by 'democracy surplus', or fragmentation of parliamentary power.

---

[15] M. Ahtiisari, J. Frowein, M. Oreja, *Report on Austria* (8 Sep. 2000).

[16] G. della Cananea, 'Italy', in H. Kassim, B. Guy Peters, and V. Wright (eds.), *The National Co-ordination of EU Policy, The Domestic Level* (Oxford, Oxford University Press, 2000) 104.

[17] M. Keating and L. Hooghe, 'By-passing the Nation State? Regions and the EU Policy Process' in P. Le Gales and C. Lequesne, *Regions in Europe* (London, Routledge, 1998).

[18] C. Scott, 'Accountability in the Regulatory State' (2000) 27 *JLS* 38.

II THE CONTRIBUTION OF NATIONAL PARLIAMENTS

The degree of control by national parliaments over EU affairs depends essentially on two variables: the balance of power inside the national system between parliament and government; and the degree of parliamentary control over the conduct of foreign affairs, in effect an aspect of the first, larger question. Different parliaments conceive their roles very differently and prioritize different aspects of their functions, with the result that their contribution to accountability and the seriousness with which they undertake their scrutiny function may vary greatly. It has, for example, been said of the Italian Parliament that it accords pre-eminence to control of policy through legislation. This raises the question whether law-making is a form of accountability. Law-making is another aspect of parliamentary government surrounded by myth: in this case, the myth of parliamentary sovereignty. In all modern systems of government, law-making is largely a function and a monopoly of government, its policy advisers, and of those concerned with legislative drafting. The contribution to accountability made by the law-making process is that government is put to the trouble of an explanation and may on occasion be forced to re-think. To put this differently, the formal stages of the law-making process afford an opportunity for parliament to participate in policy-making, but only occasionally does it play a significant role; in most systems, parliamentary input into policy-making comes primarily through political parties. A cynical view of Italy's long period of fragmented political parties, weak coalition government, and consequential reliance on votes of confidence is of a system of government accountable rather to political parties than to Parliament as a whole.[19] The scrutiny function is, in Italy, a late arrival on the scene; parliamentary questions are a new introduction, and there is no equivalent to the EP's subject-based committees or the departmental select committees of the UK Parliament.[20] Such a restricted view of parliamentary accountability at domestic level would obviously rebound on the Italian parliament's grasp over the field of European affairs.

The second significant variable is the *competence* of the national parliament, which may, as already indicated, be restricted by the genesis of the EU as an international regime. In most Member States, this led initially to the inclusion of Community affairs in the foreign-affairs portfolio, a situation symbolized

---

[19] A. Manzella, 'La transition institutionelle' in S. Cassese (ed.), *Portrait de l'Italie actuelle* (Paris, La documentation française, 2001), 60–1.

[20] P. Furlong, 'The Italian Parliament and European Integration—Responsibilities, Failures and Successes' (1995) 1 *J. of Legislative Studies* 35, 44. See similarly P. Leyland and D. Donati, 'Executive Accountability and the Changing Face of Government: UK and Italy Compared' (2001) 7 *European Public Law* 217, 234.

at Union level by the primacy in the Council of Ministers of the General Affairs Council, composed of the Foreign Ministers of the Member States. The empire of foreign affairs is historically a core executive function, over which parliaments have had difficulty in extending their control. In France, foreign affairs remains a presidential function, although, by Articles 52 and 53 of the French Constitution, the National Assembly has gained powers of ratification and scrutiny. In Italy, the predominance of the Ministry of Foreign Affairs in EU affairs is definitely a facet of the state monopoly in external affairs, under which head Europe has always been classified. The Italian Parliament is only beginning to dent this monopoly by insisting on six-monthly reports from the Government on its European policies and by strengthening its committee system,[21] a critical aspect of parliamentary control. The United Kingdom Parliament has similarly failed to establish plenary control over the foreign-affairs and treaty-making powers, historically both aspects of the royal prerogative.[22] Significantly, in 1978, the House of Commons used the opportunity of contested Treaty change to force the European Parliamentary Elections Act on an unwilling Labour government, providing that measures which extended the powers of the European Parliament would require legislative ratification.

Some parliaments have reacted more forcefully than others to the challenge of law-making at European Union level. The most stringent control is through mandate, but this is exceptional and the Danish Folketing is the only successful example of this model. The Folketing has assumed the power to mandate ministers in policy-making and, on accession to the EU, this rule was simply extended:

The Danish system of parliamentary control in EU policymaking, with the [European Affairs Committee] as the central body, is actually a system focusing on the proposals, decisions and actions of individual ministers (and thereby indirectly then whole cabinet). According to the constitution, not only the Prime Minister but also the individual ministers, are directly accountable to the Folketing. [The Constitution] states that: 'A minister shall not remain in office after the Folketing has appointed a vote of no confidence in him'. Therefore all control instruments available to parliament and MPs . . . can also be used to monitor the EU activities of individual ministers.[23]

There seems to be a measure of consensus among the Nordic commentators that the mandate procedure represents a satisfactory compromise between accountability and Denmark's need to participate fully in EU policy-

---

[21] Della Cananea, n. 16 above, 108–9.

[22] R. Rawlings, 'Legal Politics: The United Kingdom and Ratification of the Treaty on European Union (Part One)' [1994] *PL* 254.

[23] E. Damgaard and A. Sonne Norgaard, 'The European Union and Danish Parliamentary Democracy' (2000) 6 *Journal of Legislative Studies* 33, 48.

making.[24] Voters are said to believe too that ministers have been 'quite efficient in relation to their elected representatives with regard to overall EU issues'.[25] Again, it has been said that 'parliamentary control of government is quite effective, although the permanent committees could play a larger role.... [T]he EU has directly provided the Danish parliamentary principal with crucial and relevant information'.[26] It is, however, questionable whether the mandate model could be replicated across the EU, more especially after enlargement. Notably, neither Sweden nor Finland has chosen an identical solution. After a constitutional report, the Swedish Riksdag rejected the idea of mandate; instead, if either the government considers the matter to be of importance, or one-third of the European Union Affairs Committee's fifteen members demand a meeting, Swedish government representatives must attend the committee to discuss Sweden's policy stance. In Finland, the Eduskunta has to be consulted and informed. Its European Union Committee meets weekly and issues opinions, of which the minister must take very full account. They do not, however, amount to a binding mandate. Whether this less rigorous scrutiny measures up to Scandinavian standards of democracy, and how it will work in practice, remains to be seen.[27]

Denmark's achievement is often attributed to the existence in the Folketing of a powerful European Affairs Committee, the first of three indicators thought to be significant in establishing parliamentary control over European affairs. The second indicator is adequate access to information in the shape of EU documents. Problems with access to information have become a matter of increasing concern to national parliaments, often because of difficulties with translation. Third, though more tentative, the existence at national level of political parties hostile to European integration has been seen as a factor in raising the consciousness of national parliaments, as well as contributing more generally to popular debate.

The significance of a European Affairs Committee lies partly in the fact that it denotes severance of EU and foreign affairs. Its existence also lends to the

---

[24] See D. Arter, 'The Folketing and Denmark's "European Policy": The Case of an "Authorising Assembly"', in Special Issue, 'Parliaments in Western Europe' (1990) 13 *W. European Politics* 110; I. Jarvad, 'The Committee of European Affairs of the Danish Parliament (the Folketing): How to Maintain Some Parliamentary Control of the Legislative Power of the Combined Executives in the Council of Ministers' in P. Craig and C. Harlow (eds.), *Lawmaking in the European Union* (London, Kluwer International, 1998); J. Jensen, 'Prior Parliamentary Consent to Danish EU Policies' in E. Smith (ed.), *National Parliaments as the Cornerstone of EU Integration* (London, Kluwer Law International, 1996).

[25] Damgaard and Sonne Norgaard, n. 23 above, 54.

[26] Ibid.

[27] See, however, opinions expressed in the Special Issue, 'Delegation and Accountability in European Integration, The Nordic Parliamentary Democracies and the EU' (2000) 6 *J. of Legislative Studies* 33.

subject a high profile and degree of co-ordination. It can help to close the accountability gap caused by the fragmented structure of the Council of Ministers, whereby no single minister at national level has full responsibility for European Affairs, or acts as national representative on all occasions. Foreign Ministers traditionally occupy a commanding position, while Prime Ministers and Heads of State attend the European Council. The Council of Ministers, however, operates in formations: Ecofin, responsible for economic and monetary policy, is a weighty formation of finance ministers, while national agriculture ministers attend the Agricultural Council, and so on. This creates fragmentation, overlap, and even rivalry inside the committee systems of national parliaments where they do not possess a specialist committee on European affairs. Practice is extremely variable and national parliaments have been surprisingly slow to set up effective monitoring machinery. (The first European Affairs Committee, set up by Belgium, was actually wound up for lack of business in 1979.)

What sparked a change in attitudes everywhere was the advent of the Single European Act, with its startling transfer of competence to the EU,[28] and the TEU, Maastricht being the worms' final turning point. Maastricht was critical because ratification difficulties in Denmark and France breathed life into anti-European movements and exposed some national parliaments as out-of-touch. Accustomed to see themselves as the legitimate representatives of public opinion, they were disconcerted to find themselves viewed as part of a pro-European elite bent on destroying national institutions. Sensing that power was slipping rapidly from their hands, national parliaments began to examine their own procedures, developing a more aggressive attitude. Not only did they began to question and hold governments to account, they turned their attention also to the European Parliament, as rival or possible partner.

The French Assembly had been handicapped from the outset by a constitutional prohibition on the number of parliamentary committees which could be appointed. Under the 1968 constitution, no more than six may exist at any one time, the motive being to protect the French government from parliamentary interference.[29] In 1979, however, the two chambers moved to circumvent this obstacle by setting up parliamentary *délégations* of eighteen members, selected on party lines, which would report on EU matters to their respective chambers. These had limited success due, on the one hand, to government unwillingness to provide the necessary information, on the other, to the limited powers of *délégations*, which can act only as a transmission belt for information to, and at the request of, the subject-related

---

[28] J. Lodge, 'The European Parliament' in J. Lodge (ed.), *The EC and the Challenge of the Future* (London, Frances Pinter, 1989).

[29] J. Frears, 'The French Parliament and the European Community' (1975) 14 *Journal of Common Market Studies* 140, 141.

parliamentary committees. Significantly, successive governments have refused to transform the *délégations* into true committees. After Maastricht,
however, the French Assembly moved decisively to attempt greater control.
The process of ratification of the TEU presented the National Assembly with
an opportunity it was quick to seize. The opening was made by the Conseil
Constitutionnel, which ruled that constitutional amendment was necessary
before the Government could ratify, on the ground that suffrage rights,
confined by the French constitution to French citizens, were to be offered
in municipal elections to 'citizens of the European Union'. Article 88–3 was
the price exacted for the requisite changes. This Article, regarded as an
important step towards accountability, provides that:

The government submits to the National Assembly and the Senate, by way of their
transmission to the Council of the Communities, proposals of Community acts
incorporating provisions of a legislative nature. During sessions, or outside of them,
resolutions can be voted in the framework of the present article, according to terms
determined by the rules of each assembly.

A leading French newspaper called this article 'a complete break with the
French tradition of the executive being the sole player in international
negotiations'.[30] Although the government attitude to Article 88 remains
cool, an interim assessment suggests that the Assembly is unlikely to allow
the government 'the kind of unfettered freedom that was a feature of the
past'.[31] The Chambre des Députés had in fact responded rapidly and
decisively; its *Délégation* now meets regularly and scrutinizes forthcoming
EU legislation systematically. In this activity, it has found a powerful ally in
the Conseil d'Etat, expert adviser to the government on textual drafting. The
Conseil has insisted on receiving proposed EC texts early and forwards to the
Assemblée on a regular basis those which merit attention, explaining why.[32]
Proof of its new authority lies in the fact that French delegates have now
insisted, in imitation of the UK Parliament, on introducing the principle of
parliamentary 'reserve'.[33] The *Délégation* has also insisted on the right to be
informed and comment on IGC proceedings,[34] a concession first granted in

[30] *Le Monde*, 25 June 1992. And see M.-F. Verdier, 'La révision constitutionnelle du 25
juin 1992 nécessaire à la ratification du traité de Maastricht et l'extension des pouvoirs des
assemblées parlementaires françaises' [1994] *Revue du droit public* 1137.
[31] F. Rizutto, 'The French Parliament and the EU: Loosening the Constitutional Strait-
jacket' in Special Issue, 'National Parliaments and the European Union' (1995) 1 *J. of
Legislative Studies* 46, 57.
[32] N. Questiaux, 'Implementing EC Law in France' in Craig and Harlow (eds.), n. 24
above, 486.
[33] C. Lequesne, 'The French EU Decision-making: Between Destabilisation and Adapta-
tion' in Andersen and Eliassen (eds.), n. 1 above, 79.
[34] M. Westlake, 'The European Parliament, the National Parliaments and the 1996
Intergovernmental Conference' (1995) 66 *Political Quarterly* 59, 63.

1996. Reserve has become a much commoner practice: as stated earlier, five Member State parliaments were recorded as placing a reserve on Council discussion of the European arrest warrant early in 2002.

Germany underwent a series of largely unsuccessful experiments, in which comprehensive information on all European projects was supposed to be forwarded to the Bundestag, a requirement in practice largely disregarded.[35] This has been attributed at least partially to the absence in the Bundestag of serious opposition to European integration. The present Standing Committee on EU Affairs was put in place in 1991, after an interim experiment with a subcommittee of the committee on Foreign Affairs (Article 45 of the German Constitution).[36] A feature of the current German arrangements is that eleven MEPs have 'observer' status, an unusual instance of national parliament co-operation with the European Parliament, which may reflect the function of 'regime support'. After Maastricht, when the constitutional basis for ratification was famously questioned in the Federal Constitutional Court,[37] a new Article 23 had to be inserted into the German Constitution to authorize the further transfer of powers to the EU. This Article codifies the rights and powers of the two chambers of the German parliament in EU matters, imposing a constitutional duty on the federal government to keep them comprehensively informed 'as early as possible' of all proposals with possible implications for Germany. Article 23 was completed by legislation which links the various German parliaments, in an effort to overcome the structural problems of federation.[38] Although, in the celebrated *Maastricht* Decision,[39] ratification survived challenge in the Bundesverfassungsgericht or Federal Constitutional Court, the Court imposed limitations in the name of national parliamentary democracy, ruling that Article 23 envisaged the *active participation* of the Bundestag in EU activities. Added force was given to the position of the Bundestag by the insistence of the Bundesverfassungsgericht that 'functions and powers of substantial

---

[35] Art. 2 of the Act of Ratification of the EC Treaties. And see M. Hilf and F. Burmeister, 'The German Parliament and European Integration' in E. Smith (ed.), *National Parliaments as the Cornerstone of EU Integration* (London, Kluwer Law International, 1996). See also K. Goetz and J. Hesse, 'Early Administrative Adjustment to the EC. The Case of the Federal Republic of Germany' (1992) 4 *Jahrbuch für Europäische Verwaltungsgeschichte* 18; A. Hyde-Price and C. Jeffery, 'Germany in the European Union' (2001) 39 *Journal of Common Market Studies* 689.

[36] T. Saalfeld, 'The German Houses of Parliament and European Legislation', Special Issue, 'National Parliaments and the European Union' (1995) 1 *Journal of Legislative Studies* 12, 20–5.

[37] N. 11 above. And see P. Kirchhof, 'The Balance of Powers Between National and European Constitutions' (1999) 5 *European Law Journal* 225.

[38] See G. Ress, 'The Constitution and the Maastricht Treaty: Between Cooperation and Conflict' (1994) 3 *German Politics* 49.

[39] N. 11 above.

importance must remain for the German Bundestag'. Although the Court did not preclude the extension of EP powers, it did express disapproval of the gradual erosion of national parliamentary sovereignty through an uncontrolled process of Treaty amendment. This point gains added force from the fact that national parliaments play no formal part in drafting Treaty amendments at the IGC; although in practice their influence may be considerable, at IGC proceedings they have only observer status. It has been forecast that the influence of the Bundestag will remain limited in European affairs, the balance of power resting firmly with a not-too-accountable federal government.[40] This might change, however, if right-wing or anti-European parties were to be more strongly represented in the Bundestag.

The United Kingdom Parliament also reacted rather slowly. The House of Lords, with a greater degree of autonomy from government, is to be congratulated on acting well before the House of Commons. The House of Lords Select Committee on the European Communities, set up in 1972 with a wide remit to consider policy as well as draft legislation, concentrates on prior control of policy, preferably at an early stage in the debate. The expert series of reports on a wide range of subjects—several cited in this book—has gained respect, and its reports are widely circulated in Brussels. Commission representatives have been known to attend the committee when it takes evidence from the public and NGOs. This interchange could provide a significant precedent. The House of Commons early established the 'parliamentary reserve', prohibiting ministers in the Council of Ministers from giving assent to any proposal subject to scrutiny or awaiting consideration by the House.[41] Detailed scrutiny of the texts was, however, another matter. The first Commons scrutiny committee treated EC legislation as delegated legislation, greatly restricting the powers of scrutiny.[42] An important report from the Procedure Committee, highlighting problems of access to documentation,[43] brought a wide revision of procedures, none too soon. The Scrutiny Committee currently reports on every EU document 'of legal and political importance', consistently publishing well-informed and reasoned reports, based on ministerial evidence and statements. Reports can be and are referred on for debate, either on the floor of the House or in one of three new European Standing Committees. The new procedures have, over the period they have been in operation, greatly strengthened the hand of the House of Commons.

Thus a picture emerges of national parliaments increasingly on the alert, anxious to participate in EU affairs and keen to strengthen machinery for

---

[40] Hilf and Burmeister, n. 35 above, 76.

[41] Resolution of the House of 3 Oct. 1980 HC Deb, vol. 991, col. 843, now Resolution of 24 Oct. 1990, HC Deb., vol. 178, col. 399.

[42] D. Judge, 'The Failure of National Parliaments?' (1995) 18 *W. European Politics* 79, 85.

[43] Select Committee on Procedure, 'European Community Legislation', HC 622-I (1989/ 90). See also 'The Scrutiny of European Business', HC 51 (1995/6).

scrutiny of government. As stated, however, a second precondition for success is an adequate flow of information, a point now dealt with by Articles 1–3 of Protocol 8 on the Role of National Parliaments in the European Union, added to the TEC at Amsterdam. This requires the Commission to forward all consultation and Green and White papers 'promptly' to national parliaments, while Commission proposals for legislation 'shall be made available in good time'. Access remains a cause for complaint, and is only just beginning—if it is beginning—to be resolved. At regional, national, and EU level, parliaments and parliamentary committees complain of problems of access; documentation reaches them late, is incomplete and badly translated, a perennial problem for the EU at every stage of the law-making process. Not all national parliaments have Brussels offices which can supply alternative versions. Practical problems of this kind undercut the work of the national parliaments and help to offset the increased interest of members.

III 'GIVE US THE TOOLS'

Five very different sets of powers are at the disposal of the European Parliament as a lever in enforcing accountability. There are the law-making powers, in connection with which Shirley Williams has argued that a parliament which does not possess the plenary *legislative power* is neither fully sovereign nor fully legitimate.[44] Renaud Dehousse stresses the EP's power in the *appointments* process, predicting that the requirement in the Maastricht TEU of a 'vote of approval' for the President of the Commission (TEC Article 214(2) paragraph 3) would mark an important new step towards responsible government in the EU.[45] Martin Westlake emphasizes the centrality of the *budgetary and financial* powers,[46] of great historical significance in the evolution of parliamentary power throughout the western world. Martin Shapiro[47] focuses on the EP's *committee* structure, without which no parliament can hold government to account. Finally, in the aftermath of BSE, Martin Westlake notes the increasing power of committees of *inquiry*.[48]

[44] S. Williams, 'Sovereignty and Accountability in the European Community' (1990) 61 *Political Quarterly* 299.

[45] R. Dehousse, 'Constitutional Reform in the European Community. Are there Alternatives to the Majoritarian Avenue?' (1995) 18 *W. European Politics* 118.

[46] M. Westlake, ' "The Style and the Machinery": The Role of the European Parliament in the EU's Legislative Processes' in Craig and Harlow (eds.), n. 24 above, 145.

[47] M. Shapiro, 'The Politics of Information: US Congress and European Parliament' in ibid.

[48] M. Shackleton, 'The European Parliament's New Committees of Inquiry: Tiger or Paper Tiger' (1998) 36 *Journal of Common Market Studies* 115.

Law-making

It has been suggested that the contribution of the law-making process to accountability may in practice be that it forces government to explain, thus bringing into the open, albeit at a late stage, policy differences. This is not the standpoint of the EP. The EP has had to struggle hard to achieve adequate input into EU law-making and it rates its achievements in terms of sovereignty. At the first stage, the Commission proposed and the Council decided. At the second, the only power available to the EP was the right to be consulted, although case law from the ECJ soon established that the formalities of consultation, whenever required by the Treaties, had to be respected.[49] A convention soon arose also that the EP would invariably be consulted, except on highly technical texts.[50] The co-operation procedure of TEC Article 252, first introduced by the SEA, has been described as 'the procedure on which the Parliament "cut its teeth" as a "serious" legislator, and first began the process of learning to use intensified input into the legislative process as an opportunity to have a real influence upon the pattern and content of policy making'.[51] Co-operation procedure allows the EP to propose amendments, but leaves the last word with the Council, which may reject them (in practice, quite as far as many national parliaments dare go). It has to be remembered that the Council often resorts to 'old-style procedures' of legislation (consultation or no parliamentary output) in an apparent effort to bypass the heightened accountability of the codecision.

The absence of a final power of veto presented a challenge to the EP, which got much nearer to what it wanted with the codecision procedure first introduced at Maastricht. TEC Article 251 gave the EP a power of 'negative veto' over Council proposals, but only if the conciliation procedure, introduced at the same time to avoid deadlock, broke down. In case of failure, the Council could act unilaterally, presenting a new draft to the EP, which had to be simply rejected or accepted. This was a long step to the full legislative accountability of Council to the European Parliament. It has been said that codecision operated to create a common commitment on the part of the institutions to consensual law-making, rather than a confrontational situation in which Commission and/or Council, the joint policy-makers, are 'accountable' for legislative policy to the European Parliament.[52] In fact, the EP only

---

[49] Case 138/79, *Roquette Frères* v. *Council* [1980] ECR 3333 (The Isoglucose case); Case 139/79, *Maizena* v. *Council* [1980] ECR 3393.

[50] R. Corbett, F. Jacobs, and M. Shackleton, *The European Parliament* (4th edn, Harlow, Longman, 2000), 177.

[51] J. Shaw, *Law of the European Union*, 3rd edn. (Basingstoke, Palgrave, 2000) 257.

[52] M. Shackleton, 'The Politics of Codecision' (2000) 38 *Journal of Common Market Studies* 325, 331–3.

once used its 'negative veto', on the Voice Telephony Directive in 1994, voted down by absolute majority after a failed conciliation.[53] Under the variation introduced at Amsterdam, codecision procedure took another long step forward. Conciliation procedure, though theoretically still possible, is likely to become a thing of the past. The 'positive assent' of Council acting by QMV[54] and the EP by a simple majority is now required for the legislation to pass, putting the European Parliament in a position of parity with a majority of national systems. Negotiation can now start at the point where proposals are published by the Commission and agreement can be ratified by Council and EP after a single reading, shortening the process and making it more efficient.

There is a bias towards consensus in the EU Council, starting with the need in Council to avoid a veto, and ending with the need for 'positive assent' from both 'chambers of the legislature'. The effect on accountability of a consensual and collaborative law-making system is assumed to be similar to coalition government. Accountability comes through the need for prior agreement and typically takes the form of negotiated compromise. In this way, oppositional debate of policy, and the elements of blame and censure, which some see as central to accountability can largely be avoided.

Appointment

Under the original scheme of the Treaties, the Member States appointed the Commission and its President. After the first direct elections, however, the EP assumed to itself a right to set down a vote of confidence on the first occasion when a new Commission met the Parliament, amending its internal rules of procedure to accommodate the development. The TEU formalized this procedure by providing for *consultation* of the EP prior to appointment of the President (TEC Article 214). At Amsterdam, the powers of the EP were further strengthened by the substitution of the word 'approval'. This provision, apparently seen as an uncontroversial concession to the EP, in fact opened a chink in the Member States' monopoly of the appointment process, which the EP has used skilfully to heighten its political power.[55] The EP now approves the appointment of the President and Commissioners at a 'confirmation hearing', where they must appear before the appropriate committee. A practice originally conceded somewhat grudgingly by the Commission, this

---

[53] S. Boyron, 'Maastricht and the Co-decision Procedure: A Success Story' (1996) 45 *ICLQ* 293.

[54] QMV stands for Qualified Majority Voting, when votes are weighted according to population and an overall majority of 62 out of 87 votes required (TEC, Art. 205(2)). See further S. Hix, *The Political System of the European Union* (Basingstoke, Macmillan, 1999), 69–74.

[55] Corbett *et al*, n. 50 above, 234–8.

is now a routine procedure beginning to take on the colours of a US Senate hearing, taken very seriously by the EP. At the time when the Santer Commission was seeking approval, for example, a written questionnaire was sent to each Commissioner-designate. This acted as basis for a three-hour interview with each Commissioner, with full verbatim transcripts. Although Fiona Hayes-Renshaw and Helen Wallace suggest[56] that the EP's questioning of nominees 'left a bad taste in the mouth and tarnished the reputation of the nominees', a procedure smacking less of accountability and more of inter-institutional politics, this is a criticism which could be levelled at the Congressional committees of the US Senate.

More pertinent is the parliamentary power to dismiss the Commission, though not individual Commissioners, through a censure motion passed by a two-thirds majority. To date no motion of censure has succeeded. The first failed censure vote of 1992 challenged the Commission for concessions on agricultural policy made to the GATT and seen by the EP as contrary to EU interests. Clearly, this was an attempt to secure accountability, entirely consonant with classic doctrines of ministerial responsibility. The Santer Commission survived a motion of censure set down by the European Socialists by 292 to 232 votes. This can again be read as a reasonably successful exercise in accountability, since the Commission was forced to accept and co-operate with the Committee of Independent Experts. Resignation of the Commissioners was triggered by the negative character of the Interim Report of the Committee of Experts, although the threat of a majority for a vote of censure in the EP was undoubtedly the determining factor. At the time, it seemed to make the relations between the EU executive and its parliamentary body rather more like that obtained between government and parliament in democratic systems, though this was a parliamentary performance stronger than many national parliaments could put on. It represented a significant step towards strengthening the accountability of the Commission to the European Parliament and reinforcing democratic legitimacy in the EU.[57]

The EP has also steadily acquired powers of appointment in other areas. It is consulted on the appointment of the Court of Auditors and has put these powers into practice. It appoints the European Ombudsman, the first appointment providing an opportunity for a somewhat unedifying display of north/south politics. The EP plays no part whatsoever in the appointment of judges of the ECJ and CFI (TEC Article 223) and has to date wrung no concession in this respect, though it has demanded an equal share with the Council on a number of occasions.[58] It is, on the other hand, to be

[56] F. Hayes Renshaw and H. Wallace, *The Council of Ministers* (Basingstoke, Macmillan, 1997), 202.

[57] Ibid., 237.

[58] See Art. 25 of the Constitution of the European Union, EP Doc A3–0064/94, drafted by the Herman Committee.

'consulted' on the appointment of the President of the European Central Bank, a function which, on the occasion of the first appointment, it took most seriously, using the opportunity of a split nomination by the Council greatly to enhance its own powers. Specialized staff were temporarily seconded to the Committee on Economic and Monetary Affairs. The European Socialists' Group prepared and published research on the background of the two candidates, Wim Duisenberg and Jean-Claude Trichet. Questionnaires were issued, on the basis of an agreed parliamentary agenda, to be used as the basis of the hearing. The twin themes were *credibility*—the new President must possess sufficient credibility to satisfy the financial markets on the success of the launch of EMU—but also *accountability*. Shortly before the hearings, the EP published a report, provocatively entitled 'Democratic Accountability in the Third Stage of EMU', embodied in a formal Resolution. In the name of accountability, the EP demanded from the ECB a regular flow of information, a quarterly meeting, and an annual debate with the Director and European Parliament. In addition, the EP asked for the power to approve nominees to the Bank's executive board (which makes its own appointments). Not only were the majority of these demands conceded, but the EP also gained a measure of legitimacy for its tactics from successful candidate Wim Duisenberg playing politics rather cleverly, and announcing that, if not approved by the EP, he would withdraw from the contest.[59]

Financial and Budgetary Powers

Even before the major battle over audit and accountability in the Santer Commission, Martin Westlake was predicting that the EP would turn its attentions from law-making to the 'previously dormant' budgetary process, where he foresaw a 'major new front' as opening up.[60] The Community budget is a large one: in 1999, the total amounted to euros 83978 million. Table 4.1 gives an indication of the scale of the EU budget.

The allocation of revenues is often the subject of intense political conflict and of fierce bargaining, involving disputes over the destination of the regional structural funds, which absorb around 15 percent of the total budget, and the way in which the agricultural subsidies are disbursed. The budget is also at the centre of a power struggle between the institutions, with the European Parliament adopting the stance that it should play a key role in financial allocation, as national parliaments typically do. One should bear in mind when evaluating this demand that the European Parliament, unlike

---

[59] M. Westlake, 'The European Parliament's Emerging Powers of Appointment' (1998) 36 *Journal of Common Market Studies* 431, 436.
[60] Westlake, n. 46 above.

the majority of national parliaments, is not directly representative of the taxpayer and has no responsibility for supply. Of the EU institutions, it is the Council which has the strongest incentive to restrict Community expenditure, though inside the Council there is a deep split between Member States which have always been net recipients and those, notably Germany, which have usually been net contributors. Partly for this reason, the EP uses its budgetary powers in a creative fashion largely to increase its influence over policy. It might, for example, invite the Council to develop new policies, for which it will vote funding. It often votes further resources to projects which it feels the Council is under-funding, as, for instance, transport. Not only can this type of behaviour bring the EP into conflict with the other institutions, but it may result in budgetary inefficiency. The European Court of Auditors (ECA) has on several occasions noted the failure of the Commission to spend its allocated budget, only to receive the reply that no Commission capacity for the programme existed, or that plans had never been agreed with those concerned. In short, the EP, on these occasions, is not using its budgetary powers to enhance accountability but to make gestures inside a game of inter-institutional politics.

For the EP, an important stage in the struggle for power over Community finance was reached in the early 1970s, resulting from Budgetary Treaties with the Council in 1970 and 1975. In 1975, the EP gained the significant power to grant formal discharge of the budget, supported by the power of the ECA to make a Declaration of Assurance on which discharge is based. Three EP committees deal with financial matters: an active and powerful policy-making Committee on Economic and Monetary Affairs; a Committee on Budgets to deal with the allocation of the Community budget, to which the Commission makes regular interim reports; and the Committee on Budgetary Control, which prepares the way for the annual discharge of accounts, to which the ECA makes its annual reports.[61] After further years of struggle, the EP has finally gained a further concession of some importance, especially in the controversial area of agriculture. TEC Article 270 prohibits the Commission from acting outside the parameters of the budget, an assurance that the overall budget will not be exceeded without recourse to the EP. The EP has secured a measure of budgetary control and a power of audit over the affairs of agencies, as well as the powerful and largely autonomous ECB. It is the combination of audit power with the expanding powers over appointment that commentators believe may be used by the EP to exact political responsibility from the bankers. Again, Dominic McGoldrick prophesies that the budgetary powers will be used to gain control, through a new inter-institutional agreement or Treaty amendment, over the Common Foreign

---

[61] See Table 4.2 for institutional input. For further detail, see Corbett *et al*, n. 50 above, Table 17, at. 116.

Table 4.1   Simplified financial perspective, 2000-3, in million euros

	2000	2001	2002	2003
Agriculture	40920	42800	43900	43770
Structural funds	32045	31455	30865	30285
Other internal uses	5930	6040	6150	6260
External action	4550	4560	4570	4580
Administration	4560	4600	4700	4800
Pre-accession aid	3120	3120	3120	3120
Total (with reserves)	89600	91110	98360	101590

Source: European Commission, *The budget of the European Union: how is your money spent?* Brussels, 2000.

Table 4.2   Institutional input into the EC budget

January	Each institution prepares its own operating budget.
	The Commission prepares the general European Union annual budget.
March	Council examines comments of ECA and makes recommendation to European Parliament.
	European Parliament's Committee on Budgetary Control examines the report of ECA.
	DAS is granted during the Spring session.
April	Trialogue meeting between Council, Commission, EP on budget priorities.
May	The Commission adopts and presents the preliminary draft budget.
July	Council/European Parliament conciliation meetings.
	Council examines Commission preliminary draft and adopts draft budget in first reading.
	Council position sent to EP by September.
October	European Parliament examines draft budget at first reading.
November	The ECA scrutinises implementation of last year's budget and publishes Annual Report.
	Council/European Parliament conciliation meeting.
	Draft budget examined by Council at second reading.
December	Draft budget examined by European Parliament at second reading.
	President of European Parliament adopts Final Budget or declares it rejected.

and Security Policy, an area from which national parliaments and the European Parliament were deliberately excluded by the European Council.[62]

The EP is not shy of using its budgetary powers; it has three times totally rejected the budget, and frequently votes to withhold sections of the budget until satisfied that it is being properly implemented. The EP is also ready to impose stringent conditions as to use. Discharge has also been refused, at least temporarily. Yet here again, the budgetary procedure impresses commentators as a 'process of mediation and consensus-seeking'. It has been said that there is in committee 'a high premium on committee consensus', because this will enable the committee to take the plenary Parliament, without strong party alliances, along with it.[63]

Inquiry

In recent years, quasi-judicial inquiries have emerged as an important technique for securing accountability, and have often been preferred to parliamentary investigative committees. For Martin Westlake, the right to establish a temporary committee of inquiry granted at Maastricht (TEC Article 193) is an important step towards obtaining accountability. The article envisages a scrutinizing and investigatory function into 'alleged contraventions or maladministration in the implementation of Community law'. Appropriately, in the light of findings of the European Court of Auditors over the years, the first such committee was set up to look into transit fraud in the European Union.[64] A Special Inquiry into the spread of BSE has also reported[65] and a similar temporary committee of inquiry has just been set up to look into conduct of the foot and mouth disease crisis.[66]

The BSE inquiry was the first occasion on which the new procedures, authorized by inter-institutional agreement and giving powers of access to information held by the EU institutions,[67] were tested. During the inquiry, the committee used the new procedures to 'invite' the participation of the

[62] D. McGoldrick, *International Relations Law of the European Union*, (London, Longmans, 1997), 168.

[63] Westlake, n. 46 above, 222.

[64] European Parliament, Report of the Committee of Inquiry into Community Transit System, A4-0053/97 (19 Feb. 1997).

[65] European Parliament, Report of Temporary Committee on Alleged Contraventions or Maladministration in the Implementation of Community Law in Relation to BSE, without Prejudice to the Jurisdiction of the Community and National Courts, A4-0020/97, 7 Feb. 1997.

[66] Temporary Committee on Foot and Mouth Disease (Chair: E. Redondo Jímenez), PS-TAPROV (2002) 0002.

[67] Decision of the European Parliament, the Council, and the Commission of 19 Apr. 1995 on the detailed provisions governing the exercise of the European Parliament's right of inquiry, 95/167/EC [1995] OJ C43/38.

British Government, through the Foreign Secretary and Agricultural Minister. The British Government made its view of the request very plain by designating as its spokesman the Permanent Secretary at the Ministry of Agriculture and not the minister.[68] The inquiry was nonetheless relatively successful and, as we saw in an earlier chapter, brought some changes. It succeeded in focusing a spotlight on the Comitology, using its powers to call independent experts to challenge the scientific expertise of Comitology experts and to correct imbalance in the scientific committees. Admitting to poor administration, President Santer announced that food-hygiene policy would be moved from Agriculture and would become the responsibility of Consumer Affairs. Later, when the Commission brought forward a proposal to replace the veterinary inspection powers of the Agriculture DG by an agency combining legislative and inspectorial powers, the EP followed up, using its power to withhold budgetary credits to force the Commission to withdraw its proposal.[69] A vote of censure followed, but was in turn withdrawn. Negative effects have also been noted. In the course of the affair, a national, quasi-judicial, inquiry was set up by the UK Government in parallel to that established by the EP.[70] The two inquiries did not apparently collaborate or even interact. Had the two parliaments been able to operate a joint inquiry, the EP would have had access to the evidence of UK ministers, while the national inquiry would have been better informed and empowered at the EU level. Together, they could have taken a firmer grip on the complex and unco-ordinated process of EU policy-making. The criticism of a former EP President that, because the Commission was the only body which could be held accountable, it was censured by the EP for failings for which it was not properly responsible, could have been avoided.[71]

To summarize, Maastricht, named as a turning-point for national parliaments, also set the EP on a steep learning curve. On both tiers of the EU system of government, parliaments quickly set out to acquire the tools needed for the job. Machinery for accountability is being put in place, usually in the shape of committees which can move more quickly to pinpoint problems and target those responsible. At Union level, the budget procedures are being pushed to their limits by the EP. In the EP, committees of inquiry are in their infancy and there is much scope for growth and improvement. There is much to be learned here from the experience of the EU affairs committees in

[68] See M. Shackleton, 'The European Parliament's New Committees of Inquiry: Tiger or Paper Tiger' (1998) 36 *Journal of Common Market Studies* 115.
[69] G. Chambers, 'The BSE Crisis and the European Parliament', in C. Joerges and E. Vos (eds.), *EU Committees: Social Regulation, Law and Politics* (Oxford, Hart Publishing, 1999), provides a fuller account.
[70] The Phillips Inquiry, set up by the Secretary of State for Agriculture on 22 Dec. 1997, and chaired by a judge, reported to the House of Commons: Inquiry into BSE, HC (19) **http://62.189.42.105/report/**.
[71] Klaus Hänsch MEP, cited by C. Lord, 'Assessing Democracy in a Contested Polity' (2001) 39 *Journal of Common Market Studies* 641, 652.

national parliaments. The EP has begun to identify shortcomings of committees of inquiry, starting with the limited powers to subpoena witnesses, and will no doubt continue to press for change at every IGC. They will no doubt come up against the barriers and obstacles used by national governments to limit accountability to national parliaments. Greater co-operation is required between EP committees of inquiry and those set up at national level to deal in parallel with the same incident. The possibility of joint inquiry, provided for in the statute of the European Ombudsman, should be considered. In general, however, parliaments seem at last to have grasped the challenges to their authority and status and are interested in learning how to use the machinery at their disposal to good effect.

IV A 'PRISONERS' DILEMMA'?

Arguably, there is always an adversarial element in accountability, the purpose of which is to encourage admissions of responsibility and to hold people to account for their actions. Arguably too, this adversarial element is hard to reconcile with the prevailing ethos of the EU, aimed broadly at securing consensus, though also intensely rivalrous. Inside the European Parliament, we have not so far witnessed the development of a strong, transnational network of political parties.[72] This does not mean that there are no party politics in the European Parliament or that in the EP as an institution 'government by grand coalition' is the order of the day. Even if it was once true to claim that the two largest political groupings operated as a coalition, this is no longer the case.[73] Nonetheless, the term 'consensus democracy' in the technical sense of a system of governance in which decisions can emerge only if they have overwhelming political support,[74] and 'consociationalism', meaning a system of governance 'deliberately designed to accommodate as many, if not all, national preferences, cultures, styles and traditions [through a] system of articulation and accommodation between national interests',[75] have both been applied to the EU system of governance.[76] It is hardly

---

[72] S. Hix and C. Lord, *Political Parties in the European Union* (Basingstoke, Macmillan, 1997).

[73] The subject of a forthcoming study by S. Hix, A. Noury, and G. Roland, 'A "Normal" Parliament? Party Cohesion and Competition in the European Parliament, 1979–2001'.

[74] Derived from A. Lijphart, *Democracy in Plural Societies: A Comparative Exploration* (New Haven, Conn., Yale University Press, 1977).

[75] S. Hix, *The Political System of the European Union* (Basingstoke, Macmillan, 1999), 201–3.

[76] P. Taylor, 'Consociationalism and Federalism as Approaches to International Integration' in A. Groom and P. Taylor (eds.), *Frameworks for International Co-operation* (London, Frances Pinter, 1994). See also D. Chryssochoou, 'Democracy and Symbiosis in the European Union: Towards a Confederal Consociation?' (1994) 17 *W. European Politics* 1.

surprising to find traces of this culture in the EP. Some are used to working in a society where consensus or consociationalism is deeply entrenched; indeed, Lijphart's theory was worked out in the framework of the pluralist democracy of the Netherlands[77] (a society which, incidentally, is well able to accommodate a strong version of the doctrine of ministerial responsibility). Coalition government is also deeply engrained in the consciousness of many MEPs, influenced by the model of their own national parliaments, in some of which coalition government has been the norm for a period of nearly a half-century. There are added incentives for coalition or consensus modes of thought in the EP, in the absence of elected government at EU level, the commonest motivation for confrontation in national parliaments and systems of government. More positively, there is a strong sense of commitment to a common enterprise amongst the EU institutions, which goes a long way to offset inter-institutional rivalry. Historically, too, the construction of an elite consensus has been an essential element in European integration.

Martin Westlake describes the parliaments of the EU as 'partners and rivals' and notes their tendency to 'talk past one another'.[78] It is, however, beginning to be admitted that parliaments could, by collaborating with each other, achieve greater success in securing accountability for EU affairs. Equally, it is beginning to be admitted that a place must be found in policy- and law-making for national parliaments at the Union level. Declaration 13 on the role of national parliaments in the European Union, appended to the TEC at Maastricht with Declaration 14 on the Conference of the Parliaments, introduces the idea that national parliaments should participate in Community affairs. While Declaration 14 merely 'invites' parliaments to meet occasionally in plenary conference, Declaration 13 is more practical in character. It asks for the exchange of information between national parliaments and the EP to be stepped up, creating an obligation for Member State governments to ensure that documentation reaches the parliaments 'in good time'. It also stresses the need for enhanced inter-parliamentary co-operation, 'through the granting of appropriate reciprocal facilities and regular meetings between members of parliament interested in the same issues'. It has to be said that many national parliaments have been slow to encourage such contacts, sometimes with good reason.

By Amsterdam, the thorny issue of a role for national parliaments had moved up the ladder. TOA Protocol 8 again speaks to the desire of the institutions to 'encourage greater involvement of national parliaments in the activities of the European Union and to enhance their ability to express their views on matters which may be of particular interest to them'. At the practical

---

[77] A. Lipjhart, *The Politics of Accommodation: Pluralism and Democracy in the Netherlands*, Berkeley, University of California Press, 1968.

[78] M. Westlake, 'The European Parliament, The National Parliaments and the 1996 Intergovernmental Conference' [1995] *Political Quarterly* 59, 70.

level, the Protocol merely reiterates the need for better information: consultation papers to be sent promptly, made available in every Community language; adequate time allowed for consultation 'so that the Government of each Member State may ensure that its own national parliament receives them as appropriate'; and so on. These exhortations tend in practice to founder on the impediment of language, the chief obstacle to speedy circulation of documentation by the Commission and to co-operation between parliaments. Marginally more significant are the steps designed to co-opt national parliaments into the law-making process. The inter-parliamentary Conference of European Affairs Committees (COSAC) may nowadays scrutinize proposals forwarded to it by Member State governments; it is empowered make *joint* contributions to the legislative process, more specifically in the area of freedom, security, and justice or concerning the rights and freedoms of individuals. It may in addition address to the institutions 'any contribution which it deems appropriate on the legislative activities of the Union, notably in relation to the application of the principle of subsidiarity, the area of freedom, security and justice as well as questions regarding fundamental rights'.

The EU institutions, more especially the EP, which has a direct interest in the outcome, are undoubtedly keen to find a place for national parliaments in the EU policy-making process. There are, however, very real problems. The dilemma which goes to the heart of the relationship is spelled out in TOA Protocol 8, which was, after all, drafted for and signed by Member State governments. The Preamble to the Protocol demonstrates fear on the part of the European Council, representing national *governments*, of being seen to trespass on sensitive *parliamentary* terrain. In a significant caveat, the High Contracting Parties recall 'that scrutiny by individual national parliaments of their own government in relation to the activities is a matter for the particular constitutional organisation and practice of each Member State', while the Protocol concludes with the assertion that 'contributions made by COSAC shall in no way bind national parliaments or prejudge their position'. Thus the Protocol exposes two perplexing sets of linked questions, the first pragmatic, the second more theoretical, about the position of national parliaments in EU affairs.

At the practical level, it has to be said that neither the EU institutions nor the national parliaments have any clear idea of how national parliaments may be included in decision-making. Nor have they so far shown much intelligence or initiative in the matter. The practical problems are admittedly great. National parliaments are large, typically composed of several hundred representatives. They are divided internally by political party, with the majority party either dominant or strongly represented in the national government, hence in the Council of Ministers. It is not very clear why it should prove easier and more effective for national parliaments to brief, or even mandate, the chairmen of their European Affairs committee, normally a representative of national parliaments at COSAC, than the ministers they send to Council. Perhaps the explanation lies in group dynamics; parliaments share some common aims and objectives, governments others. Yet, as this chapter has tried to indicate, there is no single parliamentary model, and parliaments—even the separate chambers of the same parliament—do not necessarily share a common culture. Although there is a common core to their activities, parliaments do not necessarily prioritize the same functions or work in even a broadly similar fashion. Even in areas singled out by Protocol 8 specifically for parliamentary attention, it is doubtful whether a common inter-parliamentary position would emerge: could there, for example, be a common position on a directive designed to eliminate racism and xenophobia within the EU, agreed between national parliaments in the control of broadly conservative parties and those with a moderately liberal, social democratic agenda? In short, the policy fault lines which emerge in the Council are likely to be at least partially replicated in national parliaments. On some issues indeed, the problem may even be magnified by the existence in a national parliament, or across national parliaments, of a left/right division which does not have to be represented by a national government in the Council of Ministers.

The second set of questions revolves around the logically prior issue of what role national parliaments ought to play in EU decision-making. Once again, there is no common position; indeed, it would be more accurate to say that there is very considerable disagreement. Some parliaments prefer to focus their attention on the activities of the national government; others would extend this to the national government's performance in the Council; others again would like to go much more deeply into monitoring EU policy.[79] While some national parliaments may still see themselves as largely in the business of providing regime support for their government at Community level, others are concerned to win a greater role in Community law-making, while others again see their main function as being to ensure effective scrutiny of Community policy and law. To add to the complexity, politics in the European Parliament are not a mirror image of national politics and national political parties are not replicated there.[80] Nor do national parliaments necessarily share common positions, culture, and ethos with regional parliaments, with which the national political turf has to be shared.

The chief beneficiary of greater parliamentary participation in EU affairs would undoubtedly be the European Parliament. It is therefore not surprising

[79] P. Norton, 'National Parliaments and the European Union: Where to from Here?' in Craig and Harlow (eds.), n. 24 above, 213.
[80] Hix and Lord, n. 72 above.

to find the EP trying to secure for itself a central role in promoting parliamentary input into EU policy-making. Over the last decade, as the powers of the EP have, as indicated earlier, been greatly enhanced and it is learning to use them, it has also tried to position itself at the hub of a wheel of inter-parliamentary relationships. The first and only Assizes held by the European parliaments was held under the aegis of the EP, with a representation of fifty-three MEPs to 173 representatives of national parliaments. For Westlake, the EP was successful in managing to tie the conference to its own agenda, though he adds that 'for this reason not all national parliaments saw the Assizes as a success'.[81] In similar fashion, the EP holds a dominant position in the COSAC, or conference of representatives of parliamentary committees on EU affairs, which meets on a six-monthly time cycle in the country holding the Presidency. It is represented by a vice-president responsible for relations with national parliaments and participates on a regular basis in setting the agenda, which makes it 'the one permanent member of the preparatory group'. Again, 'almost all the national parliaments have an administrative unit responsible for liaison with the European Parliament and the latter has a division responsible for relations with national parliaments'.[82]

Its position at the hub of the wheel is crucial for the EP, for the legitimacy of which direct election, increased participation in the legislative process, enhanced visibility, and even the manifest accountability of the Commission have, to the apparent surprise of the EU institutions, done very little. The EP still depends heavily on national parliaments for its legitimation; indeed, for some theorists, indirect legitimation, with legitimacy borrowed from nationally elected governments and parliaments, is the best the EU system of governance can hope for.[83] If Simon Hix and Christopher Lord in their full-length study of EU politics are less pessimistic, they do conclude that, in the absence of a transnational political system, legitimation through national political systems and institutions is likely to remain necessary for some time to come.[84] As some national parliaments and some political parties undoubtedly realize, however, it is not necessarily in the interest of national parliaments to act as spokes in a wheel of EU parliaments.

If, as suggested, consociationalism is the preferred method of EU policy-making, then we can see the ideal reflected very clearly in the role designated

---

[81] Westlake, n. 78 above, 61.

[82] Corbett *et al.* n. 50 above, 286.

[83] S. Andersen and T. Burns, 'The European Union and the Erosion of Parliamentary Democracy: A Study of Post-parliamentary Governance', in S. Andersen and K. Eliassen, *The European Union: How Democratic Is It?* (London, Sage, 1996).

[84] Hix and Lord, n. 72 above, 219–20.

to parliaments by the Commission's White Paper on Governance.[85] The main objective of the White Paper appears to be enhanced consultation and increased opportunities for participation in EU policy-making. In taking this line, the Commission can be seen as drawing on and expanding the European Council's instructions at every one of its recent meetings, including Maastricht, where the subsidiarity doctrine, requiring the EU to take action 'only if and so far as the objectives of the proposed action cannot be sufficiently achieved by the Member States', was first introduced by TEU Article 3b. Protocol 30 of the Treaty of Amsterdam, which further explicates the doctrine of subsidiarity, exhorts the Commission to 'consult widely before proposing legislation and, wherever appropriate, publish consultation documents'. Yet the underlying objective of the Commission's proposals in the White Paper is not subsidiarity but a legitimation of EU policies through concepts of participatory democracy (an idea reserved for discussion in the final chapter of this book). In conformity with these undeclared objectives, consultation is not confined to national parliaments but extends to regional parliaments and even beyond to the Committee of Regions and civil society in general. Only the European Parliament, as an EU institution, has enhanced status in this funnelling of opinion into the Commission. This way of looking at things is deeply problematic for accountability, which, as we saw in Chapter 1, may depend for its effectiveness on a measure of externality and autonomy. It obviously becomes hard for those who have taken part in policy-making or in a decision to censure or blame the decision-maker.

A move to participatory democracy, necessarily signalling a move away from representative democracy, is likely seriously to damage the standing of national parliaments, which may find themselves placed in a type of prisoner's dilemma.[86] In order to secure the accountability of national governments and, more particularly, of the EU institutions, national parliaments need the close collaboration of the EP. To engage in collaboration is, however, unsafe for national parliaments, since they have not so far been successful in clawing back powers and responsibilities lost to the EU and its non-democratic institutions.[87] As their own input into policy-making diminishes in proportion to inter-governmental activity at Community level, so they stand to lose

[85] European Commission, White Paper on European Governance (COM(2001)428) [2001] OJ C287/1. The White Paper is addressed more fully in the final chapter of this book.

[86] S. Gustavsson, 'Preserve or Abolish the Democratic Deficit?' in E. Smith (ed.), *National Parliaments as Cornerstones of European Integration* (Dordrecht, Kluwer Law International, 1996).

[87] D. Chryssochou, S. Stavridis, and M. Tsisizelis, 'European Democracy, Parliamentary Decline and the Democratic Deficit of the European Union' (1998) 4 *Journal of Legal Studies* 109, 115.

output legitimacy.[88] Only if they can be certain that collaboration will not result in greater legitimacy for the EP can national parliaments afford to embark on a policy of collaboration, since heightened standing and greater legitimacy for the EP may have the undesired result of speedier transfer of competences to the second, Union tier of policy-making. In contrast, strict enforcement of the subsidiarity principle could bring the benefit of enhanced accountability of national governments at national level. The relevance of the consociational method of EU policy-making pencilled in by the Commission White Paper is that it may stimulate turf wars between national and regional parliaments.

It would seem to follow that, only if national parliaments can use their own enhanced power at the EU tier to secure the stricter observance of the subsidiarity principle, while at the same time confining its use to *national* level, should they indulge in co-operative enterprises with the EP. On balance, it would be unwise for them to be pulled up the spokes of the European Union parliamentary wheel. What they should do instead is to ensure that the rim of the wheel is strong and in good repair. Relationships *between* national parliaments are much less threatening and are in urgent need of development. Something very like this has been hinted at by Robin Cook, when British Foreign Secretary. (It should be noted that Cook is currently Leader of the House of Commons.) Cook calls for a forum in which national parliaments could meet to discuss problems of subsidiarity.[89] The risk national parliaments face is that such a forum would again operate to provoke turf wars between the three tiers of parliaments, the outcome being a huge and unwieldy 'forum', built to accommodate regional parliaments. This could minimize parliamentary input into policy- and decision-making, while seeming to enhance it. It would also undermine the scrutiny role of parliaments. Yet if national parliaments are to retain their central place in European democracy, it is essential that they should find innovative ways to collaborate with each other. Even without the help and resources of the EP, a programme of close co-operation between European parliaments is urgently needed.

---

[88] S. Katz and B. Wessels, 'Introduction: European Parliament, National Parliaments, and European Integration' in S. Katz and B. Wessels (eds.), *The European Parliament, National Parliaments, and European Integration* (Oxford, Oxford University Press, 1999) 8.

[89] *The New Statesman*, 14 Aug. 1998.

5

Accountability through Audit

I DESIGNING MODERN AUDIT SYSTEMS

A key problem in evolving a satisfactory system of audit in the EU is the absence of an international audit tradition and any accepted style of international audit. International organizations or systems of governance, because they do not reflect the institutional patterns of the nation state, may need a specialized audit system. The audit of international institutions has, however, evolved as almost an entirely internal function. In practice the audit boards of international organizations may be composed, as with some UN bodies, of a committee of state representatives, for obvious reasons, a system likely to be both ineffectual and inimical to accountability. There is no international audit corps yet in existence, as there could be under the auspices of a body such as the International Monetary Fund, which might eventually be instrumental in promoting and establishing an international audit agency with agreed audit standards. Currently, the World Bank, IMF, and other international organizations are interested in standard-setting and so far as possible promote their own audit standards by building them into aid schemes. There is, on the other hand, barely a mention of audit as an element in the otherwise comprehensive OECD 'PUMA' project on public management briefly mentioned in Chapter 1 as a significant actor in transnational standard-setting.[1]

The activities of the 'Big Six' multinational firms of accountants which operate throughout the world are largely confined to the private sector. Nor is there any general legal obligation to report suspicion of fraud or corruption to the national authorities.[2] There are, however, international professional bodies which help to set standards internationally. The International Organization of Supreme Audit Institutions has provided a useful definition of

---

[1] See OECD, *First Report, Ethics in the Public Service,* **www.oecd.org/puma/ethics/pubs/eip96/execsum.htr**. But the OECD publications for 2001 contain a set of 17 papers on budgeting in the public sector dated from 1993–2001.

[2] S. Strange, *The Retreat of the State, The Diffusion of Power in the World Economy* (Cambridge, Cambridge University Press, 1996), 146. The involvement of Andersen in the fall of the giant US energy company, Enron, illustrates the point.

public audit in a statement agreed at an international congress, remarkable for its breadth.[3]

[T]he specific objectives of auditing are the proper and effective use of public funds; the development of sound financial management; the orderly execution of administrative activities; and the communication of information to public authorities through the publication of objective reports.

It was from the Institute of Internal Auditors that the Committee of Independent Experts borrowed its definition of internal audit, influential in the reform of the Commission's practices discussed in a later section of this chapter. In the absence of an international audit system, centred on an approved corps of independent auditors, working, as suggested, under the auspices of the IMF or WB, or established as an international agency, there are three main options open to international organizations. First, they may employ external auditors, as does the International Posts and Telecommunications Union, which asks the Swiss federal auditors, on whose territory it operates, to audit its books. Not only is this practice rare but it is unlikely to recommend itself to the EU institutions, very conscious of their dignity and standing in the world, while at the same time inhibited from preferring a single national tradition in building up their institutions. Secondly, the UN practice of appointing political representatives, with all its defects, might be followed. To a certain extent, as we shall see, this is the way in which audit evolved in the Community and its appointments system does reflect the international style. Indeed, in some of the Member States, notably Germany, political affiliation is a criterion for appointment, and this may be indirectly reflected in appointments to the European Court of Auditors (ECA). Finally, the practice of nomination of expert representatives by the constituent members could be adopted. This is the solution actually used today for the ECA.

This book has followed a conventional approach to accountability by choosing to focus first on the institutions of political control in the EU, in practice parliaments, and their general efficacy. Michael Power has indeed suggested a direct correlation between different national attitudes to political accountability and national traditions of audit.[4] Although in national audit systems, political accountability is almost invariably ensured by a report to the parliament, the uses made by parliaments of their powers may vary very considerably; by no means every national system sets its parliament in a strong position of control over public finance. The present chapter can nevertheless be seen as a straight continuation of the classical approach to

---

[3] LIMA Declaration of International Organization of Supreme Audit Institutions, Oct. 1997.

[4] M. Power, *The Audit Society, Rituals of Verification*, (Oxford, Oxford University Press, 1999), 45.

accountability identified in Chapter 1: from parliament and political responsibility to parliament and financial accountability. In such a system, the fact that audit officers report to a parliamentary committee and cannot themselves impose sanctions justifies an investigatory role, as in the case of the British Auditor and Comptroller-General, technically an officer of the House of Commons, and the National Audit Office over which he presides. Accountability will necessarily be far more problematic for international bodies without a representative parliament capable of exacting accountability, and we shall see that the European Parliament has had to fight hard to secure a footing for itself in the EU audit process.

On the other hand, a continental lawyer might see this chapter, which deals with audit as a means of accountability, as a shift away from political responsibility to the *legal* control of government by courts, an analysis wholly unfamiliar to an administrative lawyer practising in an Anglo-Saxon country, where audit typically falls outside the world of lawyers. Indeed, lawyers are, with a few notable exceptions, just starting to realize their role in ensuring accountability. This may help to explain a remark from the UK Public Accounts Committee that the ECA was 'employing too many lawyers and not enough accountants, and that its work tended to be done by way of legal scrutiny in the Continental tradition rather than along the more pragmatic lines of UK accounting'.[5] In contrast, several of the Member States' audit procedures are judicial, or at least quasi-judicial, in character: the final audit body is a designated 'court', its procedures are 'contradictory' in character, and its task is, very much like that of a court in judicial review, to arrive at a judgment on the *legality* of financial acts and actions. This model, originating in the French Cour des Comptes,[6] and replicated in varying degrees in Belgium and the Mediterranean Member States, is strongest in Greece and Portugal, where courts of audit are constitutionally equal to the supreme court. Inside these two main groupings, there are other distinctions and divisions: in Germany, for example, there is much emphasis on conformity with standards and procedures regulated and set out in laws.

There are, according to the British National Audit Office (NAO), four types of audit institution in use within the European Union: the court model, with its judicial function; the 'collegiate body', with no judicial function; the independent audit office under the control of an autonomous officer; and a government-operated national audit office. Given its title, it is perhaps not surprising if the European Court of Auditors is widely but erroneously believed to be a court; in fact, as the NAO points out, it falls within the second category of *a collegiate body with no judicial role*. To an Italian

[5] Public Accounts Committee, 'The Court of Auditors of the European Community', HC 92 (1981–2).

[6] For a short description of the French system, see 'France', in National Audit Office, *State Audit in the European Union* (London, NAO, 1996; updated).

commentator, the court-like functions of the ECA seem to be less ample than those of the French and Italian courts of audit, as the ECA possesses no adjudicative functions and has no remedies, in the shape of court orders, at its disposal.[7] This classification does not exhaust the possibilities: some states have national and regional audit bodies, separately accountable and distinct in character, as is the case with the British NAO and Audit Commission. The Austrian Rechnungshof, by way of contrast, is a combination model, headed by a president, and audits at central, regional, and local level.[8] In the Swedish system of decentralized administration, we would expect a rather different system of audit to be in place. Sweden divides the audit function between government and parliament. The Riksdag sets up a parliamentary audit agency, with twelve professional auditors who audit central government departments on the Riksdag's behalf. The decentralized agencies are account-able to a government national audit commission which reports back to the agency and on to a relevant ministry.[9]

In all national systems, control of public finances tends to be a shared responsibility of government and parliament, though the shares may not be equal. An important and variable element is the authority vested in the finance ministry. In both the UK and France, the Treasury or Ministry of Finance exercises an iron grip on public finances, in practice successfully overriding devolution to regional level. The Treasury appoints the depart-mental accounting officer or *contrôleur*, who is responsible to the Treasury. This is a significant point, as Fidelma White and Kathryn Hollingsworth observe. A firm tie with a powerful Ministry of Finance means that manage-ment and audit 'are basically pushing in the same direction'.[10] By the same token, the ECA has specifically attributed its difficulties in establishing a firm role for itself to the absence in the EU of any equivalent to a finance ministry which can work with it to establish control of spending.[11] This important observation needs to be borne in mind when assessing attempts to reform the EU audit systems and restructure the system of financial control within the European Commission.

Audit comprises a number of elements, not all of which need be present in any one system. There is first a government budgeting exercise to estimate expenditure. Normally, this needs the approval of parliament, though this is not a universal requirement; in Italy, prior to 1978, no annual budget was

---

[7] G. Cogliandro, 'I Controlli' in M. Chiti and G. Greco (eds.), *Tratatto di Diritto Amministrativo Europeo* (Milan, Giuffrè, 1997), 278.

[8] 'Austria', in NAO, n. 6 above.

[9] F. White and K. Hollingsworth, *Audit, Accountability and Government* (Oxford, Clarendon, 1999), 137–40.

[10] Ibid., at 194.

[11] Report in response to the conclusions of the European Council of 18 June 1983 [1983] OJ C287/1.

presented to the Parliament, which gave approval only to individual measures.[12] At the level of execution, audit again has several stages, some of which may be internal to the institution, others vested in the auditor. Expenditure may need to be hierarchically justified by a departmental accounting officer, as it is in the United Kingdom, where the Permanent Secretary fills this role,[13] or it may need specific prior approval by an internal audit authority. The role of *ex ante* control is 'to verify in advance the legality of each item of revenue or expenditure and provide the management authority with an assurance that measures concerning, in particular, the safeguarding of the assets and the regularity of the accounting are adequate'.[14] This is the process generally known in European systems as the 'visa'. The visa function gives the financial controller *ex ante* control over expenditure and some systems of audit attach much importance to it: for example, until 1994, the Italian Corte di Conti had responsibility for auditing almost every individual decision or payment order, authorizing some five million expenditures annually, with only trivial amounts excluded.[15] Clearly, this is a slow and cumbersome system, and it has been suggested in the EU to be the main cause of mismanagement and serious delay, especially in the delivery of international aid, notably in cases of disaster. Modification of the visa system in the Commission was a key recommendation of the Committee of Independent Experts.[16] The second stage of audit is *ex post facto*. Accounts are drawn up and a 'certification audit' conducted. This is essentially confined to the accuracy of the income and expenditure account, although it may also look again at the lawfulness and procedural correctness of the expenditure. The object of certification audit is primarily as a protection against corruption and obvious illegality; it is concerned with the propriety of the expenditure but less concerned with waste or efficacy, though European auditors confirm that internal audit includes compliance with the principles of sound financial management. National audit systems share much in common. All audit systems recognize certification audit. There may be a difference of emphasis between the approach of the National Audit Commission in Britain and the French Cour des Comptes, but essentially both carry out the basic certification function of audit. Some of the Member States, notably Italy, place greater weight on legality and less on tracing the ultimate destination of funds.

[12] V. della Sala, 'Hollowing out and Hardening the State: European Integration and the Italian Economy' (1997) 20 *W. European Politics* 15.

[13] See, for an important example, F. White, I. Harden, and K. Donnelly, 'Audit, Accounting Officers and Accountability: The Pergau Dam Affair' [1994] *PL* 526.

[14] B. Desmond, *Managing the Finances of the EU, the Role of the European Court of Auditors* (Dublin, Institute of European Affairs, 1996), 3.

[15] 'Italy', in NAO, n. 6 above, 164.

[16] Committee of Independent Experts, *Second Report on Reform of the Commission— Analysis of Current Practice and Proposals for Tackling Mismanagement, Irregularities and Fraud*, Brussels, 10 Sept. 1999 (FR), Recommendation 35, 12.

There are essentially three main techniques of audit in use today. The first, which probably coincides with the public perception of audit, consists of a *total audit* of every item of income and expenditure. In a system as complex as that of the EU, this has to be ruled out as impractical. The second technique is that of *sampling*, whereby a small percentage of transactions is thoroughly scrutinized and the results extrapolated to cover the accounts as a whole. The sampling or 'spot-check' method is widely used in the EU where it is known as 'monetary unit sampling'. The operation of spot-check or sampling techniques in the EC is further discussed later in this chapter.[17] The third is *systems audit*, by which is meant the setting in place of a management system on which the auditor can place reliance. This involves the establishment of systems which permit the auditor to be confident that every stage of a transaction or series of transactions is properly monitored and that the actors can be called to account by a supervisory body. The auditor can then check the stages to see that each has been properly carried out, without himself checking every transaction. This is sometimes described by the metaphor of an 'audit trail'. The establishment of an audit trail is the first priority of modern audit systems.

However, the last decades of the twentieth century have seen audit being shaped into a keener and more effective tool for the management of public administration. A new and extended technique of 'Value-for-Money' audit (VFM) has been gaining ground,[18] which is intended to evaluate and shape the performance of the institution audited in terms of economy, efficiency, and effectiveness. A Report from the English Audit Commission, responsible for auditing the books of local authorities, explains how it is done:[19]

A public audit should be much more than just a check on probity and regularity. As well as being handled in accordance with the law, funds should be spent wisely. This means obtaining the best possible value for the money spent, and the success with which this is done should be assessed during the audit. [VFM] methodology identifies good practice . . . using comparisons of performance. . . . Auditors identify practical ways of improving services which help local managers target their efforts.

Not only does VFM audit allow auditors, by recourse to comparators of performance, to identify practical ways in which managers may better target their efforts but it allows them gradually to extend their remit deep into policy-making. It is this aspect of audit which has made it most attractive to public managers.[20]

[17] Power, n. 4 above, 69–74. And see below, p. 125.
[18] E. Normanton, 'Reform in the Field of Public Accountability and Audit: A Progress Report' (1980) 51 *Political Quarterly* 175.
[19] D. Cooksey, *Annual Report of the Audit Commission* (London, HMSO, 1993), 1.
[20] M. Power, *The Audit Explosion*, (London, Demos, 1994).

VFM audit originated in the Anglo-Saxon world, proving extremely attractive to market-oriented, right-wing governments, and spread rapidly alongside the methodology of New Public Management on which they also pinned their hopes for reform of bureaucracy. A recent study of performance audit and its origins in several European systems[21] has shown that it is now in place in many continental public audit systems. In the Netherlands, the Rekenkamer was empowered to pay attention to 'the goal-orientedness' of state management as early as 1976, and this has since become the general term for performance audit. In 1992, reference to VFM became more specific, when 'auditing the effectiveness and efficiency' of the public service and its policies was introduced. Audit in Finland also extends beyond legality and compliance with the budget to 'the economy, efficiency and effectiveness of the management of tasks'. Similarly, in Sweden, audit by the National Audit Office focuses on 'the connections between operations and finance', the objective being 'to point out central problems in efficiency... In a wider perspective, the financial conditions are linked to judgements on quality and the resources used'. All these audit systems are drawn from the northern, investigatorial group. Performance audit has, however, also penetrated the French Cour des Comptes, though the terminology seems to be understood slightly less generously than it is understood by Anglo-Saxon counterparts. The French Court is empowered to ensure that public resources (*crédits*) are 'put to good use' (*bon emploi*), a test apparently aimed at consistency. The body audited must be able to point to reasonably clear objectives and show that it has adopted the means best calculated to achieve its objectives. Interpreted fairly, this test, which lawyers might see as broadly approximating to their legal test of 'proportionality', would preclude direct intrusions into policy. In its special audits, however, the Cour des Comptes frequently applies the criterion of good management practice, and it is said that there has been a strong development of the ethos of VFM audit. The criterion of legality has also been treated expansively, 'to embrace goal attainment'.[22]

It seems that in this respect audit at Union level may have fallen behind the practice of the Member States. Powerful audit procedures are only beginning to be set in place, and VFM audit is in its infancy. This seems to be only partly attributable to the fact that a policy-making role of this type might be difficult to accommodate within the framework of the court-like approach to audit; we have just seen, indeed, that the French Cour des Comptes is willing to embrace VFM. As late as 1996, a member of the ECA, trying to draw a line, gave a rather clear picture of external audit in the EU as including:[23]

---

[21] C. Pollitt *et al.*, *Performance or Compliance? Performance Audit and Public Management in Five Countries* (Oxford, Oxford University Press, 1999), 82–5, from which all the following examples are drawn.

[22] Ibid., at 100–1.

[23] Desmond, n. 14 above, 4.

comprehensive audits, which involve auditing the accounts, examining the legality of revenue and expenditure, and the soundness of the management of these funds. Its ultimate aim is to provide an assurance as to the legality and regularity of the operations carried out, and to evaluate the results achieved in relation to the resources allocated.... It is not the function of an external auditor to make judgements of a political nature on the policies that managing authorities intend to pursue. The auditor's task is to comment on the implementation and concrete results of the policies and to call for any changes that may be deemed necessary by indicating *where* and *why.*

But the ECA has for some time been anxious to extend its activities into VFM auditing, building on the word 'sound' in TEC Article 188(c). The ECA hopes that the introduction of VFM audit can stiffen Commission accountability in financial matters; it would also favour the extension of accountability for the execution of policy through the introduction of NPM techniques. The Commission, on the other hand, seeks to retain its position as the motor of the EU and to preserve the discretion to which it has became accustomed.[24] The difference of opinion surfaces in the *Annual Report for 1998*, published after the Interim Report of the Committee of Experts. Not for the first time, the ECA insisted that:[25]

many of the audit findings that appear in this report confirm that, despite the reforms that have been made, the Commission all too often continues to use as the prime indicator of financial management performance the extent to which the appropriations allocated in the annual budget have been utilised. This cannot be the best indicator of performance. The Community institutions, and in particular the Commission, add value by implementing the Union's policies in favour of its citizens and the success of the Commission should be measured by the extent to which these policy goals are attained with the minimum of cost. Thus managers need to set their performance targets in terms of outputs, outcomes and the costs involved in achieving these. *As a precondition, the objectives set for all Community activities must be as clear, as precise and as measurable as possible and appropriate tools must be put in place to measure their achievement.* This change of culture and practice must be placed at the heart of the financial management reform process.

No clearer articulation of the goals of NPM could be found.

II AUDIT IN THE EUROPEAN UNION

Technically, the European Union does not have a budget, because of the way in which the Second and Third Pillars are administered, although certain of

---

[24] B. Laffan, 'From Policy Entrepreneur to Policy Manager: The Challenge Facing the EC' (1997) 4 *Journal of European Public Policy* 422.
[25] Court of Auditors, *Annual Report Concerning the Financial Year 1998* [1999]/OJC349/ 1, para. 0.3 (emphasis added).

its expenditure can be charged to the EC institutions (TEC Articles 28 and 41). It is the EC institutions and their programmes for which the EC budget caters. Although it amounts to no more than around 1.2 per cent of the Community GNP, the EC budget is still very large, amounting in 1999 to 83,978 billion euros. As mentioned in Chapter 2, the largest programmes are the Common Agricultural Policy and the programme of regional subsidy or structural funding. Figure 5.1 gives a general picture of the Community budget.

The first Audit Board of the EC had been designed for the ECSC and, in the context of these new, large programmes, proved weak and ineffectual. Once the EC had acquired an autonomous budget in 1970, the existing arrangements for audit seemed rudimentary to the EP, which published a report arguing the case for a European Audit Office.[26] Four years later, a Court of Audit was set up and its powers consolidated by regulation.[27] No one ever sat down to make a blueprint of a new system of audit for the EU, suited to its particular needs. It has simply been left to evolve, occasionally helped forward by inter-governmental conferences and given a substantial boost by the Second Report of the Committee of Independent Experts.

It is convenient to divide the EU audit procedures into three distinct stages, with a view to seeing how each stage conforms—or does not conform—with the modern ideas of audit described above:

- The initial accounting function is *internal*. It is carried out by the Commission, occupying in the EU context the place of government departments, though not, as noted, of an English- or French-style Treasury.
- The second phase of audit is *external*. Today, the ECA is the external auditor.
- The third, political stage is, in a democratic society, normally the responsibility of a parliament.

Stage 1: Internal Audit

Internal audit is supposed to operate as:[28]

an independent and objective assurance and consulting activity that is guided by a philosophy of adding value to improve the operations of the organisation. It assists

---

[26] European Parliament, *The Case for a European Audit Office* (Brussels, European Pub. 1973).

[27] Financial Regulation of 1977 applicable to the general budget of the European Communities [1977] OJ L356, as amended by Council Regulation 2335/95 [1995] OJ L240/12. The Financial Regulation is presently under review: Commission Working Document, Recasting the Financial Regulation, SEC(1998)1228 (22 July 1998).

[28] Independent Experts, FR, n. 16 above, para. 4.12.1., citing Institute of Internal Auditors, draft definition of internal audit.

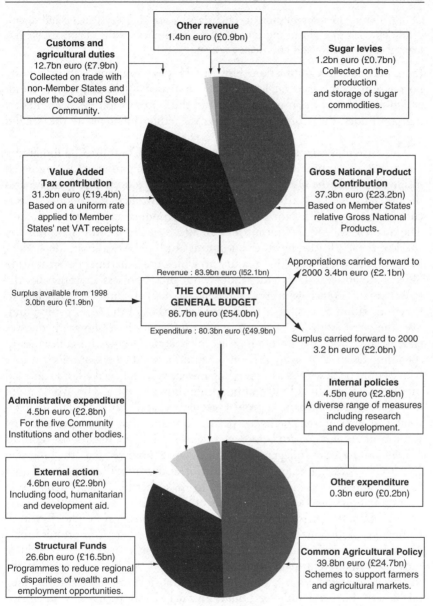

Other revenue
1.4bn euro (£0.9bn)

Customs and agricultural duties
12.7bn euro (£7.9bn)
Collected on trade with non-Member States and under the Coal and Steel Community.

Sugar levies
1.2bn euro (£0.7bn)
Collected on the production and storage of sugar commodities.

Value Added Tax contribution
31.3bn euro (£19.4bn)
Based on a uniform rate applied to Member States' net VAT receipts.

Gross National Product Contribution
37.3bn euro (£23.2bn)
Based on Member States' relative Gross National Products.

Revenue : 83.9bn euro (l52.1bn)

Appropriations carried forward to 2000 3.4bn euro (£2.1bn)

Surplus available from 1998
3.0bn euro (£1.9bn)

THE COMMUNITY GENERAL BUDGET
86.7bn euro (£54.0bn)

Expenditure : 80.3bn euro (£49.9bn)

Surplus carried forward to 2000
3.2 bn euro (£2.0bn)

Internal policies
4.5bn euro (£2.8bn)
A diverse range of measures including research and development.

Administrative expenditure
4.5bn euro (£2.8bn)
For the five Community Institutions and other bodies.

External action
4.6bn euro (£2.9bn)
Including food, humanitarian and development aid.

Other expenditure
0.3bn euro (£0.2bn)

Structural Funds
26.6bn euro (£16.5bn)
Programmes to reduce regional disparities of wealth and employment opportunities.

Common Agricultural Policy
39.8bn euro (£24.7bn)
Schemes to support farmers and agricultural markets.

Figure 5.1

an organisation in accomplishing its objectives by bringing a systematic and disciplined approach to evaluate and improve the effectiveness of the organisation's risk management, control and governance system.

In respect of the Commission, however, this is aspiration only and bears no relation to the facts, at least as they appeared to the Experts. It is not a picture of the way that internal audit in the Commission has been operating, nor does the Commission share the ethos inherent in the second sentence.

The current system, strongly criticized by the Committee[29] and under reconstruction, is briefly as follows. The book-keeping function is conducted inside each DG, the Director acting as accounting officer. The DG prepares the budget. DG XX used to act as Financial Controller and conduct *ex ante* control, giving the visa for expenditure and conducting the internal audit. The dual role of DG XX meant that, in effect, one unit of the Commission checked the legality of the others' decisions but DG XX was not independent in the way in which the UK Treasury, to which the departmental accounting officers are answerable, is independent, nor did it possess anything like the power of the French Ministry of Finance. This is because DG XX had to function within the collegial framework and ethos of the Commission and, over the years, both DG XX and its Commissioner have shown themselves endemically incapable of standing up to their more powerful colleagues in spending DGs. Moreover, there is a sense in which the Commission as a whole could be described as a spending ministry; its collegial ethos is directed more towards policies of integration, promotion of the EU, and avoidance of loss of face, than to financial probity, regularity, and efficiency. The ineffectiveness of these arrangements has been a constant cause of complaint by the ECA in its *Annual Reports* before it came up against the magisterial reproofs of the Committee of Independent Experts, which observed that 'the Financial Controller does not enjoy the position of authority with respect to other Commission services which is needed to make her/his independence truly operational. In practice, the position of DG XX as just one directorate-general among others, and the corresponding position of the Financial Controller as just one high-level nominee among others, compromises her/his ability to translate audit findings into management action'.[30] The single most important reform to result from the *Reports* was the transfer of the internal audit function to a unit directly responsible to the President, a step taken with the direct authorization of President Prodi with a view to enhancing both the authority and autonomy of the internal-audit process. This reform was both a direct outcome of the accountability process and an input into future accountability.

[29] Ibid., chap. 4.
[30] Ibid., para. 4.11.1.

The Commission had always placed much importance on the *ex ante* control of the 'visa', though, in contrast to some of the national systems described above, its *ex ante* control was cursory: it operated from a sampling base of around 10 per cent of cases. The Independent Experts, however, described the visa as antediluvian[31] and, in a White Paper on reform, the Commission proposes the substitution of what is described as a 'state-of-the-art' internal system of financial controls. DG XX also conducted the certification audit. Partly due to this combination of functions, internal audit procedures tended to be ineffectual.

The deficiencies were clearly revealed by the Independent Experts' investigation into the Tourism Unit in 1999.[32] Technically housed in DG XXIII, the Unit had the involvement of three Commissioners and a staff of fourteen, of whom five were permanent officials and three detached national experts. The Unit had a budget of nearly 18 million ecus to administer, its primary task being to organize a European Year of Tourism. A Steering Committee of Member State representatives under Commission chairmanship was set up to administer the project, which in turn set up local sub-committees at project level. To offset lack of staff, the Unit contracted out 'technical management' of the European Year of Tourism to a private company, 'Euroconseil', after a call for tenders sent to sixty firms. The Unit also contracted out a number of research studies. This is a system fraught with risk of mismanagement and financial irregularity, as it is not subject to clear lines of hierarchical control. In the terminology of modern audit and management, it requires that a risk assessment be undertaken, and steps taken to set in place an effective 'audit trail'. That no functional supervisory structure was in place is probably the fault of the Head of Unit, ultimately dismissed for embezzlement, corruption and favouritism, after disciplinary proceedings. What is surprising, however, is the inertia of the internal Commission watchdogs. In 1992, a report from the ECA finding irregularities prompted no action. In 1993, DG XXIII, the nominal supervisor, came together with DG XX, the internal auditor, to conduct an internal inquiry, referring their findings to the special fraud unit (UCLAF) for investigation. For more than five years, nothing was done. We will pick up this trail later, when considering fraud.

Contracting out of services, as in the case of Euroconseil, is acknowledged by auditors, who may not have access to the contractor's books, as a major source of risk. In the Commission, it is supposed to be regulated both by internal staff rules and by tendering procedures, but it is relatively easy to circumvent the rules. Informal staff practices, which often breach the Staff Regulations, have grown up as a response to under-staffing of the permanent Commission services. Temporary staff who are not subject to the demanding

---

[31] Ibid., para. 4.11.1. See also *Annual Report of ECA for 1998*, n. 25 above.

[32] *First Report on Allegations regarding Fraud, Mismanagement and Nepotism in the European Community* (Brussels, 15 March 1999) (IR).

official recruitment procedures may in practice take up important positions in the Commission or be put in control of budget lines. Temporary staff can use their Commission contacts on leaving to obtain preference in tendering for contracts. Here again, the laxity of the procedures, a constant source of concern to the ECA,[33] was highlighted for unfavourable comment in the investigation of the EC Office for Humanitarian Aid by the Independent Experts.[34] ECHO is a directorate responsible to the Secretary-General of the Commission and in charge of around 3.5 million ecus. It operates through partner organizations, often voluntary-sector bodies (NGOs), which tender for contracts. In 1993–4, ECHO awarded four contracts for aid in Africa and former Yugoslavia, on the face of things to three different companies. What the Commission had not bothered to notice was that two of the companies were controlled by the third, based in Luxembourg and shown to have had a longstanding relationship with numerous Commission services, either directly or through associates. It has to be said that both the relationships and the *ad hoc* companies which resulted are a consistent part of the way in which the Commission operates its public-procurement procedures. In time it emerged that the aid contracts were 'entirely fictitious'; none of the operations reported had ever taken place. Instead, the bulk of the money had been used to finance a group of eleven staff who worked as a financial unit within the administration of ECHO in Brussels. Legally employed by the contractors, they had mostly been proposed to them by ECHO. The investigation showed that senior Commission officials had connived in setting up a false accounting system, enabling aid money to be diverted into private bank accounts of relatives of ECHO personnel.

It is a matter of priority for the Commission to install systems audits or, to put this differently, construct audit trails for the EU. But this is not as easy as it may sound. Inside the Commission, audit trails are being set in place, but across the European Union and its boundaries, systems audit is intensely problematic. Just as, in Chapter 3, the complex network of administrative authorities was identified as a major factor negating political accountability, so the same rambling structure inhibits audit accountability. Transactions often pass across the geographical borders of Member States and of the European Union, implicating third nations, private corporations, agencies, NGOs, and international organizations, making an audit trail almost impossible to establish. The huge EU aid programme, running into billions of ecus and often spent on its behalf by international aid agencies, is one example of a chain of devolved responsibility; the structural funding and agricultural subsidy systems are others. This places the Commission squarely into the

---

[33] Court of Auditors, *Special Report No 8/98 on the Commission's services specifically involved in the fight against fraud, notably the 'unité de coordination de la lutte anti-fraude'* (UCLAF) together with the Commission's replies [1998] OJ C230/1.

[34] IR, n. 32 above, Ch 4.

position of a 'manager of networks', a role which, according to Leslie Metcalfe, it does not take sufficiently seriously and is unwilling, or does not know how to perform.[35] (This assessment incidentally tallies with the findings of OLAF's new supervisory committee which, with the firm support of the European Parliament, hopes to change the prevailing Commission culture to one of greater managerialism.)

The MED programme, investigated by the Independent Experts, provides a particularly strong example of lax supervision by the Commission over networks and long chains of responsibility. Five linked aid programmes had been set in place by the Commission. Each involved regional authorities, universities, private enterprises, research centres, and the media. There were four levels of management: the Commission; autonomous private bodies registered under the law of three different European countries, responsible for administrative and financial management; technical assistance offices (TAOs); and, last but not least, 496 individual and differing projects. The whole was held together by a network of committees, some with Commission participation, others without.[36] What kind of audit trail would be needed to render this ramshackle network transparent, accountable, and amenable to audit with the limited EU resources? The MED programme was halted after a Special Report from the ECA had found grave irregularities.[37] Later, internal Commission audits confirmed and particularized these initial findings, something which should have happened earlier. The outcome was a new regulatory framework, setting out explicit obligations. The ECA also flagged up the extent to which resources in the Commission allocated to the overall management and control of the programmes were inadequate.[38] The ECA itself moved to repair missing links in the audit chain, calling on the Commission, together with concerned national authorities, 'to ensure that the organisational structures and financial procedures of the networks are compatible with national rules and procedures'.[39] TAOs, called on, and often set up, to manage projects on behalf of the Commission, have been a particular cause of complaint. The Independent Experts were told that there might be around 100 of these floating entities, though a later estimate is in the region of 250, absorbing a total of some 330 million euros in administrative costs.[40] Several, including the TAO which ran the Leonardo youth training programmes under the direction of Commissioner Edith

[35] L. Metcalfe, 'The European Commission as a Network Organisation' (1996) 26 *Publius: The Journal of Federalism* 43.

[36] IR, n. 32 above, paras. 3.1.1–3.1.18.

[37] European Court of Auditors, *Special Report No 1/96 on the Mediterranean Decentralised Programmes* [1996] OJ C240/1.

[38] *Annual Report for 1998*, n. 25 above, paras. 5.90–5.100, at 5.101.

[39] Ibid., at paras. 5.96–5.98.

[40] S. Grey, 'Tackling Fraud and Mismanagement in the European Union' (London, Centre for European Reform, 2000), 13.

Cresson, have been accused of impropriety and nepotism. Such allegations would be hard to prove, since there is no public register of TAOs and no right of public access to their records. There is a close parallel here with the unreformed Comitology,[41] where lack of transparency made public accountability well nigh impossible.

According to the Independent Experts,[42] internal audit should provide a powerful management tool, helping to instil a sense of responsibility in line managers. Its function is not necessarily public accountability and publicity but a management tool for remedial action in case of weaknesses and irregularities. Clearly, this was not happening. The Experts' recommendations only echoed a sequence of annual reports of the ECA, which has on many occasions asked for operational DGs to 'carry full responsibility for the execution of commitments and payments, together with strengthening of the internal audit procedures'.[43] There is no other term for the inefficiencies, irregularities, delays, and omissions to take recuperative action than maladministration, and of a grave kind.

The Working Paper of Commissioner Neil Kinnock, appointed by President Prodi as Vice-President with a specific mandate for administrative reform, contains suggestions for reform, many of which are now in place. As already noted, the visa procedure is to be abandoned as soon as the legal steps can be finalized. DG XX has been replaced as internal auditor by an autonomous body reporting directly to the President and Vice-President,[44] a change which should go some way to distancing the internal auditor from the spending body, while at the same time lending it presidential authority over the spending directorates. An Audit Progress Board, chaired by the Budget Commissioner, will monitor the follow-up of audit reports. Alongside, DGs and project managers will take direct responsibility for financial decisions in their remit, advised primarily by new Finance Units within each DG. This can help to establish a coherent structure for managing the Commission's finances, though it stops far short of setting in place the controls available at national level, and notably to the British Treasury. These new structures are intended to run alongside new anti-fraud procedures, which will place investigations in the hands of OLAF, an independent body with which the ECA can work closely.

These improvements do not, however, tackle the Commission management deficiencies revealed in cases such as the ECHO, MED, and Leonardo schemes. which exist when outside agencies are involved, some of which have been taken out by improving the quality and precision of the specific

[41] Above, 67–71.

[42] FR, n. 16 above, para. 4.10.2.

[43] *Annual Report for 1988*, n. 25 above, paras 1.23 and 1.24.

[44] European Commission, 'Reforming the Commission', Part I, COM(2000)200 final/2, 19–24.

contracts issued by the Commission. Here again, the Commission will be trying to vest in contractees real authority and clearly defined responsibilities. This is very much the targeted 'performance indicator' approach of British Next Step Agencies.[45] With TAOs, the Finnish Commissioner, Erkki Liikanen, has been attempting to restore some order to the situation; the solution is seen to lie in a new system of independent agencies, again, it seems, somewhat similar to 'Next Steps Agencies'. The Commission is currently engaged in establishing a structure for this new venture. It is, however, by no means clear that an adequate audit system has been set in place, or that the Commission has the manpower and technical ability to establish and monitor a satisfactory structure for successful systems audit.

Stage 2: External Audit

The European Court of Auditors, set up in 1977 in response to requests from the EP, now consists of fifteen members, one from each Member State, appointed by the Council after consultation with the EP, for a renewable term of six years. Candidates must either 'belong or have belonged in their respective countries to external audit bodies' or be 'especially qualified for this office' (TEC Article 188b, paragraph 2). It is stressed that 'their independence must be beyond doubt' and that the ECA shall, 'in the general interest of the Community, be completely independent in the performance of their duties', neither seeking nor taking instructions from any government or from any other body. As with other appointments in the EU, these are not always free from controversy, and the professional competence of those appointed has on occasion been questioned. The EP can use its consultative position in appointment of members of the ECA to work against the Council, and it can try to block the appointment of national auditors felt to be unsuitable. The appointments of a French and a Greek auditor were resisted with some success by the EP in 1989, though in 1993 a similar protest was simply ignored by the Council.[46] In 1996, the ECA was composed of seven members from national or regional audit offices or courts of audit; six members of national or regional parliaments; three ex-members of the European Parliament; two former senior government officials; one former secretary-general of the ECA; one private-sector auditor. Not everyone here would necessarily possess accountancy qualifications.

The ECA elects its own President and 'portfolios' are allocated by him as in the Commission or in a *cabinet*; these determine the area of activity in which

---

[45] Sir R. Ibbs, *Improving Management in Government: The Next Steps* (London, HMSO, 1988).

[46] R. Corbett, F. Jacobs, and M. Shackleton, *The European Parliament*, 4th edn. (Harlow, Longman, 2000), 251.

members will operate.[47] Each member also has a *cabinet* of advisers, and around 250 auditors carry through the work programme under supervision. Comparison with national audit systems will immediately suggest how small this team is when the complexity and multiplicity of the EC's financial transactions are considered. Like the European Commission, the ECA acts as a college and issues its reports anonymously in the name of the whole Court, though it can, since Nice, sit in chambers. In practice, however, the work programmes are decided in five small sub-sections and then agreed by the Court, which would have difficulty in challenging the specialist sub-group. This structure is not one which can ensure that every programme is appropriate or that every investigation is of equal quality, but no means of cross-check or monitoring has as yet been devised. Problems of inconsistency are accentuated by the different understandings of audit obtaining in the different national delegations. White and Hollingsworth note the failure to develop a common style or *modus operandi*. There is as yet 'no common European culture of financial control, but rather a number of overlapping and competing national traditions, with correspondingly different interpretations of what the role of an external audit body should be'.[48]

The ECA has competence to examine the accounts of all EU revenue and expenditure and that of all bodies set up by the EU unless expressly excluded (TEC Article 188c, paragraph 1). In general, it operates on a documentary basis, having a power to call for documents. It is also authorized to call for assistance from national audit offices, many of which by now have special arrangements in place to deal with EU affairs. In addition TEC Article 188c, paragraph 3 permits 'spot checks' inside the institutions and also in Member States, where these shall be carried out in liaison with the national audit bodies or, if these do not have the necessary powers, with the competent national departments; spot sampling can also be carried out on the affairs of agencies and any body which benefits from structural funds. The ECA must certify that the accounts are in order by means of a statement of assurance (DAS) that the accounts are reliable and legal and regular (TEC Article 188c, paragraph 1). The ECA is also empowered (TEC Article 188c, paragraph 2) to examine 'whether the financial management has been *sound*'. Sound financial management is generally construed as empowering VFM audit though, as already noted, there is disagreement between the ECA and Commission over the extent to which policy can be questioned.

The ECA publishes an annual report, which is laid before the Council and European Parliament, and has in addition power to publish special reports

---

[47] For an outline of the procedures see National Audit Office, *Finance, Audit and Accountability in the European Union* (London, NAO, 2000).

[48] White and Hollingsworth, n. 9 above, 175. And see House of Lords, Select Committee on the European Communities, 'Financial Control and Fraud in the Community', HL75 (1993/4).

dealing with specific sectors; it has recently decided to publish the majority of its reports in this fashion. It is in these special reports that the contested VFM recommendations are mainly to be found and which experts see as most useful.[49] Perhaps for this reason, special reports from the ECA are not necessarily published.[50]

There are two serious defects in the first two stages of EC audit procedure: spot-check sampling and the contradictory nature of the procedure. Huge numbers of transactions are carried out—more than 18 billion individual transactions annually—and, if we accept the ECA findings for 1998, *more than one in seven* of these transactions was procedurally irregular.[51] To audit these thoroughly would be a Herculean task and, in the event, lack of manpower means that, even with help from national audit offices and with the benefit of reports commissioned externally, the ECA can only operate through a system of 'spot sampling'. The samples are ultimately extrapolated on a percentage basis in the DAS. Of the individual units of account taken as the base figure, around 600 samples of payments and commitments are examined for regularity and legality. For more than one reason, this is deeply problematic. The number of transactions which can be handled (on average about 600 out of 360,000 transactions) is too small a base from which to extrapolate. This problem is accentuated by the fact that, in the particular circumstances of the EU where, as already indicated, the financial and audit systems involved in any given transaction differ widely, any given sample or incident used as the basis of a spot check may be atypical. Accountants and auditors argue that the method is also vitiated by the dubious quality of the data on which it is based.[52] This raises another problem, seldom admitted but actually endemic in EU affairs, that national statistical data are of variable quality and difficult to collate, being based on different methods of collection. The sampling method met with heavy criticism from the Independent Experts (it will be remembered that the Chairman, Mr André Middelhoek (Holland), and Mr Pierre Lelong (France) were both former Presidents of the European Court of Auditors and Mrs Inga-Britt Ahlenius was a Swedish auditor). Following the Santer crisis, the ECA is trying to take back control over and to expand its sampling procedure, though whether this can be done without an increase in technically qualified personnel is a moot point. The place for sampling, according to the Independent Experts,[53] was in the visa process, which could be rationalized by greater reliance on 'statistical

---

[49] House of Lords, Select Committee on the European Communities, 'The ECA: The Case for Reform', HL 63 (2000–2001) conclusion 8.

[50] Published Reports are to be found on the Court's website at **www.eca.eu.int**.

[51] *Annual Report for 1998*, n. 38 above, paras. 2.41–2.52.

[52] Power, n. 4 above, 89, citing interviews.

[53] FR, n. 16 above, Recommendation No. 5, 136.

sampling and the results of systems audits and the quality of a department's
financial management'.

The second weakness lies in the 'contradictory' procedure used by the ECA
in deference to its position as a court. Contradictory procedure means giving
interested parties a sight of draft reports and an opportunity to respond, either
at an oral hearing, as in the adversarial legal proceedings of the common-law
world, or, more commonly, through the documentary procedures more usual
in civilian legal systems. In either case, contradictory procedure introduces the
need to exchange documents throughout an investigation. In the case of
the ECA, drafts of the *Annual Report* have to be sent to the Commission,
which circulates them to the relevant DGs. The replies are collected centrally,
shown to the Commission, re-drafted, and shown to a meeting attended by
the audit unit, the Secretariat-General, and OLAF. There then has to be a
meeting (*la réunion contradictoire*) between the Court and Commission
before the final wording is agreed. Such a bureaucratic and time-consuming
process offers endless opportunity for criticism to be watered down and
wording changed, blunting the impact of reports, delaying outcomes,
and undercutting the autonomy and authority of the Court's report. It is
not surprising to find this procedure the target of severe criticism by the
Committee of Independent Experts, which said of the process as it then
operated at the stage of internal audit that:[54]

'sensitive' reports drafted by DG XX auditors have been the subject of lengthy
contradictory procedures, often with the effect, and, one suspects, the intention, of
delaying the report—and any consequent action—by periods of several months. In
this process, the purpose of audit—the detection and rectification of irregularities,
the identification of systematic weaknesses and proposal of corrective action—does
not necessarily take first place, being potentially overshadowed by the wish of both
parties to come out of the process looking as good as possible.

The Experts found that problems identified in internal audit were, in several
of the cases they investigated, negotiated out of final reports during the course
of the contradictory procedure between DG XX and the unit audited.
A different perspective comes, however, from researchers Christopher Pollitt
and Hilkka Summa. They blame the auditors, noting an antipathy to self-
assessment in the ECA, whose *Annual Reports* are long and bland, summariz-
ing the year's work but containing little information on cost, quality, or
impact of audits and, more important, no indication of performance indicators.[55] Here a contrast emerges between the court-style and managerialist

[54] Ibid., para. 4.11.
[55] C. Pollitt and H. Summa, 'Reflexive Watchdogs? How Supreme Audit Institutions
Account for Themselves' (1997) 75 *Public Administration* 313, castigating in particular the
Annual Report for 1995 [1995] OJ C340/1, which ran to 328 pages of summary.

audits, with the latter reflecting a conscious desire to reassure the public about the auditor's own managerial credentials.

Disagreement over VFM audit has been a crucial component of cool relations between the ECA and the Commission. In 1988, for example, the ECA, noting an unexplained fall in VAT income, criticized the Commission for failure to carry out its primary duty of ensuring the correct transposition of EC directives in this field. The *Annual Report* called the Commission's methods amateurish; it intervened only in cases where complaints were received from individuals; there was no methodical system of investigation and examination of the VAT regulation, and no effective monitoring system of implementation. The ECA demanded wholesale regularization of Commission procedure.[56] Again, in 1995, the ECA was saying with some assurance that '[t]he European institutions are required to follow up the observations contained in the European Parliament's resolution and take steps to safeguard the European taxpayer's money by improving the quality of management systems and adopting the necessary measures to protect Union finances'.[57] These passages illustrate the way in which VFM audit extends control by auditors, together with the economic values associated with audit, into the central domain of administrators. It is not a technique with which the Commission, jealous of its policy-making prerogatives, is ever likely to be comfortable.

An Irish member of the ECA has given a rather clear picture of external audit in the EU as including:[58]

comprehensive audits, which involve auditing the accounts, examining the legality of revenue and expenditure, and the soundness of the management of these funds. Its ultimate aim is to provide an assurance as to the legality and regularity of the operations carried out, and to evaluate the results achieved in relation to the resources allocated. . . . It is not the function of an external auditor to make judgements of a political nature on the policies that managing authorities intend to pursue. The auditor's task is to comment on the implementation and concrete results of the policies and to call for any changes that may be deemed necessary by indicating *where* and *why*.

Despite this effort to draw a 'bright line', White and Hollingsworth note that 'the Commission has tended to resist the Court's increasing focus on VFM issues, claiming that these raise policy questions which are for the Commission and Council. Its view has been that the Court should be concerned primarily with regularity and legality'.[59]

---

[56] *Annual Report for 1988*, n. 43 above, paras. 1.27–1.46.
[57] *Annual Report for 1995*, n. 55 above, 32.
[58] Desmond, n. 14 above, 4.
[59] White and Hollingsworth, n. 9 above, 180.

How far has the Court of Auditors been successful in improving the performance of EC institutions, more particularly the Commission, in their use of, and the way they account for, EC funds? In her thoughtful evaluation,[60] Bridget Laffan sees a steady improvement both in the standing of the ECA and the inter-institutional relations on which it necessarily relies to create a successful accountability system. Recalling the anecdotal evidence of a far from warm relationship between previous Presidents, notably Jacques Delors, and the ECA, after an ECA report to the Council in 1992 on profligate EU spending, Laffan suggests that relations with the Commission have improved in recent years. Yet the improved relationship does not apparently reflect an improved *performance*, as reflected in ECA reports or in the reports from the Committee of Independent Experts.

Stage 3: Political Accountability

Initially, there was no EU institution capable of exacting political responsibility for financial irregularity, since the Community budget at first fell within the remit of the Council. The EP had to struggle to establish control, and formally entered the budgetary process with two financial treaties concluded in 1970 and 1975. The procedures are now set out in TEC Article 272.[61] A key moment for the EP was its acquisition in the 1975 reorganization of the sole power to grant discharge. Discharge of the accounts is a formal act, marking their formal closure. Two years after the power was introduced, Budget Commissioner Christopher Tugendat related the power directly to accountability when he remarked that '[r]efusal to grant discharge is a political sanction which would be extremely serious; the Commission thus censured would, I think, have to be replaced.'[62] Closely linked to the fight for parliamentary control were the ECA's efforts to establish itself, which culminated in the grant of institutional status by TEU Article G(6). In addition, at Maastricht, the ECA received the crucial power of delivering to the EP a 'Statement of Assurance' (DAS) as to the reliability of the Community accounts (TEC Article 248(1)).

All reports from the ECA go to the Council and to the EP exercising its budgetary functions, though the EP still has to share its budgetary powers, which include the power to reject the budget, with the Council, an uneasy relationship reflected in the 'budgetary co-operation meetings' between the Budget Commissioner, Council President, and Chair of the EP Budget

---

[60] B. Laffan, 'Becoming a "Living Institution": The Evolution of the European Court of Auditors' (1999) 37 *Journal of Common Market Studies* 251.

[61] For a concise account see NAO *Finance, Audit and Accountability*, n. 47 above, where useful Tables of the budgetary cycle are to be found. And see Corbett, Jacobs, and Shackleton, n. 46 above, chap. 13 and 252–5.

[62] Cited in ibid., at 241.

Committee, during the plenary session at which the EP adopts the budget. For White and Hollingsworth, in a comment mainly directed at the early stages of book-keeping and audit, the chief effect of the DAS procedure has been on the relations between the ECA and the Commission. ECA Special Reports do not have to be formally laid before or considered by the Commission, though in practice the Commission responses are published. Thus the DAS has been an important factor in ensuring access by the ECA to the internal audit and its supporting documentation. It has also led to an improved performance from the ECA. On the other hand, they conclude that 'it is hard to see the DAS as a major step forward in improving the management of Community finances, or the effectiveness of the Court. The requirement to provide an assurance can, of course, do nothing directly to improve the quality of financial control or the reliability of the Community's accounts'.[63] The main problem may once again lie in the EU architecture; where the culprit is not the Commission but national or subnational authorities, it is hard to see the Commission as more than technically responsible. The House of Lords in a recent report pinpointed the time taken for discharge, which means in practice that the EP 'are dealing with a report so far away from real time—a report that has already been leaked to the press in the process—that it is very like trying to digest a very old meal'.[64]

In Laffan's view, the ECA and EP are partners: they 'settled into stable and cooperative relations with the Parliament from the beginning'[65] and support and rely each other to increase their standing and powers. Yet no sanctions are designated by the Treaty and, although the EP has once refused discharge, no resignation followed, partly because the Commission was right at the end of its term of office and later the accounts were discharged. It may therefore be more accurate to see the EP, the Commission, and the ECA as a triangular 'accountability club'.[66] The Commission can support the EP against the Council. The EP can assist the Commission (e.g., by helping to simplify the complex regulatory framework which inhibits the Commission from taking control over the notably fraud-prone CAP). The ECA provides the basic material on which punitive and reforming action can be based. This description could have been enhanced by the elevation to institutional status accorded by the Maastricht Treaty. But giving evidence in 1986 to a House of Lords Select Committee, Mr Keemer, who had worked both with the ECA and UK National Audit Office, complained of the lack of follow-up from the supervisory institutions. He thought the EP the only institution to take its duties seriously. The EP had 'developed quite a useful follow-up procedure. Pretty well every special report of the Court of Auditors is followed up by the

---

[63] White and Hollingsworth, n. 9 above, 179.
[64] HL 63 (2000–2001) paras. 9, 61. And see above 68, Table 4.2.
[65] Laffan, n. 60 above, 261.
[66] Ibid.

Budgetary Control Committee of the European Parliament, and sometimes by other specialist committees'.[67] There was as yet no regular follow-up in the Council, particularly criticizable because it had established no procedures to consider Special Reports from the ECA.

III THE EUROPEAN UNION AND FRAUD

Underlying the inter-institutional struggle has been a second and more publicly visible set of concerns about EU finances. Fraud in the European Union is very much a concern of the media, and the perception that fraud is rife there has seriously undercut the legitimacy of the European Union. Selected revelations from reports of the ECA attract wide media publicity and have undoubtedly contributed to public concern. But more temperate and better informed observers share the perception: a widely publicized House of Lords inquiry has described fraud in the EC as 'a public scandal',[68] while in 1997 the EP was alleging that several billion ecu had been siphoned out of the budget through fraud.[69] In the same and successive years, the ECA identified as 'irregular' about 4.5 billion euros (5 per cent of EC payments). UCLAF (OLAF) figures confirm that, in 1997 and 1998 respectively, payments to the value of 164 and 284 million euros in agricultural payments and 42 and 57 billion in regional aid were irregular. Not all of these involved fraud, though a total of 1,343 investigations was generated and about 1 billion euros (1 per cent of the EC budget) was said to be involved. The fall of the Santer Commission helped to intensify anxiety and, as we have seen, audit reform occupied a central place in the *Second Report from the Committee of Experts*. Desire for action on fraud and lack of financial accountability had worked their way to the top of the European political agenda. In 1992, the Commission's Director of Legal Services, speaking at a conference,[70] identified the problems of fraud in the EU as emanating mainly from the structural funding (54 per cent) and the Agricultural Guarantee Fund (28 per cent), with the external affairs budget contributing a further 6 per cent and research and technology 4.7 per cent, all programmes which over the years have received attention from the ECA and also from the Committee of Independent Experts. Figure 5.2 shows Community spending by area in 1998.

Over the years, the most difficult programme to oversee has been the Common Agricultural Policy (CAP). In 1999, the Agricultural Guarantee

---

[67] HL 102 (1986–7) 14, para.54 (Mr Keemer).

[68] HL 75 (1993–4), n. 49 above.

[69] European Parliament, *Report of the Committee of Inquiry into Community Transit System*, A4–0053/97 (19 Feb. 1997).

[70] E. Mennens (ed.), 'Fraud on the Financial Interests of the Community', in M. Delmas-Marty, *Vers un droit pénal communautaire?* (Paris, Editions Economica, 1993).

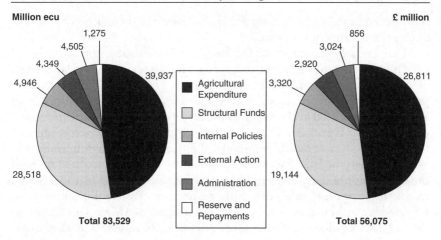

Figure 5.2
Source: European Community Finances, HM Treasury, Cm 4382, June 1999

Fund (FEOGA) alone absorbed 48.5 per cent of the Community budget (in the region of 40,735 euros, a rapidly rising figure). This leaves the Agriculture DG with the unenviable task of checking payments worth more than 37 billion ecus, paid out in fifteen Member States through 150 or so paying agencies, to several million individual payees and entities. The main problem lies in the fact that the scheme is administered by national administrations, which may see the disbursement of EU funds to their own nationals as a benefit, making this scheme particularly prone to fraud and correspondingly difficult to investigate; in 1994, for example, the ECA was unable to complete the accounts of the FEOGA on the ground that the Member States were 'unable to provide the information needed' in respect of 1,663 million ecu in guarantee payments.[71] Difficulties are heightened because FEOGA policy is a deeply controversial aspect of the controversial CAP. It is hardly surprising to find FEOGA figuring on the Commission's SEM action plan as an area in need of better management and control. Another major head of fraud is the classic customs fraud, where a fraudulent declaration of origin is made with the intention of placing goods entering the European Union into a more favourable excise category. The budget as a whole has become a major target for organized crime, with more than fifty criminal organizations identified as active, many from the former Soviet Union and Central and Eastern Europe, stimulating an active secondary industry of money laundering.[72] Agricultural

---

[71] ECA, *Annual Report for 1994* (1994)
[72] 'Protection of the Financial interests of the Communities, Fight Against Fraud', European Commission, *Annual Report for 1997* COM(98)276; European Parliament, *The Community Transit System*, DOC.PE 220–895: FIN, Brussels, 19 February 1997.

subsidies and transit transactions are big business and there is much evidence of organized crime in this area.[73]

A few concrete examples culled from reports illustrate the difficulty of constructing an 'audit trail' for this type of transaction and, at a later stage, of conducting successful police investigations and exacting accountability through the criminal process.[74] In the 'case of the Polish cows', cattle from Poland were declared at the German border as designed for 'external transit' to N. Africa via Barcelona. The duly issued customs document was confirmed by Spanish customs officials and returned to Germany, though in reality the cattle never left the EU. This fraud could not have been perpetuated without the connivance of individuals in Poland, as well as in several Member States. In the 'meat carousel case', live cattle destined for Eastern Europe went to Italy, thence to Malta, back to Italy, and out again to Africa. This scam cost the EU 18.15 million ecu in evaded levies plus 24 million ecu in wrongly paid out export grants. Securing repayment is an endemic problem for the Commission.

OLAF: The Flying Squad

The TEU added to the Treaties a provision (TEC Article 209a) imposing on Member States the obligation to take the same measures to counter fraud affecting the financial interests of the EU as they take to counter fraud affecting their own financial interests and requiring them to 'organise, with the help of the Commission, close and regular cooperation between the competent departments of their administrations'. If brought into effect, this provision would enable the type of audit trail requisite for modern auditing to be set up on a trans-European basis, greatly facilitating the task of the ECA and introducing the possibility of 'joined up audit'. An earlier case recorded in the reports of ECJ proceedings,[75] which established the important principle that EU fraud is to be treated in the same way as national fraud by Member States, shows why the new Article was necessary. The case involved a cargo of maize, declared as Greek, delivered in Belgium in May 1986. The validity of the declaration was supported by the Greek authorities, but Commission investigators obtained proof that the maize came from Yugoslavia and asked the Greek authorities to prosecute. Greece took no action, necessitating infringement proceedings in the ECJ. This single investigation had covered private companies, customs services, police and pros-

---

[73] 24th Financial Report of the EAGGF Guarantee Section, COM(95)483 final; European Commission, 'The Fight Against Fraud', COM(96)173 final.

[74] Examples from Mennens, n. 70 above, 131.

[75] Case 68/88, *Commission* v. *Greece* [1989] ECR 2965. See also HL 75 (1993–4), n. 68 above, 44–5 (Mr Rozema).

ecuting authorities across three countries; by no means all had been co-operative. An official experienced in auditing the CAP and EAGGF has blamed the problems on the EAGGF procedures, with weaknesses at every stage. The starting-point is:

- vague and badly drafted legislation;
- implemented through a process lacking in rigorous controls and inspection;
- followed by delays in reporting and uncertainty as to where the reports should be made; with finally, an absence of sanction in case of irregularity or fraud.

The Commission is not without weapons to deal with some of the problems, including powers to request Member States to 'co-operate, provide information and to take national control measures', although, on the evidence of the Independent Experts, it has not always used them to good effect. This is the sort of problem which the 'accountability club' needs urgently to tackle and which the new structure for UCLAF has in hand.

In 1987, a 'flying squad', or internal co-ordination unit, the UCLAF, was established,[76] to help co-ordinate and carry out complex investigations. This development has been strongly supported both by the EP, which has trebled the number of staff in six years in a time of stasis and retrenchment, and by the Council, which has supported new regulations establishing anti-fraud measures, including provision for 'on-the-spot' checks in Member States.[77] In 1999, UCLAF was overhauled, renamed OLAF (*Office européen de lutte anti-fraude*) and made directly responsible to the President and Vice-President responsible for reform (presently Neil Kinnock).[78] It was put into the charge of a supervisory committee which reports both to the Council and EP. A new Director General was appointed, three director appointments made, and the personnel increased to 300. The independence of OLAF's staff is not yet fully resolved, however, since they enjoy no special status. Techniques of New Public Management are very much in evidence. OLAF is in the course of laying down a management plan to include a policy on investigations, which can first be implemented and then monitored. OLAF is also moving fast to network. It has already moved to employ judicial advisers, specifically with a view to close relations with the fast-growing agency, Eurojust, and

[76] Decision of 27 Nov. 1987, COM(87)572 and COM(87)PV891.

[77] Council Regulation 2988/95 on the protection of the European Communities' financial interests [1998] OJ L36 16; Council Regulation 2185/96 concerning on-the-spot checks and inspections carried out by the Commission in order to protect the European Communities' financial interests against fraud and other irregularities [1996] OJ L292. Conventions between the Member States on further fraud measures are in the pipeline but not yet ratified.

[78] Regulation 1073/99 (25 May 1999) [1999] OJ L136/1. See NAO, n. 47 above, 33–4.

is in the process of setting up a new database to supply information on investigatory activity through the EU. This, the Supervisory Committee hopes, will be capable of being used for risk analysis, a modern audit technique with which the Commission has not apparently so far come to grips.[79] But although high hopes are entertained of OLAF and the first report of the Supervisory Committee seems encouraging, the signs are that all is not well. A recent press release states that a new dossier of corruption allegations submitted by Paul van Buitenen in August 2001 has received no response, while EP's anti-fraud rapporteur, Gabriel Stauner, told the press that 'the climate was already reverting to the bad old days'.[80]

National authorities were also described by the Experts as being 'less than fully enthusiastic' in their support,[81] and serious variance in the efficiency of national audit procedures has been identified: in the 1998 *Annual Report*, the ECA noted that 'the separate accounts kept by the Member States contained significant errors',[82] while evidence from a member of the ECA to a House of Lords inquiry questioned 'how far national audit institutions are actually able to police the expenditure of Community funds once the money has been paid over to national governments'.[83] In one example, 88.9 million ecus allocated for aid in youth unemployment were spent in training Greek civil servants; this could not have been done without the connivance of the Greek public service.[84] In the ECHO case, described earlier in this chapter, UCLAF set in train a raid on the offices of a private company in Luxembourg allegedly involved in the affair. UCLAF had no independent police powers, however; without the co-operation of the Luxembourg police, it could search premises only with the owners' consent. In the event, the documentation had 'gone missing'; it was later collected by an EU official and driven across borders to Belgium for safe-keeping. UCLAF asked the French and Belgian authorities to consider prosecution, but were met by Commission refusal to waive diplomatic immunity—surprising as it may seem, an endemic problem in the investigation of frauds against the Community budget! The criminal was dismissed only in 1998 after the CFI had confirmed in a staff case[85] that he had 'knowingly and persistently engaged in unauthorised outside activities which completely negated guarantees of independence and gave rise to serious conflicts of interest'. Finally, when in 1998 the case was passed to the Luxembourg police for action, they took no action for almost two

---

[79] *First Report of the Supervisory Committee of the Anti-fraud office (OLAF)*, OJ C365/1.
[80] *Daily Telegraph*, 27 Feb. 2002, 'New threat by official who told of EU fraud'.
[81] FR, n. 16 above, para. 5.9.12.
[82] Ibid., para.1.11.
[83] HL 102 (1986–7), n. 67 above, 11, para. 22 (Mr Jo Cary).
[84] ECA, *Annual Report for 1995*, n. 55 above, para. 5.50.
[85] Case T–74/94 (19 March 1998) anonymised and apparently still pending.

years. (Apparently the Commission is considering civil proceedings against the police in respect of a delay which means that more than one million ecus, paid into offshore bank accounts, remains untraced.)

The loopholes in the system are further highlighted by a case involving the fraudulent use of the agricultural intervention system, which permits sales of agricultural goods at concessionary prices. Irish intervention butter had been sold by a French company to the former USSR. At some point the butter was diverted from the authorized destination to Poland. When the Commission, acting on a complaint, decided to take up the matter, the investigation had to cover Latvia and Poland. The ECA report revealed a number of Commission errors. The file was not properly maintained or authenticated, and there was no proof of the fact of arrival. Despite the fact that 'the responsibility of the Commission was engaged at the highest level', no proper legal basis for the transaction had ever been suggested. This may partly have derived from the complexity of the EU regulations; a complex point of law as to their retrospective operation arose on which France, two Commission DGs, and the ECA took different positions. No adequate punitive action had been taken and the Commission had instead relied on a negotiated settlement very much to the advantage of the Member States involved. The ECA asked that 'the Commission should re-examine all possibilities for corrective action in this case'.[86] But when the attitude of the two Member States involved in the negotiations is examined, the Commission's behaviour becomes less surprising. Neither did much to co-operate with the investigating authorities. When the Agriculture DG thought a *prima facie* case of orchestrated fraud was established, Ireland failed to request France to act under the international mutual aid arrangements, with the consequence that the French company escaped liability. The ECA was left rather wearily urging that 'the current administrative reform should include measures to ensure that the administrative and management weaknesses, noted in this case, cannot re-occur'. But the case is by no means unique. Bridget Laffan once said of an ECA audit of the fruit and vegetable regime in the Mediterranean countries that it was 'a litany of mismanagement and ineffective controls'.[87] Aspects of this chain fall outside the EU competencies, so that harmonization has to come through inter-state agreements and conventions, some of which are already drafted, though few are in force, complicating the problem. The Independent Experts, however, confirmed a general lack of co-operation *even within the Commission*, where the operational services tended to regard UCLAF as 'an antagonist with whom cooperation is to be kept to an indispensable min-

---

[86] President's letter on Exportation of intervention butter to the former Soviet Union (Case Fléchard), F1BOO29EN11-OPP-DEC028-00VO-FLECHARD-OR.doc (11 May 2000).

[87] Laffan, n. 24 above, 428.

imum'.[88] This is a point of significance since, of the 252 cases opened in 1999, over 100 involved expenditure managed directly by the Commission.

Public Interest Disclosure

Inside the Commission, investigation of fiscal irregularity is made harder by old-fashioned and often poor systems of personnel management. In the Santer affair, many of the irregularities were already recorded, though to little effect, in reports from the ECA. What brought them squarely into the public domain was 'whistle-blowing' by an official in the internal-audit section (DG XX) who became so concerned by the serious accounting irregularities that he saw in the Commission that, rather than pursue the matter internally, he decided to pass internal Commission documentation straight to the European Parliament. After the resignation of the Santer Commission, the officer was charged with breaches of the Staff Regulations, reprimanded, and transferred to a post in Personnel. He complained to the European Ombudsman on the ground that his freedom of expression had been infringed. The Commission sought to justify the disciplinary proceedings on the ground that the official had, by publicizing the internal documents, infringed the procedures set in place to protect other people charged with disciplinary offences—against many of whom, it must be remembered, neither disciplinary nor criminal proceedings had been attempted! The EO dismissed the complaint, however, agreeing that the penalty fell within the parameters of the Commission's lawful discretion, and indicating some sympathy with its explanation of the posting, on the ground that 'there may have been, to some degree, a breakdown of confidence between [the official] and his hierarchy which could have caused problems in the day-to-day management'.[89] Some critical remarks attached to his decision suggest that he may have been less satisfied than the outcome would suggest.

The discovery that the Staff Regulations, in contrast to those of many national public services, contained at the time of the disclosures *no protection for whistle-blowers* is rather surprising. It is still more extraordinary that, a year after the Independent Experts had reported, at the time of the EO's report, none were yet in place. New OLAF regulations, introduced in 1999, clarify the channels for reporting suspected irregularities to superiors or, alternatively, to the Secretary-General and OLAF, but it was not until November 2000 that the Commission announced new procedures to protect

[88] FR, n. 16 above, para. 5.9.11

[89] Complaint 1219/99/ME against the European Commission, *Annual Report of the European Ombudsman for 2000* (Strasbourg, EO 2001), 91–4. There is a hint in the Further Remarks of the EO that he does not entirely approve of the existing situation. With the excuse of the new Charter of Fundamental Rights, he proposes to open an own-initiative inquiry.

whistle-blowers.[90] The whistle-blowing episode occurred at a time when, to cite the Independent Experts once more, it was 'difficult to find anyone who has even the slightest sense of responsibility' in the Commission,[91] and against a background where, of eighty disciplinary cases between 1994 and 1999, no action was taken in thirty-seven; thirteen employees were dismissed, and forty-three disciplined. Nor, as Stephen Grey reminds us,[92] has there been:

a successful prosecution of an EU official for fraud and there may not be many in future unless the EU's anti-fraud safeguards undergo a truly radical overhaul. Neither have there been many internal prosecutions. Only a handful of officials are disciplined annually for any offence. Incompetence is only punishable if it is proved deliberate. The lack of internal or external control encourages sloppy management and, on rare occasion, serious fraud.

The ECA also records that disciplinary proceedings are reserved for situations of 'gross dishonesty and/or criminal behaviour or flagrantly unprofessional conduct'. This apparently includes whistle-blowing. In these circumstances, the EO's complacency in the face of clearly retributive conduct on the part of the Commission seems indefensible, and his use of the rather severe jurisprudence of the Community Courts upholding restrictions on the right of officials to publish without permission[93] to justify the Commission's failure adequately to protect a *bona fide* whistle-blower is inexcusable.

In general, the Commission ethos seems outdated and out of line with the values laid down for public-service managers by the Nolan Committee or the OECD. Public interest disclosure finds a place everywhere in national public service regulations and in the equally sensitive area of money-laundering. In both cases, where obligations of confidentiality owed by employees to employers or professional advisers to clients come into conflict with the wider public interest in revelation of criminal activity or irregularity, there has been a rapid extension of procedural protections for those in danger of dismissal or disciplinary action. Admittedly, the increasing emphasis on transparency poses an accountability dilemma, as instant media

---

[90] The issue is mentioned in European Commission, 'Reforming the Commission', COM(2000)200 final/2, Brussels 5 Apr. 2000, 18. For implementation see House of Commons Select Committee on the European Union, *Financial Management of the European Union*, HC 437 (1999–2000), Fig. 10.

[91] IR, n. 32 above, para. 9.4.25.

[92] Grey, n. 40 above, 4.

[93] Cases T–34/96, T–163/96, *Bernard Connolly* v. *Commission* [1999] ECR II–463. The case is concerned more with freedom of opinion than with whistle-blowing. The applicant, a senior official at the Directorate of Monetary Affairs, published a book entitled '*The Rotten Heart of Europe: The Dirty War for Europe's Money*', held capable of undermining the 'dignity of his post'.

publication may indeed infringe the privacy and procedural protections of individuals. On the other hand, the dilatory conduct of the institutions in pursuing corruption and maladministration in the cases under discussion seems fully to justify the whistle-blower's approach to the European Parliament.

Critics of the internal audit process have fastened on the 'contradictory procedures', demanding that OLAF be permitted to act more like an investigator and less like a court. Concentrating on the element of sanction, however, Grey recommends a stronger mandate for OLAF and national police forces and the routine lifting of diplomatic immunity, coupled with the regular use of in-house disciplinary procedures. But even if the predictable hostility from both the institutions and staff unions could be overcome, it is questionable whether these recommendations could be implemented. Contradictory procedure and other procedural protections are strongly protected by the ECJ and any attempt to undermine or side-step them is likely to lead to interminable litigation.[94] Indeed, the investigation under discussion shows that the EO has succumbed to the use of contradictory procedure, a development likely to prolong already lengthy investigations.

Reforming Criminal Procedure

The Tampere Summit[95] ushered in a new enthusiasm for joint action to heighten co-operation and reduce the possibility for budgetary fraud. A study group working on the feasibility of harmonization of criminal laws in EU fraud cases had reported in 1996,[96] following a programme on which the independent Association for European Penal Research had been working for many years. The programme condemns the territorial integrity of national criminal-law procedures, and is working towards a fusion of adversarial and inquisitorial criminal procedure in a uniform contradictory procedure. Member States are to have a single territorial area for budgetary fraud with common procedural rules, enforced by a European public prosecutor operating from a Brussels office staffed by prosecutors seconded from national

[94] But see now Case C–315/99P, *Ismeri Europa Srl* v. *Court of Auditors of the European Communities*, 10 July 2001, where the CFI and, on appeal, the ECJ declined to find procedural improprieties in the conduct of an investigation into the MED programme.

[95] Tampere European Council, Presidency conclusions, 15 and 16 Oct. 1999: Document 200/99.

[96] M. Delmas Marty (ed.), *Corpus Juris Introducing Penal Provisions for the Purpose of the Financial Interests of the European Union* (Paris, Economica, 1997), M. Delmas Marty, 'Combating Fraud—Necessity, Legitimacy and Feasibility of the Corpus Juris' (2000) 37 *CML Rev.* 247. See further J. Spencer, 'The Corpus Juris Project and the Fight Against Budgetary Fraud' (1999) 1 *Cambridge Yearbook of European Legal Studies* 77. The project originated in the European Legal Area Project set up by Francesco de Angelis, then Director of Financial Control in DG XX of the Commission.

public prosecutors' offices. Member States will have to enact a common offence of fraud and corruption against the Community budget. It is hoped that the reorganization of OLAF, designed to reinforce links with Eurojust, and through Eurojust with national prosecutors' offices, will do much to set in place a coherent strategy for combating fraud against the Community budget and, harder but more important, to make it effective. For the first time, a criminal-law manual is in production, and the employment of specialized magistrates from Member State countries with a knowledge of national laws will put OLAF in a stronger position. Yet the structures on which these proposals rely for their success, typical of the compromises of inter-governmental bargaining, contain the seeds of future failure, and it remains to be seen whether they can be more successful than the present national arrangements in ensuring speed and success. The EP is sceptical, noting with concern that 'the protection of the European Union's financial interests has not yet improved perceptibly in practice and that the persistent blocking of the recruitment of qualified staff for OLAF could even cause irreversible damage'.[97]

An incidental effect of the efforts to introduce joined-up accountability in combating fraud and financial irregularity in the EU could be that important prosecutorial activities will be removed from the control of the national authorities.[98] The Corpus Juris proposals are said to be 'breathtaking in their scope; they constitute nothing less than the seeds of a European Criminal Code'.[99] They involve the harmonization of a number of totally incompatible prosecutorial systems. This warning is intensified by the extension of the Tampere proposals at Laeken to the area of anti-terrorist offences and the introduction of Eurojust, a new agency which may prove to be unaccountable.[100] It is distressing to find proposals of such import put together and developed by academic and official working parties. Proposals for new criminal proceedings go to the very heart of the rule of law principle. They fundamentally affect human rights and civil liberties, and may in the long run contain a threat to civil liberties at least as grave as the threat of

[97] European Parliament, Resolution on the Commission's Annual Report fror 1999, 'Protecting the Communities' financial interests—the fight against fraud' (COM(2000)718—C5-0066/2001–2001/2036(COS)) [2001] C365/27 Annex III.
[98] E. Bell, 'A European DPP to Prosecute Fraud?' [2000] *Criminal Law Review* 154, 165; L. Kuhl. 'The Criminal Law Protection of the Communities' Financial Interests against Fraud' [1998] *Criminal Law Review* 259. For the latest proposals, see Green Paper on criminal-law protection of the financial interests of the Community and the establishment of a European Prosecutor, Brussels (11 Dec. 2001) COM(2001)715 final.
[99] Editorial, 'The Tampere Summit: The Ties that Bind or the Policemen's Ball' (1999) 36 *CML Rev.* 1119,1123. See also W. van Gerven, 'Constitutional Conditions for a Public Prosecutor's Office at the European Level' in G de Kerchove and A. Weyenbergh (eds.), V*ers un éspace judiciare pénal européen*, (Paris, Editions ULB, 2000).
[100] Chap. 2, above 46; Chap 3, above 77.

fraud. Developed under the third-pillar regime, notable for its impervious-ness to democratic accountability, these policy initiatives emanate for the most part from the ministries and bodies within the Member States respon-sible for crime prevention; to such bodies the Corpus Juris initiative offers an unparalleled opportunity to avoid the stricter controls at national level.[101] Indeed, both Houses of the United Kingdom Parliament have issued negative reports on the Commission's Green Paper on precisely these grounds. The House of Commons concluded:[102]

We consider that the proposal raises more problems than it solves and we note with particular concern its effect of putting the prosecution function beyond the reach of democratic accountability, either to national parliaments or elsewhere.

There is contradiction and imbalance in the statements emanating from the European Council at Amsterdam, Tampere, Nice, and Laeken. On the one hand, the Nice Council endorsed and gave final approval to a new Charter of Fundamental Rights for the EU, a document which significantly extends the concept of rights in the EU, and which unexpectedly contains protections in the field of criminal procedure (such as a rule against double jeopardy), a hint that the EU may be looking to expand its operations in this field.[103] The same European Council set in place the machinery for a thorough look at the future governance of the European Union, a process initiated by the Commission with its White Paper, and targeted again at Laeken (see Chapter 7). All these initiatives are aimed at, and stress the need for, the democratic values of transparency, consultation, participation, and accountability. On the other hand, we find important policies, with a tangible bearing on fundamental rights and civil liberties set in place through a process of distant, secretive, and undemocratic policy-making in which input from civil society and its democratic representatives is left to the last minute and inevit-ably comes too late. It is a fine irony that, in their policy-making processes, the EU institutions should be so oblivious to the values they profess so liberally.

[101] P-A. Albrecht and S. Braun, 'Deficiencies in the Development of European Criminal Law' (1999) 5 *European Law Journal* 293.

[102] House of Commons, Nineteenth Report of the Select Committee on European Scrutiny, 'Establishment of a European Public Prosecutor', (2001/2): Report on Green Paper on criminal law protection of the financial interests of the Community and the establishment of a European Prosecutor, COM(01)715. See also House of Lords, Select Committee on the European Communities, 'Prosecuting Fraud on the Communities' Finances—the *Corpus Juris*' HL 62 (1998–9).

[103] Charter of Fundamental Rights of the European Union [2000] OJ C364/01, Arts. 47–50.

IV CONCLUSIONS: IS ACCOUNTABILITY FEASIBLE?

To construct an efficient system of audit for the EU would never be easy, and a change both of culture and practice is necessary for reform of financial management structures to be effective. Power's catalogue of elements contributing to the present 'audit deficit' includes:[104]

lack of a common Euro-audit community, imperfect links with national audit bodies, ambivalent relations with the budgeting arm of the European Parliament, European Commission hostility to criticism of internal controls in its implementation of the EU budget, an uneasy operational mixture of regularity and value for money auditing, the absence of an internal audit function in the Commission, at least until recently and a spending culture in conflict with constraint values.

The audit problems of the EU fall into two linked categories, the first concerning the internal management of the Commission, the second the disbursement of funding throughout the EU and the management of external funding programmes. The link is provided by the Commission, which has the responsibility of supervising the external programmes, a mammoth task, which can be undertaken only by a body with finely honed management skills. But the internal audit system has for a long period of time been wrongly structured, lacking independence, autonomy, and an audit culture. Incentives have notably been lacking to encourage a sense of responsibility in staff. The main weaknesses were identified by the Independent Experts and have been reviewed by the Commission, with the encouragement of President Prodi and under the close supervision of Vice-President Kinnock. Their ideas are only beginning to take shape and, more important, to be put into practice. A perennial complaint is that the Commission has not enough staff adequately to police the multiplicity of financial transactions even at the level of internal audit, though this is not to say that its performance in this respect could not be greatly improved. If the reforms recommended by the Commission in internal documents[105] become operative and prove effective, things could change very much for the better even if reports from the media suggest that they are being contested at every step. Current proposals to vest responsibility firmly in directors-general, breaking monopolies and allowing for the rotation of senior staff within directorates, are significant steps in the direction of public management theory, while the proposal that directors-general should certify their directorate's expenditure in an annual report will place them more in the situation of an accounting officer in a British department. It

---

[104] Power, n. 4 above, 48.
[105] Notably, European Commission, 'Reforming the Commission' and New Staff Policy, IP/01/283, Brussels (28 Feb. 2000). Further internal papers are discussed in Chap. 7.

has also been suggested by Grey[106] that directors-general should become answerable directly to the European Parliament, though this would impinge rather seriously on the political accountability of Commissioners.

Externally, as this chapter has amply demonstrated, the major weakness lies in the failure of the Commission to set in place adequate 'audit trails' in respect of its progammes of grants and subsidies; the Commission has been no manager of networks and has not yet amply demonstrated that it can become one. Driven on by the Council, EP, and ECA, and more recently with the expertise of the OLAF supervisory committee to help it, the Commission has at last recognized the necessity of introducing a degree of uniformity, and is currently in the process of negotiating protocols on management and audit, with Member States participating in the administration of structural funds. As yet, however, the administrative structure provides few incentives for national authorities to deal with fraud within their boundaries, even if they have the capacity to do so. The complex network of budgetary and audit systems is hard to police, and audit requires the help of national and subnational administrations, whose own audit procedures may be less than impeccable. Outside the boundaries of the EU, and across the public/private divide, there is no 'joined-up' system of audit in place to override the failings and misdemeanours of national authorities. Here the disquiet expressed by the House of Lords Select Committee at the 'seeming indifference expressed at the Council's highest level to the auditing functions and findings of the ECA'[107] is highly relevant; there is no real incentive for Member State governments to collaborate in creating cross-border audit networks—rather the reverse.

Michael Power does not, like some critics, despair of making the EU auditable. He dislikes the 'spot-check' system, seeing it as incapable of generating public confidence, and hopes for a new and more professional look at the audit techniques, with a view to designing an effective audit system to be integrated into the mechanics of parliamentary discharge of the EU accounts.[108] Fidelma White and Katherine Hollingsworth direct their criticism at the ECA,[109] describing it as an institution without a role. A more accurate description might be of a headless institution, divided by different audit traditions and with no clear institutional culture. White and Hollingsworth also see the absence of an EU Ministry of Finance as critical, and the Commission as incompetent to fill this key role. Yet they too are not altogether without hope, seeing signs of encouragement in the more aggressive role played recently by the EP and in the beginnings of a Commission reform programme. Like those who have pushed the Corpus Juris project

---

[106] Grey, n. 40 above, 11.
[107] HL 63 (2000/1), n. 64 above, Conclusions, para. 12.
[108] Power, n. 4 above, 89.
[109] White and Hollingsworth, n. 9 above, 194–6.

high on to the EU agenda, these authors see the way forward as being through harmonization, with the objective of aligning the audit methodologies of Member States and the Commission, taking into account the methodology used by the ECA. This, they believe, would herald 'the beginnings of a "Community" model of financial control and audit'.[110] The first report of the OLAF supervisory committee could be seen as a step in this direction.

In a way this is a worrying conclusion, since it assumes that harmonization of the strongly competing conceptions of audit which currently operate in Member States is possible as well as desirable, overlooking the problems latent in the EU 'consociationalist' ethos—the need 'to accommodate as many, if not all, national preferences, cultures, styles and traditions [through a] system of articulation and accommodation between national interests'. An audit system must be chosen for effectiveness and efficiency, and not because it combines elements of all or most of the audit models in use through the EU. Such a hybrid would either fail as an administrative transplant or might actually undercut the efficiency of the most effective national systems. The House of Lords asks in contrast only for *minimum standards*, accepting that 'differences between systems of control are justified so long as each system is effective'.[111] This is a more sensible approach, though it begs the crucial questions: are they or can they be made so?

---

[110] Ibid.
[111] HL 63 (2000/2001), n. 64 above, Conclusions, para. 13.

6

Accountability through Law

I ACCOUNTABILITY AND THE RULE OF LAW

The theories of responsibility discussed in Chapter 1 tend to assume a significant role for legal accountability while never precisely pinpointing what that role is or ought to be. This may be because the relationship between courts and government is seldom formulated in terms of accountability. Lawyers prefer the classical terminology of the rule of law. Dawn Oliver, however, in her thoughtful study of accountability, lays the relationship open when she defines accountability as:[1]

a framework for the exercise of state power in a liberal-democratic system, within which public bodies are forced to seek to promote the public interest and compelled to justify their actions in those terms or in other constitutionally acceptable terms (justice, humanity, equity); to modify policies if they should turn out to have been well conceived; and to make amends if mistakes and errors of judgement have been made.

This is precisely the function allocated by lawyers to the rule of law.

Liberal-democratic systems of government promote the ideal of limited government, a goal they set out to achieve by limiting the ambit of governmental competence and by neutralizing the idea of legislative sovereignty. There are a number of techniques by which this may be done. These include the device of distributing or 'balancing' power between the various branches of government, as in classical separation-of-powers theory. The influence of the separation-of-powers doctrine in European systems of government is very marked and lies behind the idea of 'institutional balance' used by the European Court of Justice as an interpretative principle of EU law. A more effective starting-point for limitation is a written constitution, likely in modern times to contain a justiciable charter of rights, as typified by the modern German Constitution with its Basic Law. Liberal constitutional

---

[1] D. Oliver, *Government in the United Kingdom: The Search for Accountability, Effectiveness and Citzenship*, (Milton Keynes, Open University Press, 1991), 28. See also 10.

theory places the constitution in a paramount position, ranking in the legal hierarchy over law as formulated by the legislature. To put this differently, legislature and government can act only within the framework of the 'constitution', a term typically construed inclusively to embrace a body of constitutional principle which 'it is the courts' inalienable responsibility to identify and uphold',[2] the operative word here being 'identify'. The rule of law formula admirably conveys the message that the loser lost 'not because the judges were against him but because the law was'.[3] With the aid of the rule of law doctrine, it is possible to argue that law is an essential ingredient of democracy,[4] hence to counter the 'argument from democracy' that judges should not dabble in law-making or policy because they are not elected. The classical metaphor of balance is fulfilled, according to which the law can be seen as encompassing and confining the judges who administer the legal system at the same time as it confines the legislature and elected politicians. Recognition in the Treaties of the powerful rule of law ideal in a paragraph asserting the attachment of the signatories to 'the principles of liberty, democracy and respect for human rights and fundamental freedoms and of the rule of law' has made it easier to conceptualize the Treaties as a 'basic constitutional charter' of a 'Community based on the rule of law'.[5] These fictions have also been of vital importance in lending the ECJ the legitimacy it has required to bring into being the 'new legal order' of EU law.

During the course of the nineteenth century, when public power (*puissance publique*) began to come systematically under judicial scrutiny, courts acquired a power to 'control' or, in the classical terminology of the common law, 'review' the legality of administrative action. Review powers were not always spelled out—as they are in the EC Treaties—in the constitution or in legislation; the US Supreme Court is by no means the only court to seize jurisdiction over the executive, as famously it did in the seminal case of *Marbury* v. *Madison*.[6] In the second half of the twentieth century, judicial review tended to expand its empire, becoming the standard means of challenge to administrative action. From this point of departure, courts were able

---

[2] Lord Woolf of Barnes, 'Droit Public—English Style' [1995] *PL* 57, 68–9. Compare M. Letourneur, 'Les principes généraux dans la jurisprudence du Conseil d'Etat' [1951] *Etudes et Documents du Conseil d'Etat* 19.

[3] M. Shapiro, 'The European Court of Justice' in P. Craig and G. de Búrca (eds.), *The Evolution of EU Law* (Oxford, Oxford University Press, 1999), 323.

[4] D. Dyzenhaus, 'Reuniting the Brain: The Democratic Basis of Judicial Review' (1998) 9 *Public Law Review* 98.

[5] See R. Cooter and D. Schmidtchen, 'Introduction', in Special Issue; 'Conference on the Constitutional Law and Economics of the European Union' (1996) 16 *International Review of Law and Economics* 277; B. de Witte, 'International Agreement or European Constitution?' in J. Winter *et al.* (eds), *Reforming the Treaty on European Union—The Legal Debate* (Dordrecht, Kluwer Law International, 1996).

[6] *Marbury v. Madison* (1803) 1 *Cranch.* 137.

to add to their portfolio the function of 'higher law judicial review' or 'the invalidation of laws enacted by the normal or regular legislative process, because they are in conflict with some higher law, typically a constitution or treaty'.[7] In respect of the EU institutions, a power 'to review the legality' of their acts is expressly conferred on the European Court of Justice by TEC Article 230. TEC Article 220 adds to this power the obligation 'to ensure that in the interpretation and application of this Treaty the law is observed'. Today this obligation rests on both of the Community Courts (ECJ and CFI).

Courts in judicial review proceedings act essentially as overseers, scrutinizing the procedures by which decisions are taken, and able, if dissatisfied, to annul or set decisions aside. (The two terms 'review' and 'control' are not entirely synonymous and the latter may suggest a greater measure of compulsion than exists. This is one reason courts are inclined to favour possession of mandatory orders.) A point has now been reached in many jurisdictions at which it is tempting simply to equate legal accountability with judicial review or control. Dawn Oliver, herself a public lawyer, prefers, however, to avoid conflation of review and accountability. For Oliver, legal accountability comprises three essential elements; first, a duty is laid on the administration 'to explain and justify its actions in legal terms if sued in the courts'; secondly, this duty must be 'enforceable by action in the courts at the instigation of those affected by the actions of public bodies'; the third element, on which Oliver touches only lightly, is the obligation 'to make amends'.[8] In this definition, the ambit of legal accountability is limited to the imposition of procedural restraints upon the administration, coupled with a right of legal action and a power to award reparation. The latter suggests that courts should have a power either to fine or to award damages against the state, a power conceded within limits by all modern European legal systems and escalating in importance over the last decade.

Richard Mulgan separates law's standard-setting function, regarded as the framework for accountability, from the enforcement procedures by which administration is brought to book. He argues that 'accountability' and 'control' are not identical terms and ought not to be conflated:[9]

Being accountable for alleged breaches of the law does not mean that compliance with the law is also an act of accountability or that the law itself is an accountability mechanism ... the legal accountability mechanism is confined to that part of the law which lays down enforcement procedures. The main body of the law, which most public servants follow as a matter of normal practice, is an instrument for controlling their behaviour but not for holding them accountable.

---

[7] Shapiro, n. 3 above, 321.
[8] Oliver, n. 1 above, 26.
[9] R. Mulgan, ' "Accountability": an Ever-Expanding Concept?' (2000) 78 *Public Administration* 555.

Mulgan's interpretation represents a narrowing down of the classical rule of law concept, in which the standard-setting function of courts is part and parcel of the machinery for control. For Mulgan, 'law' in the sense of legislation and judicial principle provides the *framework* within which public bodies operate and with which they must comply. 'Law' is thus distinct from the legal system, in the narrow sense of the machinery of justice by which the law is enforced, and public bodies brought to book, or made accountable. On this view, legal accountability is to be found through an effective judicial system capable of imposing itself on the administration through a system of enforceable judicial remedies. This is certainly a view of legal accountability with which the European judiciary and EU lawyers would empathize.

II STRUCTURING ACCOUNTABILITY

It was almost certainly never the intention of the Member States that national governments would be held responsible for breaches of EC law at the suit of individuals before national courts.[10] This was the effect of a decision of the ECJ in the seminal case of *Van Gend en Loos*.[11] In their ruling, the judges had clearly outrun the intentions of the signatories to the Treaties; to their consternation, evidenced when a majority of Member States came to court to argue against what became the Court's decision, the Member States had, in Shapiro's telling metaphor, 'let the cat loose on themselves'.[12] However inadvertently, they had rendered themselves accountable to a Community institution. It proved impossible, even if the Member States had wished to do so, to put the judicial cat back into the bag. *Van Gend en Loos* became the foundation stone on which the doctrine of the legal supremacy, together with the new legal order, were built.

As with the parliamentary and audit systems, the EU judicial system was designed as a two-tier system. EC law was the responsibility of the European Court of Justice, until 1988, when the Court of First Instance was introduced, the sole court of the European Communities. The ECJ was a court of limited competence,[13] designed as a forum to handle disagreements between Member States, or Member States and institutions, arising out of the interpretation of the Treaties. The ECJ certainly possessed a 'control function', its primary functions being to review the legality of the acts and activities

---

[10] G. Tsebelis and G. Garrett, 'The Institutional Foundations of Intergovernmentalism and Supranationalism in the EU' (2001) 55 *International Organisations* 357, 360.

[11] Case 26/62, *Van Gend en Loos v. Nederlandse Administratie der Belastingen* [1963] ECR 1.

[12] Shapiro, n. 3 above, 329.

[13] But see A. Arnull, 'Does the European Court of Justice have Inherent Jurisdiction?' (1990) 27 *CML Rev.* 683.

of the EU institutions (TEC Article 230) or hear complaints that they had
failed to carry out their Treaty obligations (TEC Article 232). The Court
also heard proceedings for infringement brought by the Commission, on
its own initiative or at the request of Member States (TEC Articles 226,
227). This would allow it to interpret the Treaties and secondary legislation
passed pursuant to the Treaties. National law was reserved for national
courts.

The fragile link between the two tiers of the judicial system was the
preliminary reference procedure of TEC Article 234. This permitted the
'courts or tribunals' of the Member States to pose questions on the interpretation of EC law which arose in the course of proceedings before them to the
ECJ, reference being *mandatory* in the case of final appellate courts. At EU
level, the mandate of the ECJ, recently confirmed and extended to the CFI by
the Nice Treaty, was to 'ensure that in the interpretation and application of
this Treaty, the law is observed' (TEC Article 220). The power of the ECJ to
hold the institutions of the EU to account was not in question, though little
guidance was in practice given by the Treaties on how this was to be done.
The grounds of review were largely borrowed, and the terminology of French
administrative law was used. The court is to 'review the legality of acts . . . on
grounds of lack of competence, infringement of an essential procedural
requirement, infringement of this Treaty or of any rule of law relating to
its application, or misuse of powers'. The remedies at the Court's disposal
were aimed at the institutions. In review proceedings, the ECJ possessed a
power to declare acts void (TEC Article 231) and a power to prescribe
'necessary interim measures' (TEC Article 243). In return, both institutions
and Member States undertook 'to take the necessary measures to comply with
the judgement of the Court of Justice' (TEC Articles 233, 228). In case of
non-compliance, the Treaties provided only for an infringement action to be
brought by the Commission (TEC Article 226); it was not until Maastricht
that the ECJ was given a power to fine recalcitrant Member States. In
addition, the ECJ was given power to award compensation against the EU
institutions (TEC Article 235), the principles on which they were to act being
'the general principles common to the laws of the Member States' (TEC
Article 288). On this famous phrase, the Court was to build a celebrated
jurisprudence, capable of putting flesh on to the bones of the Treaty vision of
a Community under the aegis of the rule of law.

Access to the Court

For Christopher Lord, legal accountability possesses two main elements: the
rules must be 'enforceable by an independent judicial authority' and the legal
system must allow 'any citizen on a basis of equality' to access a court 'with a
complaint that power-holders are seeking to evade or distort the rules by

which they are themselves brought to account'.[14] The court structure as established by the Treaties meets Lord's first condition: members of the ECJ are chosen from persons qualified for the highest judicial office 'whose independence is beyond doubt'. Access is, however, a point of greater difficulty. The institutions—at first the Council and Commission—and Member States had 'privileged access' to the ECJ. They could consult 'their' court without the need to show interest (TEC Article 230). This represents a very special sort of standing, best suited to an international tribunal. A significant problem soon emerged that there was no mention of the European Parliament, not in existence at the time when the Article was drafted; it was given no rights to appear before the Court. This was a gap which made it hard to defend its position in the legislative process and placed it at a disadvantage to the Council. By stages the ECJ allowed this position to be rectified, conceding standing in so far as was necessary for the EP to protect its 'prerogatives'.[15] The move was a bold one, attracting criticism on the grounds of judicial activism, though defensible on the twin grounds of accountability and 'institutional balance'. The relationship of deference between Member States and their Court is highlighted by the action taken at the Maastricht IGC to endorse the ECJ's solution to this problem. At Nice, the EP was finally placed on an equal footing with Commission and Council, and new institutions fill the slot of 'semi-privileged' access: the ECA and ECB can now sue 'for the purpose of protecting their prerogatives'. For private parties, the standing provisions are, in comparison to many national jurisdictions, restricted. They allow private parties to challenge 'decisions' addressed directly to them or 'of direct and individual concern' (TEC Article 230). For an international tribunal, on which the ECJ was patterned, this provision was generous, opening the door to an administrative-law jurisdiction for the Court.[16] The standing provisions of the ECJ have, however, always been problematic, making it difficult for private parties to approach the court.

Courts faced with narrow rules of standing can move in two directions. They can interpret standing tests with generosity, gradually opening it out. The ECJ could have done this by blurring the distinction between 'direct' and 'individual' interest, fusing the tests. Instead, the Court stood very strictly on the need for both forms of interest, a restrictive interpretation for which over the years it has attracted much criticism.[17] Alternatively, courts can

---

[14] C. Lord, *Democracy in the European Union* (Sheffield, Academic Press, 1998), 96.

[15] Case 302/87, *Parliament v. Council* [1988] ECR 5615 ('Comitology'); Case C–70/88, *Re Radioactive Food: European Parliament v. Council* [1990] ECR I–2041 ('Chernobyl').

[16] See M. Lagrange, 'La Cour de Justice des Communautés Européennes: du plan Schumann à l'union européenne' [1978] *Revue trimestrielle de droit européenne* 1.

[17] See the classic article by H Rasmussen, 'Why is Art 173 Interpreted against Plaintiffs?' (1980) 5 *EL Rev.* 114. And see A. Arnull, *The European Union and its Court of Justice* (Oxford, Oxford University Press, 1999), 41–8; A. Arnull, 'Private Applicants and the Action for

encourage 'public interest actions'. These seek to challenge the validity of laws or legality of administrative action, on the ground that the general public interest is in issue. Public interest actions deliberately use the legal system for purposes of public accountability. In very direct fashion, public interest actions demand that public bodies come before the courts to account for their use of public power. They are thus a significant addition to the machinery for securing public accountability. Typically, public interest actions are not brought by individuals but by interest or pressure groups claiming to represent the public interest.[18] Public interest groups rely on the rules of individual standing, which seriously limits their access to the ECJ. From time to time, the ECJ has modified the rules, as for example with a line of cases which opened access to persons and bodies invited by the Commission to participate in administrative procedures, a development helpful in heightening Commission accountability and protecting public rights of participation.[19] Some of these groups simply represent individuals entitled to participate; others, such as consumer or environmental groups, claim to represent the general public.[20] In general it is true to say that public interest litigation has not had a high profile in the EU, and although public interest groups are beginning to find their way into the ECJ and CFI, they have not so far found a warm welcome.[21] Indeed, the negative response of the ECJ to public interest litigation is rather marked in comparison to that of national jurisdictions, especially when, by comparison to access rules at national level, the rules of individual standing have remained so strict.

The ECJ's reticence causes particular problems for environmentalists, as a 'direct and individual' interest in the environment may be hard to establish.[22] In *Stichting Greenpeace*,[23] for example, the Commission had made a decision to grant financial assistance from the structural funds for the construction of power stations in the Canary Islands. The development was the subject

Annulment under Article 173 of the EC Treaty' (1995) 35 *CML Rev.* 7; N. Neuwahl, 'Article 173 Paragraph 4 EC: Past, Present and Possible Future' (1996) 21 *EL Rev.* 17; M. Hedemann-Robinson, 'Article 173 EC, General Community Measures and *Locus Standi* for Private Persons: Still a Cause for Individual Concern?' (1996) 2 *European Public Law* 127.

[18] C. Harlow, 'Towards a Theory of Standing for the European Court of Justice' (1992) 12 *Yearbook of European Law* 213; H. W. Micklitz and N. Reich, *Public Interest Litigation before European Courts* (Baden-Baden, Nomos, 1996).

[19] Case 26/76, *Metro-SB-Großmärkte GmbH v. Commission* [1977] ECR 1785. The case law is analysed in some detail in P. Craig and G. de Búrca, *EU Law. Text, Cases and Materials*, (2nd edn., Oxford, Oxford University Press, 1998), 461–89.

[20] For a classification of representative groups see C. Harlow, 'Towards a Theory of Standing for the European Court of Justice' (1992) 12 *Yearbook of European Law* 213.

[21] Micklitz and Reich, n. 18 above.

[22] L. Kramer, 'Public Interest Litigation in Environmental Matters Before the European Courts' (1996) *Journal of Environmental Law* 1.

[23] Case T-585/93, *Stichting Greenpeace Council (Greenpeace International) v. Commission* [1995] ECR II–2205.

of planning decisions, vulnerable to challenge under Spanish law in local courts. But Greenpeace wished to attack the policy of the Commission, taking the view that, without structural funding, projects like this one, detrimental to the environment, must inevitably fall. Greenpeace therefore joined with residents and local fishermen to challenge the Commission's funding decision on ecological grounds. Interpreting the Treaty Articles very strictly, the CFI ruled the application inadmissible, on the ground that the applicants were not individually affected; the development would affect them only 'in the same manner as any other local resident, fisherman, farmer or tourist who is, or might be in the future, in the same situation'. Greenpeace appealed the decision,[24] with the classic public interest argument that environmental interests are 'diffuse': they are, by their very nature, 'common and shared, and the rights relating to those interests are liable to be held by a potentially large number of people so that there could never be a closed class of applicants satisfying the criteria adopted by the CFI'. Very plausibly, Greenpeace also argued that a legal vacuum had been created; it was difficult to pinpoint responsibility for a decision shared by actors at so many different levels of governance. The ECJ was unresponsive; it upheld the CFI in asserting that the rights in question were fully protected by the national courts. This response was not entirely accurate because of the split in jurisdiction between national and EU courts.

The Mullaghmore decision illustrates one of the ways in which the split jurisdiction can undermine the accountability of public bodies, notably the Commission. Structural funding was being used to develop the Burren National Park in Ireland, an area of natural beauty and special scientific interest, by building a visitor centre to open up access and promote tourism. The Worldwide Fund for Nature (WWF) asked the Commission to take infringement proceedings on the ground that environmental impact assessments had not been made. On refusal by the Commission, WWF moved for annulment of the decision. Following precedent, the CFI ruled the application inadmissible on grounds of lack of standing.[25] Defeated, WWF applied for access to the documentation on which the Commission had based its refusal to take infringement proceedings.[26] Again the Commission refused, basing its refusal on the mandatory exception to the Code of Conduct on access to information which protects the public interest in court proceedings and investigations. This time WWF was partially successful. The case was ruled admissible since, in cases involving access to information, standing rules are generously interpreted, a relaxation perhaps based on the fact that no

---

[24] Case C–321/95, *Stichting Greenpeace Council (Greenpeace International) v. Commission* [1998] ECR I–1651.
[25] *An Taisce and WWF (UK) v. Commission*, Case T–491/93 [1994] ECR II–733 (CFI); Case C–325/94 P [1996] ECR I–3727 (ECJ).
[26] Case T–104/95, *WWF (UK) v. Commission* [1997] ECR II–313.

interest is necessary to ask for access to official documents.[27] The CFI also ruled that the Commission must make a reasoned decision. In practice, however, this does not get applicants much further, since reasoned decisions are fairly easily drafted. This case law renders the Commission virtually immune from accountability for conduct of the key enforcement procedure under TEC Article 226.[28] One way to analyse the problem is in terms of the two-tier decision-making process, which leaves a 'gap' in the accountability system. Another way to think about it is in terms of 'joined-up government', which might suggest co-ordinating the actions of the decision-makers. Joanne Scott and David Trubek[29] see the problem as one of 'multi-level governance'. The governance structures of the EU have developed 'through experimentation and pragmatic accommodation' and are still in the process of emergence. The ECJ, along with the Commission and institutions generally, is working with an older paradigm. Unless it can provide new approaches both to efficiency and legitimacy, the accountability gap cannot be bridged. This criticism, however valid, is part of wider debate over governance in the European Union addressed in the final chapter.

In any event, two recent cases point to a sharp swing in judicial opinion over standing, designed to fill the gap whereby the general legislation and regulation of the EU cannot be attacked in the Community courts. In *Jégo-Quéré*,[30] a group of fishermen affected by a prohibition on drift-net fishing contained in Regulation 1162/2001 tried to attack its validity in the CFI. The Commission based its defence on the standard *Greenpeace* argument that the regulation was a measure of general effect which could not be said to affect the applicants *individually*. The CF unexpectedly ruled that the applicants did have standing, allowing the case to be considered on its merits. This change of position would have brought the CFI, responsible for the majority of decisions on standing, into conflict with the older ECJ case law but for the fact that the ECJ seemed also to be contemplating change. In *Union de Pequeños Agricultores*,[31] an association of farmers asked for annulment of Regulation 1638/98, amending the organization of the olive-oil market, once again raising the perennial question whether individuals could be affected by a measure of general application. Jacobs A. G. advised the ECJ to change direction. Acknowledging that standing was a Treaty requirement,

---

[27] See now Art 2 of Regulation EC 1049/2001 Regarding Public Access to European Parliament, Council and Commission Documents [2001] OJ L145/43.

[28] Described above, 71–4.

[29] J. Scott and D. Trubek, 'Mind the Gap: Law and New Approaches to Governance in Europe' [2002] 8 *European Law Journal* 1, 12.

[30] Case T–177/01, *Jégo-Quéré v. Commission*, 7 May 2002.

[31] Case C–50/00, *Union de Pequeños Agricultores v. Council*, 21 Mar. 2002. The citation is from para. 75.

he nonetheless reasoned that reconsideration of the narrow rules of individual standing was possible within the framework of the Treaties:

It is clear, and cannot be stressed too strongly, that the notion of individual concern is capable of carrying a number of different interpretations, and that when choosing between these interpretations the Court may take account of the purpose of Article 230EC and the principle of effective judicial protection for individual applicants. In any event, the court's case-law in other areas acknowledges that an evolutionary interpretation of Article 230 EC is needed in order to fill procedural gaps in the system of remedies laid down by the Treaty and ensure that the scope of judicial protection is extended in response to the growth in powers of the Community institutions.

Had it been approved, this reasoning would have operated to close a gap which can at present insulate EU legislation from challenge, or make it necessary to move indirectly, attacking the actions of a national authority executed in reliance on EU law through the national courts, which may then be persuaded to refer the validity of the EU regulation or directive to the ECJ.[32] However, the ECJ has rejected this innovatory solution.[32a]

National and Community Courts

Though treated by EU lawyers as implicit in the Treaties, the close relationship which exists today between national and EU judicial systems was not envisaged by the treaty-makers. It has been constructed by the ECJ in a series of bold and inventive decisions, with the general acquiescence of the Member States and active participation of national courts.[33] A statement of principle enunciated in one of the Court's most significant early cases[34] is a pointer to where the ECJ was heading. The ECJ described the infant EEC as a:

Community based on the rule of law, inasmuch as neither its Member States nor its institutions can avoid a review of the question whether the measures adopted by them are in conformity with the basic constitutional charter, the Treaty. In particular, in Articles 173 [now 230] and 184 [now 241], on the one hand, and in Article 177 [now 234], on the other, the Treaty established a complete system of legal remedies and procedures designed to permit the Court of Justice to review the legality of the measures adopted by the institutions.

Their chosen route was extensive use of the preliminary-reference procedure set in place by TEC Article 234. This allowed an applicant to challenge the validity of EC regulation indirectly, through the device of inviting a

[32] Case C–6/99, *Association Greenpeace v. Ministère de l'Agriculture et de la Pêche*, 21 Mar. 2000.

[32a] Case C–50/00P *Unión de Pequêños Aqricultoves v Council*, 25 July 2002

[33] A.-M. Slaughter, A. Stone Sweet, and J. Weiler (eds.), *The European Courts and National Courts—Doctrine and Jurisprudence*, (Oxford, Hart Publishing, 1998).

[34] Case 294/83, *Les Verts v. Parliament* [1986] ECR 1339.

national court to refer to the ECJ questions on the validity of EC law. From the standpoint of the ECJ, it provided a useful path around the restricted individual access to the ECJ, although the remedy was admittedly imperfect, first because EC law could not be directly challenged in national courts and secondly, because reference was not a right. Thus many commentators argued that the direct access for individuals now under consideration would have been a more suitable solution from the outset.[35] Koen Lenaerts argues, however, that the principle of the new legal order had 'to be won over the fierce opposition of a majority of the then six Member States'. Without the success of the ECJ in recruiting national courts as allies in the battle for supremacy, victory would scarcely have been possible.[36] Article 243 leaves space for national autonomy, and judicial backlash would have been more far-reaching if the ECJ had moved too fast and had *not* at first left space.

Many different explanations have been offered as to why national courts, in contradistinction to national parliaments, have worked together to construct an EU legal system in which the tiers are vertically linked. Damian Chalmers propounds a consociational or partnership view of the EU legal system, in which a willingness to accommodate a plurality of interests comes together with a common will not to let the system fail.[37] Karen Alter's intergovernmentalist explanation is more sceptical. She describes national courts as 'fair-weather supporters' of the ECJ, concerned to insert themselves into the legal policy-making process in order to establish limits on the transfer of national powers to European level.[38]

Martin Shapiro turns to game theory for a plausible explanation of Member State conduct, according to which autonomy and integrationist policies are a condition that they will tolerate so long as 'overall cost-benefit calculations continue to run in their individual and collective favour'.[39] Once they do not, threats to the courts' autonomy and independence will be issued, as when, on the transference of Third-Pillar responsibilities to the EC, the Member States indicated their sentiments by explicitly curtailing the jurisdiction of the ECJ.[40] By and large, however, it is in the interest of Member States to see EU law enforced, as failure to observe the rules imperils the economic 'level playing-field'. They thus accept the risk of occasionally being on the receiving end of a judgment which finds them to

[35] E.g., H. Rasmussen, 'Why is Art 173 Interpreted against Plaintiffs?' (1980) 5 *EL Rev.* 114.

[36] K. Lenaerts, 'Some Thoughts About the Interaction Between Judges and Politicians in the European Community' [1992] *University of Chicago Legal Forum* 93.

[37] D. Chalmers, 'Judicial Preferences and the Community Legal Order' (1997) 60 *MLR* 164.

[38] K. Alter, *Establishing the Supremacy of European Law, The Making of an International Rule of Law in Europe*, (Oxford, Oxford University Press, 2001), 62.

[39] Shapiro, n. 3 above, 333.

[40] TEC Art. 68; above, 44.

be in breach of EU law. Tolerance may be heightened by the belief, current in many Member States, that they alone enforce EU law, while others ignore it. The public-choice explanation is sufficiently flexible to explain the behaviour of national courts in occasionally passing and applying ECJ decisions which have the effect of curtailing their own competence, with possible consequences for their standing in the national, political order. A dialogue may then be conducted with the ECJ through multiple references, designed to provoke a change of direction.[41] This can be read as an example of Scott's redundancy principle, whereby the national judiciary imposes judicial accountability. The general consequence of the ECJ's activist policies has, however, been an extension of judicial competence at national level; an outcome sufficiently favourable, on Shapiro's argument, to sweeten the pill of the few intrusive decisions. The possibility remains nonetheless open for national courts to turn against the persecutor if they feel threatened, and they have on occasion done so, notably when the German Constitutional Court raised objections over the performance on the ECJ in the protection of human rights.[42]

The early *Saarland* ruling[43] is undoubtedly an example of the point made earlier by Lenaerts. Here the ECJ ruled that it was for 'the domestic legal system of each Member State to designate the courts having jurisdiction and to determine the protection of the rights which citizens have from the direct effect of Community law'. This set in place a two-tier court system and guaranteed the procedural autonomy of national jurisdictions. Later, as the ECJ grew more confident, it changed its attitude. It used the reference procedure, in conjunction with the 'legally supranationalist doctrines' it was developing, such as the doctrines of direct effect and supremacy of EU law, to promote an integrated legal system.[44] Courts were therefore instructed to refer whenever a disputed point of law arose. Later, the argument became one of convenience. The docket of the ECJ was crowded; Article 234 procedure

[41] J. Weiler, 'A Quiet Revolution—The European Court of Justice and its Interlocutors' (1994) 26 *Comparative Political Studies* 510.

[42] *Internationale Handelsgesellschaft mbH*, BVerfGE 37, 271 (1974) and [1974] 2 CMLR 541. And see J. Kokott, 'Report on Germany', in Slaughter *et al.*, (eds.), n. 33 above. See also the *Maastricht* decision (Cases BvR 2134/92 and 2 BvR 2159/92 (12 Oct. 1993), BVerfGE 89, 155), Similar conflicts have arisen in other national jurisdictions: see for Italy, G Gaja, 'New Developments in a Continuing Story: The Relationship between EEC Law and Italian Law' (1990) 27 *CML Rev.* 83; Spain, D. Linan Nogueras and J. Roldan Barbero, 'The Judicial Application of Community Law in Spain' (1993) 30 *CML Rev.* 1135. And see generally the country reports in Slaughter, *et al.* (eds.), above.

[43] Case 33/76 *Rewe v. Landwirtschaftskammer Saarland* [1976] ECR 1989 at 1997. See also Case 158/80, *Rewe-Handelsgesellschaft Nord mbll and another v. Hauptzollamt Kiel* [1981] ECR 1805; Case 13/68, *Salgoil* [1968] ECR 453; Case 265/77, *Ferwela* [1982] ECR 617.

[44] T. de la Mare, 'Article 177 and Legal Integration' in Craig and G. de Búrca (eds.), n. 3 above, 227.

allowed the Court to benefit from the filter function of the national courts; reference procedure was quicker. This argument became less plausible as preliminary reference procedure lengthened, and the CFI was installed in 1988, and as the modifications to the judicial architecture approved at Nice come into operation. The goal now seems to be to loosen the reins on national courts, allowing them to decide when reference is appropriate and encouraging them to decide points of EU law themselves—a move in favour of subsidiarity.[45] It must however be said that a system based on wide direct access to the ECJ could not have produced this homogenising effect.

Harmonizing Judicial Remedies

The *Saarland* principle of procedural autonomy made harmonization of judicial remedies a difficult enterprise. It meant that, so long as a national legal system offered an effective remedy for breach of EC law, and so long as the conditions of exercise were no less favourable than those governing domestic cases, EU law was complied with. In practice, remedies in national courts differed very widely. Some courts had at their disposal powerful mandatory orders; others relied on the declaration of nullity. Unless they created an absolute barrier to legal protection, the ECJ could do nothing about the disparities. Nor was the ECJ supposed in principle to impose a *new* remedy on national courts. That is why the *Factortame* decision[46] marked such a significant step forward, because an interim injunction was authorized by the English House of Lords after a ruling from the ECJ in circumstances where the national court lacked jurisdiction to impose such an order. By the 1990s, when *Factortame* came before it, the ECJ had, however, entered a bolder and more activist phase. Commentators spoke of the virtual erosion of the rule of national procedural autonomy[47] and the advent of a 'common law' of remedies.[48] In the celebrated *Francovich* decision,[49] the ECJ again

[45] C. Barnard and E. Sharpston, 'The Changing Face of Article 177 References' (1997) 34 *CML Rev.* 1113; D. O'Keeffe, 'Is the Spirit of Article 177 under Attack? Preliminary References and Admissibility' (1998) 23 *EL Rev.* 509.

[46] Case C–221/89, *R v. Secretary of State for Transport ex p. Factortame (No 3)* [1991] ECR I–3905. There is general agreement among English commentators that this was a new remedy: see, e.g., D. Chalmers, 'Judicial Preferences and the Community Legal Order' (1997) 60 *MLR* 164; G. de Búrca, 'The Quest for Legitimacy in the European Union' (1996) 59 *MLR* 349.

[47] R. Crauford Smith, 'Remedies for Breaches of EU Law' in Craig and de Búrca (eds.), n. 3 above.

[48] R. Caranta, 'Judicial Protection Against Member States: A New Jus Commune Takes Shape' (1995) 32 *CML Rev.* 703; W. van Gerven, 'Bridging the Gap Between Community and National Laws: Towards a principle of Homogeneity in the Field of Legal Remedies?' (1995) 32 *CML Rev.* 679.

[49] Joined Cases 6, 9/90, *Francovich and Bonifaci v. Italy* [1991] ECR I–5357.

introduced a novel remedy, ruling that damages could be awarded where Member States failed, deliberately or otherwise, adequately to implement EU law. This was again a bold and innovative decision, which effectively imposes accountability on the legislatures of Member States. Not only had the judicial cat turned upon the Member States with a vengeance, but it had bitten them rather sharply. In theory, EU law was now enforceable; the judicial liability system had been completed; by adding the elements of redress and sanction,[50] the ECJ had rendered the Member States fully accountable. Again in theory, a 'private police force' of individuals and, more important, transnational corporations, had been set in place to supplement the Commission's meagre enforcement capacity.[51]

Effective Enforcement

The achievement of the ECJ in creating a system of legal accountability and opening the system to provide access to private parties is a very great one and must not be discounted. Moreover, the remarkable measure of trust and co-operation which generally exists between national courts and the ECJ provides a sharp contrast to the generally negative parliamentary relationships. The system is, however, not as accessible nor are the remedies as effective as they might seem. As Francis Snyder reminds us,[52] lawyers tend to confuse the notions of enforcement and effectiveness. Thus EU law is seen as 'effectively implemented' when it has been transposed into a national legal system; it is 'enforced' when individuals possess the *potential* for recourse to national courts. Court orders are described as 'binding', hence assumed to be effective. When courts award a judicial remedy, the law is seen as 'enforced'. For policy-makers and administrators, on the other hand, the effectiveness of law is to be determined by its outcome; law is 'effective' when it is 'enforced' in the sense of being put into operation and seen to work. This is also how the political actors and lobby groups who have worked to shape EU policy and see it 'implemented' as law understand enforcement.[53] In this full sense, EU law is, and is generally perceived to be, badly enforced. Non-compliance with EU law is a serious problem, and

---

[50] For the argument that damages in *Francovich* primarily served a penal purpose see C. Harlow, '*Francovich* and the Problem of the Disobedient State' (1996) 2 *European Law Journal* 199.

[51] E. Szyszczak, 'Making Europe More Relevant to its Citizens' (1996) 21 *EL Rev.* 351; J. Steiner, 'From Direct Effects to *Francovich*: Shifting Means of Enforcement of Community Law' (1993) 18 *EL Rev.* 3; J. Tallberg, 'Supranational Influence in EU Enforcement: The ECJ and the Principle of State Liability' (2000) 7 *Journal of European Public Policy* 104.

[52] F. Snyder, 'The Effectiveness of European Community Law: Institutions, Processes, Tools and Techniques' (1993) 56 *MLR* 19.

[53] E.g, R. Macrory, 'The Enforcement of Community Environmental Laws: Some Critical Issues' (1992) 29 *CML Rev.* 348.

enforcement has even been described as a 'chimera'.[54] In this full sense, the EU legal system does not really offer an efficient system of legal accountability. The celebrated *Factortame* litigation, for example, responsible for two seminal principles of EU law, took more than twelve years to produce an outcome and necessitated multiple visits to the ECJ and House of Lords,[55] a saga beyond the reach of all but the richest and most determined litigants.[56]

Built up on proceedings brought in local courts and tribunals, the EU legal system is supposedly easy to access. In reality, the EU courts inevitably remain distant and the complex reference procedure is slow. Over the years, the case load of the Community courts has been rising steeply and with it, the delays.[57] Table 6.1 shows that neither the backlog nor the delays in the ECJ are improving, as it was hoped that they would after the creation of the CFI. The CFI is now building backlogs, to be ameliorated, it is hoped, by the power to sit in panels introduced at Nice, while the ECJ is being presented with a surprisingly large number of appeals. There is serious concern over the 'judicial architecture', shared by the ECJ. The two courts made representations to the Nice IGC,[58] in terms which seemed decidedly muted to many commentators, impressed with the urgency of the situation.[59] So far from providing effective remedies, the EU legal system, they argue, is in terminal crisis; enlargement could bring it tumbling to the ground.

But perhaps the very urgency of the situation will stimulate reflection about the nature and value of enforcement through legal remedy. Sectoral

[54] C. Harding, 'Member State Enforcement of European Community Measures: The Chimera of Effective Enforcement' (1997) 4 *Maastricht Journal of International and European Law* 5.

[55] The most important are: *R. v. Secretary of State for Transport ex p. Factortame (No. 1)* [1990] 2 AC 8; Case C–246/89R, *Commission v. UK* [1989] ECR 3125; *R. v. Secretary of State for Transport ex p. Factortame (No. 2)* [1990] 3 WLR 818; Case C–221/89, *R v. Secretary of State for Transport ex p. Factortame (No 3)* [1991] ECR I–3905; Joined Cases C–46/93 C–48/93, *Brasserie du Pêcheur SA v. Germany, R v. Transport Secretary ex p. Factortame (No 4)* [1996] ECR I-1029; *R v. Secretary of State for Transport ex p. Factortame (No 5)* [1999] 3 WLR 1062.

[56] For this reason, a preponderance of cases is brought by corporate bodies: see C. Harding, 'Who goes to Court in Europe? An Analysis of Litigation against the European Community' (1992) 17 *EL Rev.* 105.

[57] See further C. Harlow, 'Access to Justice as a Human Right: The European Convention and the EU' in P. Alston (ed.), *The European Union and Human Rights* (Oxford, Oxford University Press, 1999).

[58] ECJ, *The Future of the Judicial System of the European Union, Proposals and Reflections* (Luxembourg, ECJ, 1996).

[59] H. Rasmussen, 'Remedying the Crumbling EC Judicial System' (2000) 37 *CML Rev.* 1071; the Slynn Report, *The Role and Future of the Court of Justice* (London, British Institute of Comparative Law, 1996); C.Turner and R. Muñoz, 'Revising the Judicial Architecture of the European Union' (2000) 19 *Yearbook of European Law* 1.

Table 6.1 Actions and Outcomes in the ECJ

The first figure refers to preliminary references, the second to direct actions

		Cases Brought	Judgments	Cases dealt with	Average length of hearing in months
1995	ECJ	251 + 109	110 + 52	289	20.5, 17.1
	CFI	128	34	265	
1996	ECJ	256 + 132	123 + 59	349	20.8, 19.6
	CFI	118	66	186	
1999	ECJ*	255 + 214	135 + 72	395	21.2, 23.0
	CFI	254	63	659	12.6
2000	ECJ*	224 + 197	152 + 84	526	21.6, 23.9
	CFI	242	55	344	17.0

*In these years, the ECJ received 72 and 79 appeals and delivered judgement in 26 and 37.

studies suggest that the normative standards established in judgments of the ECJ are not necessarily diffused across the national boundaries. Nor do they act on national authorities to make and introduce amendments or change behaviour—a crucial element in accountability. In practice, diffusion depends very much on the fit between the decision to be implemented and the national policy environment into which it has to be imported.[60] The legal system is neither the only nor necessarily the most effective way to hold public services to account.

III EXPLAIN AND JUSTIFY

In a discussion of ways in which accountability can be imposed on regulatory regimes, Giandomenico Majone prioritizes legal accountability through procedural scrutiny. Majone's framework for accountability requires that:[61]

agencies are created by democratically enacted statutes which define the agencies' legal authority and objectives; that the regulators are appointed by elected officials; that regulatory decision-making follows formal rules which often require public participation; finally, that agency decisions must be justified and are open to judicial review. The simplest and most basic means of improving agency decision-making is to require regulators to give reasons for their decisions. This is because a

---

[60] F. Beveridge, S. Nott, K. Stephen, 'Addressing Gender in the Nation and Community: Law and Policymaking' in J. Shaw (ed.), *Social Law and Policy in an Evolving European Union* (Oxford, Hart Publishing, 2000), 143–7. See generally G. Teubner, 'Legal Irritants: Good Faith in British Law or How Unifying Law Ends Up in New Divergencies' (1998) 61 *MLR* 11.

[61] G. Majone, 'Causes and Consequences of Changes in the Mode of Governance' (1997) 17 *Journal of Public Policy* 139, 160.

giving-reasons requirement activates a number of other regulatory discretion, such as judicial review, public participation and deliberation, peer review, policy analysis to justify regulatory priorities and so on.

For Martin Shapiro,[62] reasoned decisions provide the basis for all judicial review of administrative discretion—arguably, indeed, for all judicial review. This would make reasoned decisions the fundamental premise of accountability, largely coincident with Oliver's duty to 'explain and justify'. In EU law, the duty to give reasons is imposed by TEC Article 253, which obliges the institutions to 'state the reasons on which [their decisions] are based'. The ECJ has not been slow to recognize the potential of this laconic requirement. The standard formula justifying reasoned decisions stresses the control function of judicial review, but also extends to an embryonic public principle of transparency. From early days the Court has insisted that:[63]

In imposing upon the Commission the obligation to state reasons for its decisions, Article 190 is not taking mere formal considerations into account but seeks to give an opportunity to the parties of defending their rights, to the Court of exercising its supervisory functions and to Member-states and to all interested nationals of ascertaining the circumstances in which the Commission has applied the Treaty.

The door was in this way opened to wider judicial protection of procedural rights through 'process review', the term used to describe review of the structure and procedure of administrative entities by courts. Popular with judges because it protects them against charges of judicial policy-making, process review is the main medium for the protection of private interests and control over administrative decision-making; indeed, in most administrative-law systems, it is the heartland of judicial review. In practice, process review is a powerful tool to enhance accountability and, to Shapiro, a perfect facade too behind which to disguise judicial forays into the merits of decisions—a licence for courts to 'run through, replay or reconstruct the decision-making process'.[64] Shapiro uses the term 'synoptic dialogue' to describe the extreme version of control exercised over executive agencies by the American courts, though 'hard-look review' is a commoner term for the phenomenon. Synoptic dialogue commits the administration to 'respond adequately not only to all issues actually raised by interested parties, but also to all issues. In short, the demand is that the agency do a perfect job of decision-making with the

---

[62] M. Shapiro, 'The Giving Reasons Requirement' [1992] *University of Chicago Legal Forum* 179, 180.

[63] A passage recurring in (e.g), Case 24/62, *Germany v. Commission* [1963] ECR 69; Case 37/83, *Rewe-Zentrale AG v. Direktor der Landwirtschaftskammer Rheinland* [1984] ECR 1229.

[64] N. 62 above, 183.

strong implication that the agency must arrive at the perfect, or at least the best, decision'.[65]

But Shapiro is writing of the USA, where synoptic dialogue is taken very seriously.[66] European jurisdictions tend to adopt a softer approach. When Shapiro wrote, the ECJ case law on procedural protection was in its early stages, while the Codes of Conduct concerning the right of access to information (see note 77 below) were not yet in place. It had long been settled law that the ECJ would evaluate the adequacy of reasons, but its attitude towards the fledgling Commission was sympathetic. Except in flagrant cases, the Commission was assumed to be doing its best and acting in the public interest; it must broadly outline its reasoning and give a clear indication of the facts on which its decision was based, but did not need to be too specific or to discuss every point which had arisen during administrative proceedings. Shapiro was right to conclude that the ECJ would be wary both of excessive proceduralism and of a drift to substantive review, though he also thought this attitude might change.

At first, the ECJ preferred to limit review to 'manifest error' or obvious misuse of power, although an occasional case indicated that the Court had doubts. In *Tradax*,[67] for example, a company wanted a sight of the basis on which levies on imported grain had been calculated, arguing that disclosure ought to be made as a 'good administrative practice'. The Commission replied that a duty to disclose would seriously impede proper management of the common market in agricultural products. This argument was accepted by the ECJ, on the ground that 'good administration' was an indeterminate notion, too wide to amount to 'a legally enforceable rule'. There was thus no precise legal basis for the claim. Yet although the Court refused to compel the Commission to reveal information to individuals or to concede an individual right to access the Commission file, it did try informally to steer the Commission in the direction of greater transparency, asserting that 'it would be consistent with good administration for the Commission to publish for the information of the traders concerned the main data taken into account'. Over the years, the ECJ has built up procedural rights from a common core, recognized in slightly varying forms in all major European legal systems.[68] The recent case law moves procedural control sharply towards synoptic dialogue. The CFI, established in 1988 partly to deal with

[65] Shapiro, n. 62 above, 206.
[66] Though see R. Stewart, '*Vermont Yankee* and the Evolution of Administrative Procedures' (1978) 91 *Harvard Law Review* 1821 and R. Stewart, 'Madison's Nightmare' (1990) 57 *University of Chicago Law Review* 335.
[67] Case 64/82, *Tradax Graanhandel BV v. Commission* [1984] ECR 1359.
[68] For a study of the development of process review in EU law see H.-P. Nehl, *Principles of Administrative Law* (Oxford, Hart Publishing, 1998).

complex cases,[69] now handles the bulk of complex litigation against the EU institutions. Like the US courts, it takes its scrutiny function very seriously; indeed, Hans-Peter Nehl describes the establishment of the new court as an essential factor in establishing real control of Commission investigations in competition cases. After a careful evaluation of the case law, Nehl concludes that we are seeing:[70]

a more active and thorough fact finding and evaluation. [The CFI] would show enhanced responsiveness to the factual points and evidence put forward by the parties to the litigation as well as a more intrusive stance in scrutinising whether the challenged administrative acts were well-founded. . . . Against this backdrop certain process standards, such as the principle of care and the duty to give reasons, were not unlikely to develop into appropriate instruments for scrupulously reviewing administrative measures.

Today, Shapiro's prophecy of a likely judicial trend towards synoptic dialogue and hard-look process review is being fulfilled. Reasoned decision-making and conformity with procedural prerequisites is being required of the Commission and other EU agencies. Again in conformity with Shapiro's expectations,[71] the Courts are carrying process review into the realm of indirect and mixed administration. *Technische Universität München*[72] for the first time imposed a duty to give interested parties the opportunity of a hearing in composite proceedings involving both national and EU bodies. This case reveals the dynamic nature of the case law, as it introduces a new obligation on 'the competent institution to examine carefully all the relevant aspects of the individual case'.[73] It recognizes the importance of 'joined-up government' in a multi-level system.

Closely linked to the duty to give reasons is a right of access to one's personal file, justified on the triple ground of 'good administration' (ensuring accuracy); permitting interested parties to protect their legal interests; and enabling the judiciary to carry out its control function of reviewing the legality of administrative action.[74] It is not surprising to find that the two lines of reasoning have come together, to the point that access to information is beginning to be seen as one of the rights of due process recognized by EC law.[75] The link was spelled out in the important *Worldwide Fund for Nature*

[69] The CFI was set up in 1988 (TEC Art. 225) to handle staff and competition cases against the institutions; further transfers have since been made. Preliminary rulings (TEC Art. 234) were until Nice reserved for the ECJ, which also hears appeals from the CFI.

[70] Nehl, n. 68 above, 8–9.

[71] Shapiro, n. 62 above, 342.

[72] Case C–269/90, *Hauptzollamt München-Mitte v. Technische Universität München* [1991] ECR I–5469.

[73] Nehl, n. 68 above, 133.

[74] C. Harlow, 'Freedom of Information and Transparency as Administrative and Constitutional Rights' (2000) 2 *Cambridge Yearbook of European Law* 285.

[75] Nehl, n. 68 above, 39–69.

(WWF) judgment,[76] where the CFI drew the analogy between the Treaty right to reasons and general information rights.

Consonant with this attitude, the Community courts, though largely the CFI, which has primary jurisdiction in the majority of applications under the Code of Conduct for access, have been prepared to hold the institutions strictly to the Codes of Conduct on public access[77] as a vehicle for assuring legal accountability. The Courts could easily have held the codes to be internal administrative documents, which did not give rise to justiciable rights; significantly, from the outset, they resisted this narrow approach. Even in the disappointingly restrictive case of *Netherlands* v. *Council*,[78] the ECJ accepted jurisdiction before ruling that access to documents was a matter of institutional procedure, probably because the ECJ has always jealously protected its own jurisdiction, construing it widely. The point was confirmed by the CFI in the *WWF* judgment, where the Court stated that the Code was 'capable of conferring on third parties legal rights'. Having established its jurisdiction, however, the CFI did *not* go on to grant access, but confirmed the Commission's use of the public interest exception to privilege documentation received during the administrative stages of infringement procedure brought under TEC Article 226. The obligation imposed on the Commission was no more than to indicate its reasons for refusing access with sufficient detail for the court to confirm that the they properly related to potential infringement proceedings. This did not mean that the reasons had to be so specific as to allow the contents of the documents to be guessed.

Other cases have been more successful. In the early *Carvel* case,[79] the European affairs editor of *The Guardian* newspaper applied under the Code of Practice for access to a number of documents of the Justice and Agriculture Councils. On refusal, he applied for review of the Council decision. The CFI ruled that, although access could lawfully be refused under the 'public interest' proviso to the Code of Conduct, the decision must be based on a genuine exercise of discretion, weighing the individual right of access against the Community's interest in confidentiality. The documentation, plus a declaration from the Danish and Dutch governments as to what had taken place in Council, persuaded the CFI that no adequate balancing exercise had taken place. *Carvel* was a breakthrough in establishing the justiciability of the

---

[76] Case T–105/95, *WWF (United Kingdom) v. Commission* [1997] ECR II–313.

[77] Council Decision 93/731/EC [1993] OJ L340 41 and Code of Conduct, n. 51 above, 43; Commission Decision 94/90 EC on public access to Commission documents [1994] OJ L46/58; Council Decision of 14 Aug. 2000 amending Decision 93/731/EC on public access to Council documents and Council Decision 2000/23/EC on the improvement of information on the Council's legislative activities and the public register of Council documents [2001] OJ L212 9. And see above, 40.

[78] Case C–58/94, *Netherlands v. Council* [1996] ECR I–2169. Above, 38-9.

[79] Case T–194/94, *Carvel and Guardian Newspapers v. Council* [1995] ECR II–2769.

Code; it was equally important in establishing that decision-making under the Code in respect of Third-Pillar documents was subject to review by the CFI—another important breakthrough in transparency and accountability. The *Carvel* reasoning has been applied in further cases, which usually turn on the failure of one of the institutions to give sufficiently precise reasons why access to documents is refused. In the *Swedish Journalists'* case,[80] where the applicants were deliberately testing the Code of Conduct against the wider Swedish rules of openness, they had applied under Swedish law for documents used by the Justice Council, obtaining around 80 per cent. Under EU law, the Council released just 20 per cent. The CFI annulled the decision, though only on the narrow ground that inadequate reasons for refusal had been given, a 'halfway house' solution which allows for further refusal, based on more appropriate grounds. Finally, in *Hautala*[81] the CFI hinted that it might be prepared to treat access to information as a general democratic right, reference being made also to proportionality, the most important of the Courts' general principles. The proportionality principle is important in securing accountability, as it requires an administrative measure to be appropriate, and also necessary to achieve the desired objectives. This is a balancing test which allows the court to examine the evidence and weigh the 'means against the ends', consequently permitting, at the court's discretion, an unusual degree of intensity of judicial review.[82]

From the standpoint of accountability, the development by the ECJ and CFI of this procedural case law cannot be over-estimated. The courts have undoubtedly helped to introduce into EU decision-making a greater measure of transparency and heightened respect on the part of the EU authorities for individual rights and interests. Their position will no doubt be strengthened by the introduction of the European Charter of Fundamental Rights, adopted at Nice on a non-binding basis. This text has been praised by the European Ombudsman for introducing a chapter on citizens' rights creating a right to good administration (Article 41). This includes the two principles on which we have seen the Courts place especial emphasis: the right to be heard and the right of access to one's file. The Charter confirms the duty to give reasons. The Charter does not specifically protect transparency but does provide (Article 42) that '[a]ny citizen of the Union, and any natural or legal person residing or having its registered office in Member State, has a right of access to European Parliament, Council and Commission documents', surely approbation of the Court's judicial handiwork.

---

[80] Case T–174/95, *Svenska Journalistforbundet v. Council* [1998] ECR II–2289.

[81] Case T–14/98, *Hautala v. Council* [1999] ECR 11–2489 ref. For discussion of both cases see 40.

[82] T. Tridimas, 'Proportionality in Community Law: Searching for the Appropriate Standard of Scrutiny' in E. Ellis (ed.), *The Principle of Proportionality in the Laws of Europe* (Oxford, Hart Publishing, 1999), 66.

We need, though, to be careful before equating procedural justice too closely with the public accountability on which this book has focused. One view of the EU, as already indicated, is as a regulator and protector of the public interest against powerful and predatory corporations. It is therefore a matter of some importance that the Commission shall have the tools to do the regulatory job. Recent cases on procedural protections are less an exercise in accountability and more a saga of delay and obstruction by powerful corporate players. Even if, at the end of the day, the CFI does not annul a decision, the time and energy of Commission officials have been consumed. Mark Galanter sees American multi-national commercial concerns as well placed to play transnational 'law games', predicting that their dominance will result in judicialization of Commission and EU procedures.[83] Amongst competition lawyers in particular, there are genuine fears that the Commission's regulatory powers may soon be 'undermined to such an extent that it is no longer capable of successfully fulfilling its role as guardian of competition'.[84] This is a misuse of procedural protection and a travesty of accountability.

IV CONCLUSIONS

The liberal democratic theory discussed in the first section of this chapter, which sets law at the centre of constitutional machinery for securing limited government and accountability, may be justified in terms of neutrality and effectiveness, both important qualities in establishing public trust. An effective and accessible justice system is also the way to provide the element of individual redress and reparation and, where appropriate, sanction, which form essential components of accountability systems. But important choices have to be made about the proper balance between different forms of accountability and the extent to which, in any given situation, legal, political, or regulatory accountability is preferable. The principle of judicial autonomy often makes these choices hard to make.

Systems of legal accountability tend to be left to the care of the judiciary. They expand and retract as judges think appropriate, passing through active and passive periods, as the EU judicial system has done. In the early, formative years, the ECJ built from the shadowy, two-tier structure outlined in the Articles of the Treaties, a formidable machine for exacting legal accountability. After the Treaty of Maastricht, when the subsidiarity

---

[83] M. Galanter, 'Predators and Parasites: Lawyer-Bashing and Civil Justice' (1994) 28 *Georgia Law Review* 633.

[84] D. Stevens, 'Covert Collusion' (1995) 15 *Yearbook of European Law* 46, 48, citing especially the Woodpulp II cases: Cases C–89/85 and others, *Ahlström Osakeyhtiö and others v. Commission* [1993] ECR I–1307.

principle was installed in the Treaties, judicial creativity was reined back.[85] A degree of respect, evident in the early days of the system, is again shown for national, procedural autonomy. Integration has slowed, judicial attitudes have changed towards the way in which TEC Article 234 should be used by national courts, and a cautious note has crept into judgments in the area of remedies and damages.

The enormous achievement of the ECJ in constructing a system of legal accountability must not be underrated, but we should not be inhibited either from asking how far legal accountability should be allowed to go. In an important contribution to the debate over accountability, Daniel Wincott has advanced the argument that courts ought not to be overly anxious to step in to fill the 'democratic deficit'.[86] By tilting the balance of power too far towards a non-accountable judiciary, courts may weaken the political process, a regression called by Wincott the 'perversion of democracy'. In the case of the EU, the two-tier system of governance renders the process more complex. Judicial eagerness to step in and fill the accountability gap at Union level may rebound on the constitutional balance between executive and legislative organs at national level, cutting down 'domestic mechanisms of democratic accountability'. Similarly, relocation of power from national to the Union judiciary, anti-democratic only in the sense that it substitutes one form of elite government for another, can 'subvert' national democracy by shifting the balance of power to the EU.

A substantial relocation of power from parliamentary institutions towards a non-elected judiciary is a feature of transnational governance, linked to the dominance there of economic and commercial interests, comfortable with legal process because of its autonomy from political interests. Attempts to ward off accusations of bias towards economic and property interests in the judicial process are typically countered by moves to bind the judiciary through the standards of human rights. Once these are incorporated in judicially enforceable charters, the inevitable consequence is a further accretion of judicial power. At national, transnational, and international levels, these shifts are already occurring, a matter of self-congratulation for many lawyers. The erosion of democracy should not be allowed to continue

---

[85] The turning point is often said to be the judgment of the ECJ in Cases C–267, 268/91, *Keck and Mithouard* [1993] ECR I–6097, placing limits on the reach of TEC Art. 30 and refining the famous 'Cassis de Dijon' principle. See N. Reich, 'The "November Revolution" of the European Court of Justice: *Keck, Meng* and *Audi* Revisited' (1994) 31 *CML Rev.* 459.

[86] D. Wincott, 'Does the European Union Pervert Democracy? Questions of Democracy in New Constitutionalist Thought on the Future of Europe' (1999) 4 *European Law Journal* 411. See also D. Chryssochoou, 'Democracy and Symbiosis in the European Union: Towards a Confederal Consociation?' (1994) 17 *W. European Politics* 1.

without consideration whether a heightened degree of legal accountability to individuals is likely to end in inhibiting, possibly even superseding, the forms of collective political and democratic accountability which modern society has learned to value most highly.[87]

[87] P. Cerny, 'Globalization and the End of Democracy' (1999) 36 *European Journal of Political Research* 1.

7

Accountability and European Governance

I THE CHANGING FACE OF EUROPEAN GOVERNANCE

Four decades of steady if discontinuous progress towards European unity
have, at the start of this new millennium, been replaced by a feeling of great
uncertainty. The European Union has lost its sense of mission. It no longer
knows where it is going. Decades of cold war are seemingly over, leaving
behind them widespread economic and political uncertainty. Externally, the
European Union has had to confront the threat of European war on a scale
which it had hoped never to see replicated. Internally, it faces the delicate task
of incorporating a large number of new entrants, many in transition towards
economic liberalism and with fragile democratic institutions. The Nice IGC,
at which the institutional problems consequent on enlargement were to be
resolutely tackled, resulted in virtual stalemate. It failed notably to resolve
institutional problems[1] and, after the adverse referendum vote in Ireland, is
in any case not yet in force.

At the very moment when the Union has lost confidence in its system of
government, the governance of Europe has become an issue of importance.
The period of assumed consensus, in which an idealistic elite determined the
modalities of European government, without demands for any significant
measure of accountability, is undoubtedly over. Our societies are drifting into
a new era of populist government, which leaves the Union in a position of
obvious weakness. It has never been clear whether the European Union
actually has any 'citizens';[2] if, as the Commission insists, it has, then there
is a sense that it has lost touch with them. The EU professes democracy, on
which it is said to be founded (TEU Article 6(1)). A serious breach of the

---

[1] X. Yataganas, 'The Treaty of Nice: The Sharing of Power and the Institutional Balance
in the European Union—A Continental Perspective' (2001) 7 *European Law Journal* 242.

[2] See for discussion J. Weiler, 'Does Europe Need a Constitution? Reflections on Demos,
Telos and the German Maastricht Decision' (1995) 1 *European Law Journal* 219; D.
Chryssochoou, 'Europe's Could-be Demos: Recasting the Debate' (1996) 19 *W. European
Politics* 787; J. Shaw, 'The Interpretation of European Citizenship' (1998) 61 *MLR* 293.

principles of democracy (undefined) is ground for suspension (TEU Article 7). Yet the EU is not itself a modern democracy in the sense of 'a political system in which rulers are held accountable for their policies and actions in the public realm by citizens, and where competing elites offer alternative programmes and vie for popular support at the European level'.[3] Organized civil society, necessary to voice the concerns of citizens, is weak, while Europe-wide political institutions have not taken root.[4] This is not a simple matter of the ballot box but involves a more complex set of relationships, about which the European Union institutions have consistently expressed concern but with no very clear vision of how the problems can be rectified. Every IGC and every meeting of the European Council mentions the need to resolve the allegedly critical problem of 'connecting Europe with its citizens'. According to the most recent Declaration, made at Laeken,[5] 'people' want the European institutions to be:

less unwieldy and rigid and above all, more efficient and open. Many feel also that the Union should involve itself more with their particular concerns instead of intervening, in every detail, in matters best left by their nature to Member States' and regions' elected representatives. This is even perceived by some as a threat to their identity. More important, however, they feel that deals are too often cut out of their sight and they want better democratic scrutiny.

This perception, if true, affects democratic accountability in its simplest and most compelling sense.

The Member States of the European Union are said by the Swedish political economist, Sverker Gustavsson, to be faced in their search for democracy and accountability with a number of different options.[6] The journey towards suprastatism has reached a *provisional* stage in which we are faced with a dangerous degree of democratic deficit. Two diametrically opposed paths lead away from the abyss. On the one hand, suprastatism can be abandoned; we can move back into our national trenches, a solution which could mean abandoning the Single Market altogether or, more plausibly, reverting to a regime more like the World Trade Organization. Both the concept of subsidiarity as expressed in TEU Article 3(b) and the Third-Pillar arrangements are in a sense steps in this direction, the second in particular implying 'living together without marriage'. In terms of accountability,

---

[3] S. Andersen and T. Burns, 'The European Union and the Erosion of Parliamentary Democracy: A Study of Post-parliamentary Governance' in S. Andersen and K. Eliassen (eds.), *The European Union: How Democratic Is It?* (London, Sage, 1996), 227.
[4] S. Hix, *The Political System of the European Union* (Basingstoke, Macmillan, 1999).
[5] Laeken Declaration—The Future of the European Union, SN 273/01, Laeken, 15 Dec. 200, 2.
[6] S. Gustavsson, 'Reconciling Suprastatism and Accountability: A View from Sweden' in C. Hoskyns and M. Newman (eds.), *Democratizing the European Union, Issues for the Twenty-first Century* (Manchester, Manchester University Press, 2000).

both developments imply national and subnational solutions in which responsibility for accountability will return to national institutions and political accountability will be confirmed according to the national recipe. This is not a narrow chauvinistic viewpoint. Those who share the view that globalization is the insuperable enemy of democracy,[7] or think it unrealistic to expect people to govern themselves in mass modern societies,[8] or who simply fear leaving the known security of the (Westphalian) nation state,[9] will naturally prefer this outcome. On the other hand, we can try to democratize suprastatism, likely to prove a slow and immensely difficult process. These stark alternatives lie at the heart of every debate over governance, and similarly of every conception of accountability discussed in this book. It is on this terrain that the European Union's fiercest political battles have been fought, though never honestly faced or finally resolved.

In Gustavvson's condition of 'provisional suprastatism', the European Union is justified in terms of delegation, but only to the extent that the limit of the delegation was foreseen at the time of delegation.[10] This is the point now reached and authorized for Germany by the *Maastricht* decision of the Bundesverfassungsgericht.[11] We could continue in a situation which, with fairly stringent enforcement of the subsidiarity principle, would rule out the wilder policy initiatives of the Commission and restrain judicial activism in the ECJ. In practice, however, we are fast drifting towards suprastatism, with integrationists pushing for faster integration, presented as the road to democracy and accountability through the medium of a written, federal, or quasi-federal constitution for the European Union. Two further options remain to us according to Gustavvson. The first is to 'surrender representation', a solution unpalatable in principle to exponents of pluralism and majoritarian democracy, though attractive to proponents of elite government.[12] A measure of control and accountability could still arguably be retained at European level through the interplay of the institutions, the doctrine of institutional balance, and through the Charter of Fundamental Rights. The second option is to abandon accountability 'in favour of a system of government which is independent rather than

[7] P. Cerny, 'Globalization and the End of Democracy' (1999) 36 *European Journal of Political Research* 1; P. Allott, 'European Governance and the Re-branding of Democracy' (2002) 27 *EL Rov.* 60.

[8] Gustavvson, n. 6 above.

[9] R. Cooper, *The Post-Modern State and the World Order* (London, Demos, 1996).

[10] S. Gustavsson, 'Defending the Democratic Deficit', in A. Weale and M. Nentwich (eds.), *Political Theory and the EU, Legitimacy, Constitutional Choice and Citizenship* (London, Routledge, 1998).

[11] Bundesverfassungsgericht, 2nd chamber (Senat) Cases BvR 2134/92 and 2 BvR 2159/92 (12 Oct. 1993) BVerfGE 89, 155.

[12] Gustavsson, n. 10 above, citing the work of E. Grande, 'Demokratische Legitimation und Europäische Integration' (1996) 24 *Leviathan* 339.

accountable, and which derives its legitimacy from the fact that, instead of being majoritarian in character, it is based on expertise, and is beyond the reach besides of public opinion, parliaments and electorates'.[13] At least to the present author, both propositions are equally unpalatable.

Gustavvson is, however, speaking of political accountability in its most general sense of electoral accountability, a power which the peoples of the EU do not in any event possess. It may indeed be correct that majoritarian democracy is an inappropriate paradigm for the Union tier of the EU but this does not imply, as Gustavvson suggests, that the search for *accountability* must be abandoned. It is still possible, while leaving the crucial puzzle of democratic deficit unresolved, to search for accountability via non-majoritarian means.[14] Indeed, one way to interpret the very powerful movement for integration through law is as an experiment in accountability.[15] The EU could learn to live with the democratic deficit inherent in its asymmetrical structure, and experiment with new, non-majoritarian approaches to accountability.

II GOVERNMENT AND GOVERNANCE

Currently, the EU has on the table four rather different exercises in governance, which have not been properly co-ordinated. These are: the partially concluded exercise in drafting the Charter of Fundamental Rights; the Commission's White Paper on European Governance; the Commission working papers and position papers on reform of the Commission; and the Convention recently established to advise on a European constitution. It will be argued here that these do not promote a single, common objective; that they appear to be premised on rather different values; and, crucially, that they operate against the background of the two very different visions of European union. But the difference of opinion over a top-down, integrated Union and a 'Europe of the nations' lies at the heart of problems over an institutional framework for Europe, and unless the European Council is prepared to resolve it or submit it for resolution to the peoples of Europe, no draftsman is likely to be able to formulate coherent proposals.

---

[13] Ibid.

[14] R. Dehousse, 'Constitutional Reform in the European Community. Are there Alternatives to the Majoritarian Avenue?' (1995) 18 *W. European Politics* 118.

[15] Amongst the copious literature, see particularly: J. Weiler, 'Journey to an Unknown Destination: A Retrospective and Prospective of the European Court of Justice in the Arena of Political Integration' (1993) 31 *Journal of Common Market Studies* 417; A.-M. Burley and W. Mattli, 'Europe Before the Court: A Political Theory of Legal Integration' (1993) 47 *International Organization* 41.

The Model of Government

One way to explain the key difference in approach between the different exercises would be in terms of two models, here termed for convenience the models of *government* and of *governance*. James Caporaso has characterized the former as institutional and constitutional in character.[16] It is premised on an idealized model of liberal democratic government as it might operate in an autonomous nation state and, as experienced in debates over the future of Europe, there is a strong legal input, since democratic government, though prioritized by the Treaties, is always tempered by the rule of law. At its strongest, the model envisages government as confined also within the framework of a written constitution. This is a model which, in recent years, has been pushed strongly by Germany and is currently at the very top of the EU agenda. It has been confirmed by Convention President Valéry Giscard d'Estaing that 'the Convention will consider amongst the options the plan for a Europe organised along federal lines, as put forward by high-level German decision-makers in particular'.[17]

As this book has tried to indicate, however, there are many problems in trying to fit the EU and its evolving institutions within the model of government. The EU does not sit easily within the theory of formal separation of powers used as an analytic tool by many constitutional lawyers.[18] Its dual legislature is unusual, vesting plenary legislative power in a Council of Ministers which relies for its legitimacy on national elections yet is not accountable to national parliaments. Attempts to square the circle by describing Council and Parliament as two chambers of a European legislature are artificial and undercut both the institutional balance of the Union and the unique concept of 'Community method'. The situation is in terms of accountability an unhappy one, and the constitutional arrangements at Union level do nothing to alleviate the problem, since they allow both Member States and the Council to bypass such machinery for accountability as exists by resorting to inter-governmental co-operation, 'Third-Pillar methods', or possibly the procedures of 'closer co-operation', all of which undercut the authority of the European Parliament. The effect is to undo the progress made in twentieth-century democracies towards holding governments accountable for their actions in the field of foreign affairs. In Lodge's terms,[19] a yawning accountability gap has been opened, which the

[16] J. Caporaso, 'The European Union and Forms of State: Westphalian, Regulatory or Post-Modern?' (1996) 34 *Journal of Common Market Studies* 34, 37.

[17] Speech at the inauguration of the Constitutional Convention: **www.europa.eu.int/ futurum**.

[18] K. Lenaerts, 'Some Reflections on the Separation of Powers in the European Community' (1991) 28 *CML Rev.* 11.

[19] J. Lodge, 'The European Parliament', in S. Andersen and K. Eliassen (eds.), *The European Union: How Democratic Is It?* (London, Sage, 1996), further discussed in Chap. 4.

two-tier structure of national parliaments and European Parliament, jealous of power-sharing, has so far been unable to fill. A clear division of competence between the two tiers of government, currently under discussion in the Convention, might do something to alleviate this problem but it will not attack its roots.

An alternative solution to problems of accountability in a framework of separation of powers has been put forward by Peter Lindseth.[20] American in origin, his explanation draws much from experience of American executive regulatory agencies, which do have to operate within a constitutional framework of strict separation of powers. According to Lindseth, both Commission and European Union are creatures of delegation, a view which situates them for purposes of both legitimacy and accountability inside a hierarchical structure. The Commission's accountability is that of agent to principal, and it is this which 'first and foremost gives policy-making in the administrative sphere a democratic veneer, if not full democratic legitimacy'.[21] Based on a theory of executive delegation, this analysis is, of course, a good fit with American administrative law, and is also consonant with the formal theory of sovereignty used by English constitutional lawyers to explain away the supremacy of EC law.[22] In an unprecedented elevation of the doctrine of subsidiarity, Lindseth's theory clearly subordinates the Union to its Member States, technically the principals in this fictional transaction. It follows therefore that national institutions must take full responsibility for democratic accountability. Such an analysis is deeply problematic in the EU context, where there is no federal government, and no directly elected equivalent to the American President, constitutionally responsible for the executive function. As Lindseth himself admits, application of his theory in the EU might trigger a reversion to the days of elite governance when a virtually autonomous and unaccountable Brussels bureaucracy took the lead in policy-making,[23] an untenable position today.

Similar criticism can be addressed to the work of Giandomenico Majone, who also seeks the answer to the dual problems of legitimacy and accountability in classical, Madisonian doctrines of power-sharing. For Majone who, like Lindseth, sees the Commission as a species of regulatory agency, and the core activity of the EU as regulation of competition and monopoly in the

[20] P. Lindseth, 'Democratic Legitimacy and the Administrative Character of Supranationalism: The Example of the European Community' (1999) 99 *Columbia Law Review* 628. See also M. Everson, 'Administering Europe?' (1998) 36 *Journal of Common Market Studies* 195.

[21] Lindseth, n. 20 above, at 646.

[22] H.W.R. Wade, 'The Basis of Legal Sovereignty' [1955] *Cambridge Law Journal* 172; P. Craig, 'Parliamentary Sovereignty of the United Kingdom Parliament after Factortame' (1991) 11 *Yearbook of European Law* 221.

[23] See P. Craig, 'The Nature of the Community: Integration, Democracy, and Legitimacy', in P. Craig and G. de Búrca (eds), *The Evolution of EU Law* (Oxford, Oxford University Press, 1999), 32–6.

global market, efficiency is necessarily a paramount value and delay and complexity are unacceptable.[24] From such a standpoint, alternative means of accountability will be essential. In a passage redolent of American constitutionalism, Majone advocates procedural legitimacy, monitored by courts in 'hard-look review' as a non-majoritarian answer to these problems. In the United States, on which Majone bases his ideal-type, a vibrant political society is, however, in being; in the context of the European Union, where this precondition of democratic accountability is lacking, American constitutionalism could prove a dangerous blind alley.

Ironically, a diametrically opposed vision of the same hierarchical relationship puts the Union in the position of principal, with national governments and parliaments as agents.[25] In terms of accountability, both positions for different reasons demand strong control of policy at Union level. The inverted principal/agent relationship would, for example, involve conceding that co-decision procedure in legislation should become the norm, ruling out reversion to the so-called 'old procedures', thus rendering Council and Commission invariably accountable to the democratically elected European Parliament through the law-making process. Equally, it would suggest heightened control by the parliamentary machinery for scrutiny examined in Chapter 4. Both developments would, for very obvious reasons, be unacceptable alike to inter-governmentalists and, more seriously, to national parliaments, which would have to accept a significant limitation of their powers, with possible reduction of status in areas of EU competence to that of a consultative body. (This is very like the stance taken towards national parliaments by the Commission in its White Paper on Governance.) Many of the national parliaments would deeply resent such a diminution of their standing. Moves in such a direction would therefore be likely to lessen co-operation between national parliaments and the European Parliament, with a consequently detrimental effect on representative democracy in Europe.

A further difficulty with Lindseth's analysis is that it fits neither the present machinery devised to deal with the problem of inter-governmental law-making nor that currently under consideration by the Commission. At administrative level, the machinery for ensuring that EU action is compatible with national arrangements is provided by the untidy web of committees described in earlier chapters, whose task it is to feed into the EU policy-making processes information about the compatibility of EU policy with national needs and arrangements. This system, as we saw in Chapter 2, raises

---

[24] G. Majone, 'The Rise of the Regulatory State in Europe' (1994) 17 *W. European Politics* 77.

[25] J. Steiner, 'From Direct Effects to *Francovich*: Shifting Means of Enforcement of Community Law' (1993) 18 *EL Rev.* 3.

its own severe problems of accountability. Committees, in common with regulators and regulatory agencies, soon acquire a life of their own. This may in time involve them in illegitimate policy-making for which they need to be held accountable, or it may involve a form of 'agency capture', whereby the committee falls into the hands of an industry or group of experts. Although, as we saw, steps have been taken to render the Comitology more accountable, these are by no means completed nor are they adequate.

The solution propounded by the Commission in its White Paper on Governance is for purposes of accountability hardly more attractive than what we now have. The White Paper proposes[26] simpler and more efficient legislative procedures, recommending resort to Council regulations whenever uniform application of EU rules and legal certainty across Europe are considered desirable (by whom?). On the other hand, the Commission recommends frequent resort by the Council to 'outline' or 'framework' legislation, which would leave the Commission to fill in 'technical details', its reasoning being that such texts are 'less heavy-handed, offer greater flexibility as to their implementation, and tend to be agreed more quickly by Council and the European Parliament'.[27] Another way to put this might be that wide, imprecise, outline proposals leave less scope for accountability to representative bodies, while at the same time greatly expanding the scope of Commission discretion in implementation. The White Paper also suggests greater use of 'co-regulation', a method of regulating which combines legislation with 'soft law' instruments,[28] created through Commission-motored processes which would involve the 'stakeholders' in the activity to be regulated in the preparation and enforcement of the regulation. This again is somewhat less than democratic; indeed, it is an open invitation to factionalism and self-interested participation. The Commission's response to such criticisms is, however, to add the proviso that 'organisations participating in co-regulation must be 'representative, accountable and capable of following open procedures'.[29]

All this necessarily raises the question why this procedure, which so greatly dilutes the accountability of the Commission to the EU's elected assemblies, is being substituted for standard EU legislative procedures. Precisely the same question needs to be asked in respect of the 'open method of co-ordination', a technique designed by the Commission to enhance co-operative action

---

[26] European Commission, White Paper on European Governance, COM (2001) 428 Final [2001] OJ C287/1, (hereafter WPG).

[27] Ibid., 20.

[28] For explanation see K. Wellens and G. Borchardt, 'Soft Law in European Community Law' (1989) 14 *EL Rev.* 267; F. Snyder, 'Soft Law and Institutional Practice in the European Community' in S. Martin (ed.), *The Construction of Europe, Essays in Honour of Emile Noel* (Dordrecht, Kluwer, 1994).

[29] WPG, n. 26 above, 20.

through the 'exchange of best practice and agreeing common targets and guidelines for Member States'.[30] Because of its 'light touch', this method of governance is likely to prove attractive to inter-governmentalists. They should, however, be put on guard by the Commission's example of use of the method in areas of employment, social policy, and, above all, *immigration*, bringing a reminder of the technique used in Third-Pillar policy-making, whereby national parliaments, to which governments remained theoretically accountable, are presented with the *fait accompli* of EU policy. In short, these proposals entirely fail to deal adequately with concerns over accountability in the key law-making area of models of limited, constitutional government, although it will be suggested later that they can be incorporated into a new accountability system.

Once again, the EU is moving in two directions at once. On the one hand, the European Council is asking the Convention for a proposal which will establish a clear demarcation of national and Union competences within the framework of some sort of constitution or, in the language of the Convention President, a 'constitutional treaty'; for its part, the Commission is moving towards a fluid and flexible theory of governance which will end in an increase of Commission discretion at the expense of more representative and accountable political actors. It comes as no surprise to find that the White Paper contains no proposals for enhancement of Commission accountability in institutional terms—although a justification for this serious omission might be that the Commission is working within the present parameters of the Treaties and with special regard to the 'Community method', defined in the White Paper in a distinctly unusual fashion to mean little more than a division of functions between the Commission, Council of Ministers and ECJ.[31] Again, it will be suggested in the concluding paragraphs that these two viewpoints can—and must—be co-ordinated.

The exercises conducted by the two Conventions set up by the European Council first to draft a European Charter of Fundamental Rights and, secondly, to work towards a constitution for the European Union,[32] are clearly constitutional in character. They fit, and are to be understood, within the model of government. The Charter of Fundamental Rights was always seen as forming part of a wider debate about the future of Europe and the most committed proponents of the Charter are also committed to the idea of an EU constitution, seeing the Charter both as an integral part of a constitutional settlement and as a long step forward towards a written constitution. The Charter is also seen as an element in accountability, both by those who favour a greater degree of integration and those who see in a written consti-

---

[30] Ibid.
[31] Ibid., 8. And see explanatory note MEMO/02/102
[32] Laeken Declaration, n. 5 above.

tution the best hope of propelling power downwards, to a 'bottom-weighted', pseudo-federal state with clearly designated competences and limited powers for the European Union and its institutions.[33] This line of reasoning forms an important thread in the accountability debate, since the main motivation for a written constitution is, from both standpoints, to achieve the 'liberal-legal' ideal of government limited by law. The draft text produced by the Charter Convention was endorsed by the Nice IGC, but as an advisory and not a binding document, for the time being undercutting its potency in this respect.

The experiment with the Charter Convention led on, however, to an altogether more ambitious project authorized by the European Council at Laeken, in the shape of a Convention with a mandate to 'identify the key issues for the Union's future development and the various possible responses'. It is not this time suggested that the result will be the text of a draft constitution but a 'document with options and recommendations' to form the basis of discussion at the IGC of 2003. As yet in its early stages, the exercise has been described by President Romano Prodi as 'a path to a constitution for European citizens'. In a speech on the same occasion,[34] Convention President Giscard d'Estaing suggested that, if a broad consensus were to be achieved on a single proposal, that proposal would be submitted to the European Council, *as a possible blueprint for 'a constitution for Europe'*. The most important of the issues on the Convention's order paper is the thorny issue of a better and clearer division of competence between the EU and Member States, already singled out for particular attention in the Laeken Declaration. Also on the agenda are the perennial questions of more democracy, transparency, and efficiency, together with the secondary issue of simplification and reorganization of the system of legislation and 'the document prepared by the European Commission on modernising the Community method'.

In the case of the Charter of Fundamental Rights, the European Council for the first time delegated its constitution-making responsibilities to a Convention composed of representatives of the people instead of the usual delegation to public servants and functionaries. The introduction of this novel procedure, designed to legitimate the Council, could theoretically make it both more transparent and more accountable to the European public. The Commission, in principle responsible for developing law-making initiatives, had only one representative. There were instead thirty representatives from national parliaments and sixteen from the European Parliament, sufficient in principle to outweigh the votes of the fifteen governmental

---

[33] C. Dorau and P. Jacobi, 'The Debate over a "European Constitution": Is it Solely a German Concern?' (2000) 6 *European Public Law* 413.

[34] N. 18 above.

representatives. Paying lip-service to the concept of accountability through transparency and participation, the Convention carried out its work in public, organized an interactive website, and consulted with non-governmental organizations seen as representative of civil society. Marginally more democratic than the Charter Convention, the Constitutional Convention is composed of fifteen governmental representatives, with thirteen from the Enlargement States; thirty representatives from national parliaments and sixteen from the EP, with a further twenty-six from the parliaments of Enlargement States. Representatives of civil society, in the shape of the Ecosoc, the Committee of the Regions, and social partners are to be admitted as observers.[35] Again, there is to be a period for initial consultation of 'the people', through an interactive website and auditions. In reality, both experiments remain very questionable in terms of legitimacy and accountability—a fig-leaf intended to deflect attention from the requirements of *true* democratic accountability. There has been no prior consultation of national parliaments, the real institutions of democracy, on the need for either a Charter of Rights or a European constitution, while at the end of the day the only true citizen input will come through a referendum to approve or reject implementing Treaty modifications. This, though it is a form of democratic accountability, is a once-and-for-all procedure, hardly appropriate to the circumstances.[36]

The Model of Governance

The term 'governance', less familiar than government, is an imprecise term with several sets of meanings. Caporaso sees governance as a process of collective problem-solving and use of the term 'directs attention to the problems to be solved and to the processes associated with solving them, rather than to the relevant agents or to the nature of the political institutions associated with these processes'.[37] One reason the term may have been brought into use in the context of transnational and global political orders is to sever governance from the institutions of the modern nation state, regarded by internationalists as an outdated tool.[38]

[35] In addition to the President, ex-(French) Prime Minister Giscard d'Estaing, the Convention's praesidium has ex-(Italian) Prime Minister Amato and ex-(Belgian) Prime Minister Dehaene plus two Commission representatives.

[36] The European Parliament has already made its own attempt at drafting a constitution for Europe: see Reports of the Committee on Institutional Affairs (A3–0031/94) and (A3–0064/94).

[37] Caporaso, n. 16 above, 37.

[38] D. Held, A. McGrew, D. Goldblatt, and J. Perraton (eds.), *Models of Democracy* (Cambridge, Polity Press, 1999).

The Commission White Paper on Governance[39] chooses its own unortho-dox definition of 'governance', defining it in a footnote to mean the 'rules, processes and behaviour that affect the way in which powers are exercised at European level, particularly as regards openness, participation, accountabil-ity, effectiveness and coherence'.[40] By adding the last phrase, the Commis-sion has arguably incorporated its own agenda of participatory and consultative policy-making into its definition,[41] a point to which we will return. The White Paper is neither institutional nor constitutional in charac-ter, in that it focuses neither on issues of allocation of functions to the EU institutions nor on accountability in the sense of limitation and control of the powers allocated. It can, on the other hand, be fitted into Caporaso's definition of governance, though with the proviso that the problems selected by the Commission for resolution are hypothetical rather than practical. In other words, the Commission does not choose as its starting point, as it might sensibly have done, actual EU policies and procedures, such as structural funding, and then set out to resolve them as it has done, for example, in the recent remodelling of structural-funding procedures.[42] This can truly be described as an exercise in governance, meriting replication in other fields. If this policy-based approach to governance had been adopted, then the White Paper would have recognized the true nature of the EU as a trans-national system of governance and the Commission's role as an organizer of networks would have emerged; instead, the Commission has used its oppor-tunity to set off on a wild goose chase after a new form of supranational, participatory democracy.

There are several senses in which the European Union conforms more closely to a system of transnational governance than to the statal corset into which constitutional lawyers and European political actors are attempting to squeeze its developing institutions. The EU forms an integral part of a post-modern trend in international capitalism. As international capitalism organized itself as a transnational network of economic actors, who set their own normative standards and sought autonomy from national govern-ments,[43] this has been matched by the emergence, with the permission of

---

[39] WPG, n. 26 above.

[40] WPG, n. 26 above, 8.

[41] Contrast the discussion in 'Enhancing Democracy in the European Union', Work Programme, SEC(2000) 1547/7 final, 3. And see for comment D. Wincott, 'The Commis-sion and the Reform of Governance in the European Union' (2001) 39 *Journal of Common Market Studies* 897.

[42] European Commission, *Reform of the Structural Funds* (Brussels, Commission, 2000). Ways in which this could have been done are explored by J. Scott, 'Law, Legitimacy and EC Governance: Prospects for "Partnership"' (1998) 36 *Journal of Common Market Studies* 175 and 'Regional Policy: An Evolutionary Perspective' in Craig and de Burca (eds.), n. 23 above.

[43] See further G. Teubner (ed.), *Global Law Without a State* (Aldershot, Dartworth, 1997).

national governments, of an international network of regulators. The EU is, on the one hand, a liberalizing force for international capitalism, while on the other—a point on which Majone always insists[44]—it was set up as a regulator of capitalist economic forces. It has therefore followed the tendency for transnational systems of governance to fall into the hands of an autonomous elite. As Jachtenfuchs observes,[45] the EU is a prime candidate for such a development since its regulatory functions are aimed at areas of highly specialized technical knowledge, as, for example, food and products safety, pharmaceuticals, or biotechnology. This makes democratic accountability difficult, since lack of expertise in technical subject-matter is a deficiency of most parliamentary institutions. In the case of the EP, control is further undercut by its weak legitimacy and base in popular support. In other words, the positive legitimacy of expertise and regulatory specialism cannot as the system stands be outweighed by negative democratic legitimacy.

As the EU widened its ambit, expanding its policy-making into the field of environment, its possible role at the centre of an international 'policy network' began to emerge. The concept of 'policy network' is a variant of systems analysis becoming fashionable for the study of public policy.[46] Applied to the EU, it is argued that network theory enables the unit of the nation state to be transcended without an automatic transition to federalism; in other words, the statal mould can be broken.[47] The commonest application of network theory is to discrete policy areas, particularly, perhaps, the area of environment, where policy cannot be confined to a single agency but spreads across national boundaries. One way to focus policy-making in such a situation is to establish a network, grouped around one or more single-subject agencies: thus environmental agencies are found at international, transnational, national, and even sub-national level. To date, however, the European Union has not followed the pattern of modern nation states, notably the USA, in this direction. Its theory of agencies is based on the non-delegation principle, which establishes the overall responsibility of the Commission for its committees and agencies.[48] European agencies have so far not gained policy-making functions, although it is thought that their informational

---

[44] G. Majone, n. 24 above.

[45] M. Jachtenfuchs, 'The Governance Approach to European Integration' (2001) 39 *Journal of Common Market Studies* 245, 253.

[46] D. Marsh, 'The Development of the Policy Network Approach' in D. Marsh (ed.), *Comparing Policy Networks* (Buckingham, Open University Press, 1998) and D. Marsh and M. Smith, 'Understanding Policy Networks: Towards a Dialectical Approach' (2000) 48 *Political Studies* 4.

[47] K-H Ladeur, 'Towards a Legal Theory of Supranationality—The Validity of the Network Concept' (1997) 3 *European Law Journal* 33.

[48] Above, p. 75.

responsibilities could develop in this direction.[49] One way to develop the EU as a system of transnational governance would therefore be as a set of policy networks centred around agencies, and there are some signs in the White Paper on Governance that the Commission might be thinking tentatively of a move in this direction. Making reference to the range of agencies which exist at national level, the Commission states that:[50]

the creation of further autonomous EU regulatory agencies in clearly defined areas will improve the way rules are applied and enforced across the Union. Such agencies should be granted the power to take individual decisions in application of regulatory measures. They should operate with a degree of independence and within a clear framework established by the legislature. The regulation creating each agency should set out the limits of their activities and powers, their responsibilities and requirements for openness.

The only tenuous reference to accountability is in the last sentence.

There are other ways in which the EU can be seen to conform to a network model of governance. In the regulatory activities which are its main output, the Commission's function, usually exercised either through the comitology or through the network of informal working groups and advisory committees briefly described in earlier chapters, is one of harmonization. Network theory is easily transferable to study of the Comitology.[51] Again, in the agriculture and structural funding programmes, building and controlling networks is an essential Commission function, often carried out badly, as the case study of the MED programme revealed.[52] Again, administration of structural funding is typified by the 'partnership principle', in which a wide spectrum of public and private actors co-operate in the execution of projects, with Commission funding, encouragement, and supervision. The reform of structural funding might be seen as an acknowledgement by the Commission of its crucial role as an organizer of networks, in which the twin reports from the Committee of Independent Experts had revealed its deficiencies.

In a radical critique of the White Paper on Governance, Leslie Metcalfe has suggested[53] using the network concept as a basis for organizing the general administrative functions of the Commission. Hierarchical models of control and management, combined with variants of the classical models of account-

---

[49] J. Vervaele, 'Shared Governance and Enforcement of European Law: From Comitology to a Multi-level Agency Structure' in C. Joerges and E. Vos (eds.), *EU Committees: Social Regulation, Law and Politics* (Oxford, Hart Publishing, 1999).

[50] WPG, n. 26 above, 22–3.

[51] K. Ladeur, n. 48 above.

[52] Above, p. 121.

[53] L. Metcalfe, 'Reforming the European Governance: Old Problems or New Principles?' (2001) 67 *International Review of Administrative Sciences* 415. See also L. Metcalfe, 'The European Commission as a Network Organization' [1996] *Publius: The Journal of Federalism* 43.

ability, have not so far, Metcalfe argues, proved very effective in the EU, and whichever model of public management in the EU has been adopted, has proved unsuccessful and ineffective. In particular, there has been a tendency to rely on the development of common standards and bench-marking for administrative co-ordination, a method which lacks coercive powers. The White Paper is redolent of this regulatory method in the proposals for framework legislation and the 'open method of co-ordination' outlined above. According to Metcalfe, an accountability gap has been created in EU governance, which present thinking seems unable to close. The Commission needs to concentrate its energies on network management and the provision of management capability, especially for risk- and crisis-management. If such a system were installed—he does not say how—Metcalfe thinks an appropriate system of *managerial* accountability would be in place.

Instead, the White Paper concentrates on what it calls a 'reinvigoration of the Community method'. It re-states the Commission's role in European governance as the existing functions of policy initiation, execution, guardianship of the Treaty, and international representation of the EU. There is no indication here that the Commission has understood its position at the centre of a set of transnational and subnational policy and executive networks, nor that it has any real proposals as to the best methods of achieving a control of such networks, nor of how they can be adequately supervised. The lessons of the Santer disaster in the context of policy implementation have not been learned, and it is highly significant that the White Paper contains almost no reference to the Commission's proposals for reform. There is an urgent need to co-ordinate the various Commission proposals.

What type of accountability would one expect to find in the framework of a network model of governance? The best attempt at any explanation is that of Colin Scott,[54] briefly set out in Chapter 1 and referred to in later chapters. Scott suggests that debates about accountability raise three sets of questions: Who is accountable? To whom? And for what? Earlier chapters provide structural and institutional accounts of the EU with a view to providing material on which tentative answers to these questions can be based. It could be said that, in the EU context, the first question is relatively easy to answer: the principle of political accountability has been widely recognized, first in the emergence and performance of the European Parliament, and more recently by attempts to find a role for national parliaments. Scott himself includes legal accountability, although, in contrast to the definitions advanced in Chapter 6, he defines this to mean that 'all public bodies act in ways which correspond with the core juridical value of legality [and] thus correspond with

---

[54] C. Scott, 'Accountability in the Regulatory State' (2000) 27 *Journal of Law and Society* 38.

the democratic will'.[55] Scott's apparent equation of legality with the democratic will is surprising; it would be more correct to describe the legality test as
a fiction which legitimates and *provides the illusion* of democratic accountability. It is, as we have seen, however, strongly represented in the rule of law
ideology of the ECJ and has been used as a foundation for the installation of
an EC legal order capable of providing effective protection for the legal rights
and interests of private parties. Legality has also emerged in the EC legal order
as the central element in good administration accepted both by courts and
(more surprisingly) by the European Ombudsman. Though much more
strongly in the classical model of government, accountability to courts and
parliaments is recognized and does apparently feature in Scott's new model of
accountability as one of a number of horizontal devices by which accountability is guaranteed, the difference with the classical model of government
being that here parliamentary control is viewed as vertical or hierarchical.

But Scott also sees the need for a further cluster of 'extended accountability
structures', which he denominates as the models of *interdependence* and
redundancy and which are more obviously related to the model of governance. In the interdependence model, the actors are seen as 'dependent on each
other in their actions because of the dispersal of key resources of authority
(formal and informal), information, expertise, and capacity to bestow legitimacy such that each of the principal actors has constantly to account for at
least some of its actions to others within the space, as a precondition for
action'. This is a form of multi-polar accountability originating in regulatory
theory.[56] Though Scott uses the example of the British Treasury, his idea is
equally applicable to the Commission's general supervisory powers over
networks or to the external audit process operated by the ECA.

Scott's 'redundancy model' refers to the tendency to extend traditional or
'upwards' mechanisms of accountability by the 'horizontal' mechanisms of
market, notably contract, competition, and public procurement law, and
to regulatory agencies, in which 'overlapping (and ostensibly superfluous)
accountability mechanisms reduce the centrality of any one of them'.[57] This
he sees as a feature of EU expenditure programmes, such as the structural
funding, where 'redundancy is built into the accountability mechanisms
deliberately by EU decision makers, by requiring joint funding, and therefore
ensuring that both domestic and EU audit institutions necessarily take
an interest in single expenditure programmes within Member States'.[58]

---

[55] Ibid., 43. This is a stark contrast with Mulgan's view, accepted above, at 146.
[56] Ibid., at 50. See also C. Hood, 'The Hidden Public Sector: The "Quangocratization" of
the World' in F.-X. Kaufmann, G. Majone, and V. Ostrom (eds.), *Guidance, Control and
Evaluation in the Public Sector* (Berlin, de Gruyter, 1986).
[57] Scott, n. 55 above, at 52.
[58] Ibid., at 54.

Although he sees some problems, notably in programming in appropriate public-law norms of fairness, legality, rationality, etc., Scott is convinced of the potential to harness the 'dense networks of accountability within which public power is exercised ... for the purpose of achieving effective accountability or control'.[59]

Whether Scott's models are really capable of providing accountability within a system of transnational governance is, however, very questionable. The Committee of Independent Experts certainly did not think so, preferring to situate its recommendations squarely within the model of government. Arguably too, a diametrically opposite deduction might be drawn from the present study. As with separation of powers theory, multi-polar systems of accountability are seen as holding the system in perpetual equilibrium. The reality is that they allow responsibility to be dispersed and passed around the system, leading to the situation castigated by the Independent Experts, in which it is 'difficult to find anyone who has even the slightest sense of responsibility'.[60] The actors may be put in the position of the servant of two masters whose interests may differ very substantially, responsible and accountable to neither. Alternatively, the interests of the actors may fuse, in which case they will operate as a single network answerable only to themselves. This is a serious problem with scientific policy networks based around autonomous agencies and, in the BSE case, we have seen it in the context of Comitology. Again, policy-making networks, even when they satisfy Scott's principle of accountability through interdependence, are limited to *ex ante* accountability and 'dense networks' are, by definition, difficult if not impossible to penetrate.

In its White Paper, the Commission attaches to its discussion of governance a list of civic virtues without which, it suggests, good governance cannot be attained.[61] This is really a standard-setting view of 'good governance' which links the White Paper to the concept of global governance promoted by the World Bank, IMF, OECD, Council of Europe, and other bodies working to promote a unitary set of international standards conformant to Western capitalist ideas. Its values are selective, if predictable. The White Paper prioritizes: openness, participation, accountability, effectiveness, and 'coherence', an addition to the normal list which seems to refer to the idea of 'joined-up government'. Although accountability finds a place in the Commission's lists of values, the term acquires a novel meaning. The Commission tells us that:[62]

---

[59] Ibid., at 59.
[60] Committee of Independent Experts, *First Report on Allegations regarding Fraud, Mismanagement and Nepotism in the European Commission* (Brussels, 15 March 1999) para. 9.4.25.
[61] WPG, n. 26 above, 10.
[62] Ibid.

Roles in legislative and executive processes need to be clearer. Each of the EU institutions must explain and take responsibility for what it does in Europe. But there is also a need for greater clarity and responsibility from Member States and all those involved in developing and implementing EU policy at whatever level.

There is little relation here to any of the types of accountability identified either in this chapter or in Chapter 1. Instead the term has borrowed nuances from the participatory theme which infuses the White Paper on Governance, where the Commission seems to be following the OECD in using responsiveness and accountability as synonymous terms.[63] In the White Paper, the retrospective accountability generally prioritized in classical versions of the model of government is replaced by the prospective notion of participation in rule- and policy-making. Responsibility and accountability in the traditional sense of these terms, are thus blurred. Like the accountability of 'New Public Management', often conceived in terms of 'stakeholders' comprising sections of the public,[64] public accountability may be conceived in terms of a 'responsive' public service. This is a conception of accountability which sits comfortably inside the ideas of both consensus government as practised in many of the Member States of the European Union, and of the consociationalism associated in Chapter 4 with governance at Union level. Again, the concept of accountability through consultation is compatible with the idea of the Commission as a co-ordinator of policy networks.

The American town planner, Sherry Arnstein, describes most consultation exercises and procedures designated for participation as a sham: there is 'a critical difference between going through the empty ritual of participation and having the real power needed to affect the outcome of the process'.[65] She has devised a ladder of citizen participation consisting of the following eight rungs: 1. Manipulation; 2. Therapy; 3. Informing; 4. Consultation; 5. Placation; 6. Partnership; 7. Delegated power; 8. Citizen control. Only at the top two rungs of this ladder is there any genuine transference of power, while the bottom two rungs represent levels of 'non-participation that have been contrived by some to substitute for genuine participation. Their real objective is not to enable people to participate ... but to enable power-holders to "educate" or "cure" the participants'. This critique is particularly applicable to the White Paper's manipulative proposals for the regulation of civil society.[66] There is a grave danger in the White Paper's vision of accountability through participation that it will end by undercutting the authority of

---

[63] OECD, *Administration as Service: The Public as Client* (Paris, OECD, 1987).

[64] D. Farnham and S. Horton, 'Public Managers and Private Managers; Towards a Professional Synthesis?' in D. Farnham *et al.*, *New Public Managers in Europe*, 33.

[65] S. Arnstein, 'A Ladder of Citizen Participation' (1969) 35 *Journal of the American Institute of Planners* 216.

[66] WPG, n. 26 above, 14–15. And see K. Armstrong, 'Rediscovering Civil Society: The European Union and the White Paper on Governance' (2002) 8 *European Law Journal* 102.

representative institutions, making it harder for them to exact political responsibility through parliamentary scrutiny. If, as Arnstein argues, participation and consultation are purely notional, then real accountability through
representative democracy will be subordinated to a process essentially aimed
at placation and easily capable of manipulation by the Commission.

III GOOD GOVERNANCE AND MANAGEMENT

Central to any discussion of government or governance is, therefore, the
question of *good* governance and, in the EU context therefore, reform of the
Commission. This has to be spelled out of the White Paper on Governance
and does not apparently feature on the Convention agenda. Yet the twin
Reports of the Committee of Independent Experts revealed the techniques
and standards of administration as ineffective and even amateurish, and
realization that the Commission might be inadequate for its functions
antedates the Santer affair by at least twenty years, when the Spierenburg
Report set out proposals for restructuring and co-ordinating the Commission
and its Directorates-General.[67] The Single Market programme added to the
problem. Some years after Maastricht, Stephen Weatherill noted the extent to
which the EU administration lacked expertise and institutional maturity and
was reliant on participation from national authorities.[68] The Delors Presidency thought in terms of greater resources but succeeded only in establishing
that resources would be strictly limited.[69] This ought to have brought a
serious review of the Commission's responsibilities. In practice, this only
arrived with the Santer affair, the shock of which added a willingness to re-
think functions and responsibilities in the light of static resources. Pushed
forward by its President, Romano Prodi, and the Vice-President in charge of
reform, Neil Kinnock, the Commission's programme has, at least on the
surface, been relatively ambitious.

The first set of proposals,[70] placed before the Nice IGC, deals essentially
with 'government'. Aimed essentially at restructuring the Commission to
prepare for enlargement, they recommend changes to facilitate firm government by the President; it is, for example, now the President who decides on

[67] European Commission, 'Proposals for Reform of the Commission of the European
Communities and its Services' (Brussels, Commission, 1979).
[68] S. Weatherill, *Law and Integration in the European Union* (Oxford, Clarendon, 1995),
154.
[69] European Commission, 'From the Single Act to Maastricht and Beyond: The Means to
Match our Ambitions' (Brussels, Commission, 1994).
[70] European Commission, Communication from the Commission to the Intergovernmental Conference on the reform of the institutions, Brussels, COM(2000) final. See also
'Adapting the institutions to make a success of enlargement', COM(2000)34, Brussels (26
Jan. 2000).

portfolios, which he may reshuffle during the term of office, and the power of the President to ask a Commission member to resign is confirmed (TEC Article 217). At Nice, however, Member States could not agree a new appointments system which would end their privileged right of representation,[71] the only change accepted being some moves to qualified majority voting in Council. Suggestions for a presidential casting vote and power to 'determine the political orientations of the Commission' fell by the wayside. In this way, progression towards a model of cabinet government was for the time being ruled out. Instead, the *managerial* responsibility of the President for the Commission's internal organization 'in order to ensure that it acts consistently, efficiently and on the basis of collegiality' was affirmed (TEC Article 217). Consonant with the concept of the President as manager, the Commission's Communication to the IGC sought to reassure the Council of its commitment to reforms, 'concerned with modernising and improving the workings of the administration'; these were stated to be both essential and 'under way'.

The Commission proposals were published as two, joined working papers,[72] firmly based on recognition of the Commission as the 'motor of European integration', which, like the later White Paper on Governance, seek to reinforce the 'Community method'. Accepting that the Commission must henceforth focus on its 'core functions' of policy-making, political initiative, and law enforcement, the Commission set out to identify these more clearly. The Prodi Commission, in the words of Vice-President Neil Kinnock,[73] 'became the first that has ever asked itself: "Do we really need to do all that we are doing at present?" and "Can we do what we must do, and do it properly, with the resources at our disposal?" '. These questions led in two directions: first to the internal reform of the Commission, second to proposals for 'new forms of partnership between the different levels of governance in Europe'. In this way, the proposals foreshadow the hiving-off of managerial and operational functions which are a marked feature of the White Paper on Governance.

The proposals on internal reform of the Commission—central, it has been argued, to any discussion of EU governance—are, on this occasion, strictly pragmatic and practical. Cast in the methods and terminology of a diluted version of New Public Management (NPM), they aim at streamlining the

---

[71] J. Temple Lang and E. Gallagher, 'What Sort of Euopean Commission does the EU Need?' (Brussels, European Policy Centre, 20 Mar. 2002).

[72] European Commission, 'Reforming the Commission', 2Vols, COM(2000)200 final/ 2 (Brussels, 5 Apr. 2000). Available at **http://europa.eu.int/comm/off/white/reform/ index_en.htm**. See also N. Lebessis and J. Patterson, 'Developing New Modes of Governance', European Commission Forward Studies Unit, Working Paper, 2000.

[73] N. Kinnock, 'Accountability and Reform of Internal Control in the European Commission', Sunningdale lecture, 15 Oct. 2001.

Commission's work practices and inculcating the sense of responsibility for clearly-defined units of work found lacking by the Independent Experts. To carry out its tasks efficiently, the Commission needs to reconsider 'the working practices, conventions and obligations that have accumulated over decades [and] now inhibit the Commission's effectiveness'. The resulting Action Plan is intended, to cite Kinnock again,[74] to ensure that the Commission is a 'well-managed policy-producing and policy-applying administration of the highest quality, integrity and service, focused firmly on its core tasks and executing them efficiently and with independence, transparency, responsibility and accountability'. The Plans are mainly devoted to a thorough overhaul of staff policy, notably the systems of audit and financial management inside the Commission. Redolent of the audit/NPM ethos, they are based on a set of defined objectives and performance indicators, vesting responsibility in identifiable individuals, to be implemented through a series of action plans. Behind the scenes, some of the changes are already in operation, implemented, though not without substantial internal opposition, through the SEM internal audit project and other internal management programmes, monitored by committees of the European Parliament.[75] A new staff policy emphasizing training, horizontal career mobility for everyone with upward mobility for high fliers, appraisal and professionalism have been introduced, their aims and objectives again expressed in vocabulary redolent of managerialism.[76] If this were to succeed, it could, in conjunction with the much needed overhaul of the Staff Regulations, do much to change the Commission culture, introducing a managerial ethos and promoting development of the professional management skills needed for the supervision of an extended European Union. Full implementation would go some way to meeting the criticisms that the Commission bureaucracy is inadequate as manager of European programmes.[77]

The second set of proposals, dispersed between the three Papers, aims, as already mentioned, to experiment with 'new forms of partnership between the different levels of governance in Europe'. The 'open method of co-ordination', pioneered inside the area of economic union, permits the Com-

[74] Ibid.

[75] E.g., Reform Progress Report, Feb. 2001 at **http://europa.eu.int/eur-** and European Parliament resolutions COM(2000)200 (C5-0445/2000 (2000/2215) and (COM(2000)200) C5-0447/2000) 2000/2217(COS) (budgetary control) and COM(2000) 200% C5–0448/2000% 2000/2218 (constitutional affairs). See, however, the sceptical views of L Cram, 'Whither the Commission? Reform, Renewal and the Issue Attention Cycle' (2001) 8 *Journal of European Public Policy* 770.

[76] European Commission, New Staff Policy, IP/01/283, Brussels (28 Feb. 2000); Press Release 'Commission proposes a new staff policy from recruitment to retirement' (28 Feb. 2001).

[77] L. Metcalfe, 'Reforming the Commission: Will Organizational Efficiency Produce Effective Governance?' (2000) 38 *Journal of Common Market Studies* 817. Above 63–4.

mission, for example, to agree policies, down-loading implementation to national or regional level. The open method relies on NPM techniques of standard-setting, performance indicators, and 'benchmarking', with periodic monitoring. Read in conjunction with the proposals for co-regulation, this would represent a substantial move in the direction of subsidiarity. Hodson and Maher argue that:[78]

the flexibility of the open method, which allows for policy formation best suited to national needs, albeit within the context of best practice and transparency between states, avoids problems of ill-fiting Europeanisation of national policies and attendant dissatisfaction by governments and their electorates.

The developments can be seen also as helping to counter Metcalfe's criticisms of the Commission as 'organizer of networks'.

IV CONCLUSIONS: TOWARDS ACCOUNTABILITY

In Britain, with its current reliance on regulation as a technique of administration, accountability has become something of a fetish. We have allowed ourselves to become dominated by Vincent Wright's '*état évaluateur*',[79] in which the essential features of every administrative programme are reduced to numbers and evaluated, and every administrative action scrutinized with a view to allocating blame and censure. Transparency has been taken to extreme lengths, and has become a weapon with which the media presses incursions into private life, howling for punitive action and seeking exaggerated redress for the simplest of errors. With this has come a change in public-service values: from public service to management, economy, and efficiency, from trust and discretion to rules and regulation, and above all to quantifiable criteria. As Michael Power explains:[80]

the most influential dimension of the audit explosion is the process by which environments are made auditable, structured to conform to the need to be monitored ex-post . . . The standards of performance themselves are shaped by the need to be auditable . . . [Audit] models organisations for its own purposes and impacts to varying degrees upon their first-order operations . . . Concepts of performance and quality are in danger of being defined largely in terms of conformity to auditable process.

---

[78] D. Hodson and I. Maher, 'The Open Method as a New Mode of Governance' (2001) 39 *Journal of Common Market Studies* 719, 741.
[79] V. Wright, '*Le cas britannique: le démantelement de l'administration traditionnnellé*', in L. Rouban and J. Ziller (eds.), Special Issue, *Les Administrations en Europe: D'une Modernisation a l'Autre* (1995) 75 *AJDA* 355, 361 (emphasis added).
[80] M. Power, *The Audit Explosion* (London, Demos, 1994), 37–9.

This is a society which has taken accountability too far and in an inappropriate direction. The European Union, however, stands at the opposite end of the spectrum; from a management standpoint, it has grown too fast. The peculiar problems of welding together a transnational bureaucracy have made it hard to develop an ethos of management appropriate to the 'Community method' and the Commission's multifarious tasks. The problem has not really started to be addressed.

The new approach, which prioritizes 'good governance', inevitably places accountability high on the list of governance values. Rejecting the White Paper's deviant definition,[81] the approach pushes managerial and audit accountability to the top of the agenda, a development probably in line with modern trends. The media and opinion polling confirm that citizens like to be well governed, even if they prefer to leave operational details to management. In time, pressure stimulated and stirred up by a more lively European civil society, will create a real need for the Commission to move into the modern era of public administration based on audit and accountability. Unless this can be achieved, European 'governance' will surely fail and Scott's criteria for accountability in a network system will not be met. To make this last point differently, only if networks are properly managed and supervised are the conditions right for equilibrium supported by the network's many actors.

But managerial efficiency and effectiveness can never be the end of the story. Government as well as governance must be in equilibrium. Accountability and representative government go together and, at institutional level, the 'democratic deficit' of the Union renders political accountability weak. 'Giving people a greater say in the way Europe is run and making the European institutions work more transparently and effectively' are worthy objectives, but no amount of the placatory consultation recommended in the White Paper on Governance can make up for the absence of government directly responsible to a representative parliament; it may, indeed, as already suggested, operate to undercut it. But if the 'open method of coordination' were to become the centrepiece of a revived Community method, a decentralized and 'bottom-weighted' governmental system, in which the subsidiarity principle became a reality, could be installed. Lindseth's agency theory of European Union would then serve an important explanatory purpose. In becoming the agent of the Member States, the Commission would lose nothing, not even its accountability to the ECA and the European Parliament, both of which would remain intact. The credentials of the European Parliament would, however, be seen to depend not on its accountability to the European electorate, which, in the absence of elected government at European level, is a misconception, but on its position as agent of the

---

[81] Above, 184.

national parliaments. The full responsibility for policy accountability would then rest and, more important, be seen to rest with national parliaments, which could no longer afford to offer only regime support. For the first time, they would become accountable and could be evaluated on their perform-ance. As suggested in Chapter 4, however, the response of national parlia-ments could be a move to co-ordinate their legislative and scrutiny activities and to collaborate in exacting greater control. Over time, co-operation could achieve a measure of indirect control of the Council. The division of competence would depend on clear guidance from the Constitutional Con-vention, and would need to be monitored by a constitutional adjudicator whose 'genetic code', in contrast to that transmitted by the founding fathers to the present Court of Justice,[82] would be not integrationism but the impartiality spelled out by Fritz Scharpf:[83]

[T]he recognition of a bipolar constitutional order prevents the one-sided orienta-tion of judicial review towards the enumerated powers of the central government, which is otherwise characteristic of federal states. It requires the court to balance competing jurisdictional claims with a view not only to their substantive justifica-tion, but also to the manner in which the powers are exercised. The criterion is *mutual compatibility*, and the characteristic outcome is not the displacement of one jurisdiction by the other, but the obligation of both to choose mutually acceptable means when performing the proper functions of government at each level.

The outcome of this reshaping of governance in the European Union ought, if the Laeken Council's analysis of what people want is correct, go a long way to providing a system of governance which is not only more accountable but also 'less unwieldy and rigid and above all, more efficient and open'.[84] It should help to meet the popular suspicion that the Union 'interven[es], in every detail, in matters best left by their nature to Member States' and regions' elected representatives'. It should help to mitigate the sense of threat to identity. It could, if operated in a spirit of goodwill, provide better democratic scrutiny. Whether this would in any way alleviate people's feeling that 'deals are too often cut out of their sight' is, if the experience of national politics is anything to go by, extremely unlikely.

Some readers, gripped by the strange magic of globalization, transnational governance, and integration, will inevitably see this decentralized solution as a move back into national trenches and even a retrograde step back towards the perceived factionalism of national systems of government. This is em-phatically not the intention. Until the political accountability to which we

---

[82] F. Mancini and D. Keeling, 'Democracy and the European Court of Justice' (1994) 57 *MLR* 175, 186.

[83] F. Scharpf, 'Community and Autonomy: Multi-level Policy-making in the European Union' (1994) 1 *Journal of European Public Policy* 219, 225.

[84] Laeken Declaration, n. 5 above.

have, in the course of the twentieth century, become used in the nation state, is replicated at transnational level, we would be wise not to entrust transnational organizms with too much power. We should remain in a state of 'provisional suprastatism' from which it is still possible to step back. A pluralist, decentralized, confederal solution, based firmly on the principles of subsidiarity and agency, will hasten the evolution of a union of nations firmly grounded in collaboration and consensus. 'Back to the Future', in other words.

Index

Committee of Independent Experts (*cont.*)
audit and 109, 112, 116, 118, 121–2,
126, 135
Final Report 56
functions and membership 54
Interim Report 55–6
Common Agricultural Plan 129, 131–2,
181
'Community method' 176, 190
Consociationalism 101–2, 105–6
Convention on the constitution 29, 171,
172, 176, 177, 186
Cook, Robin 107
COREPER 33–4, 35
COSAC 103, 105
Council of Europe 11, 20
Council of Ministers
(*see also* European Council) 31–2,
172
Council committees 32–3, 34
General Affairs Council 86
Third Pillar and 41, 43, 172
Transparency and 43–4
working groups 31, 34, 38
Courts
Community Courts 4
access 148–53, 158
accountability and 165–7
competence 146, 147
delay 158–9
privileged access 149
public interest actions 150–1
standing to sue 148–53
Court of First Instance of the European
Communities (CFI) 147
administrative court as 163–4
delay 159
transparency and 40, 163–4
European Court of Justice (ECJ)
appointment 95
constitutional adjudication and 145–6,
147, 191
European Parliament and 93
judicial remedies 156–9
judicial review and 145–7
Member States and 154

preliminary reference procedure 147,
153–6
quota system and 61
reasons and 160, 162
Third Pillar and 44–5
national courts 81–2, 153–4, 170
judicial remedies and 156–7
procedural autonomy and 155–6
Criminal procedure (Corpus Juris
project) 46, 77, 138–40, 142
Curtin, Deirdre 35, 36

Dashwood, Alan 31
de Haan, Jacob 50
Dehousse, Renaud 92
Democracy
consensus democracy 101, 185
majoritarian 170, 171
non-majoritarian 170, 171, 174
participatory 106–7, 170, 185–6
representative 106–7, 170, 175, 190
Democratic deficit 8, 79, 82, 84, 169, 171
Dicey, Albert Venn 6, 17
Directives 72
Duisenberg, Wim 50

EC budget 116
Environment 60, 72–3, 180
European arrest warrant 80–1
European Central Bank (ECB) and
European System of Central Banks
(ESCB) 48–51
European Charter of Fundamental
Rights 29, 164, 177–8
European Commission 53–78
accountability (definition) 184, 190
appointment 58–9, 94–5, 186–7
audit and 118–23, 188
bureaucratic culture 59–61
College of Commissioners 55, 59, 60, 78
committees and (*see also* Comitology) 65
composition 63–4
delegation and 68, 173
ECHO programme of humanitarian
aid 54, 120, 134–5
enforcement of EC law 71–4